All You Need Is Love
THE END OF THE BEATLES

Also by Peter Brown and Steven Gaines

The Love You Make: An Insider's Story of the Beatles

All You Need Is Love
THE END OF THE BEATLES

PETER BROWN
STEVEN GAINES

monoray

First published in the USA in 2024 by St. Martin's Press

First published in Great Britain in 2024 by Monoray,
an imprint of Octopus Publishing Group Ltd
Carmelite House
50 Victoria Embankment
London EC4Y 0DZ
www.octopusbooks.co.uk

An Hachette UK Company
www.hachette.co.uk

Copyright © Peter Brown and Steven Gaines 2024

All rights reserved. No part of this work may be reproduced or utilized in any form or by any means, electronic or mechanical, including photocopying, recording or by any information storage and retrieval system, without the prior written permission of the publisher.

Peter Brown and Steven Gaines assert the moral right to be identified as the authors of this work.

ISBN 978-1-80096-233-0

A CIP catalogue record for this book is available from the British Library.

Printed and bound in Great Britain.

1 3 5 7 9 10 8 6 4 2

This FSC® label means that materials used for the product have been responsibly sourced.

Publisher's note
The interviews in this book have been edited and condensed for clarity.

For Brian Epstein

Contents

Introduction by Peter Brown 1

Brian Epstein 15
Paul McCartney 17
Alistair Taylor 47
Queenie Epstein 52
Nat Weiss 58
Alistair Taylor on Brian's Death 62
Peter Brown on Brian's Death 65
Allan Williams 66
Bob Wooler 70
Dick James 73
Geoffrey Ellis 77
Peter Brown on Manila 84
Vic Lewis 89
George Harrison 93
Alexis Mardas 107
Peter Brown on Maharishi 119
Pattie Boyd Harrison Clapton and Jenny Boyd Fleetwood 120
Neil Aspinall 130

David Puttnam 142
Martin Polden 149
Peter Brown on Apple 156
Alistair Taylor on Apple 158
Derek Taylor 160
Peter Brown on "Hey Jude" 171
Robert Fraser 174
Ray Connolly 181
John Dunbar 190
Cynthia Lennon Twist 198
Ron Kass on Yoko Ono 208
Yoko Ono 209
May Pang 230
Peter Brown on Allen Klein 238
Dick James on Northern Songs 240
Ron Kass 246
John Eastman 255
Alistair Taylor on Allen Klein Having Him Fired 263
Allen Klein 265
Maureen Starkey 290
Ringo Starr 301
Afterword 321

Acknowledgments 323
Index 325

I've read cracks about, "Oh, the Beatles sang,
'All You Need Is Love,' but it didn't work for them."
But nothing will ever break the love we have for each other,
and I still believe all you need is love.
 —John Lennon, radio interview with
    Howard Smith on WPLJ, 1972

Introduction

The transcripts in this book are a mosaic: elucidating, contradictory, confounding. They are culled from over one hundred hours of interviews that have never been broadcast or published before. The information and experiences, as well as the authority of the people who relate them, are unique; they can never be duplicated, simply because most of the participants are dead. In the Beatles' canon these untempered interviews are historic, set apart from all others, literally the "last words" of the Beatles' inner circle before John was killed. The reader should be forewarned that interviewees don't always remember events or people the same way, or tell the truth, and expect to find contrasting versions throughout the interviews. We leave it up to the reader to decide if some versions are self-serving or deliberately misleading. The interviews were conducted for the book *The Love You Make: An Insider's Story of the Beatles* by Peter Brown and Steven Gaines. Except for Yoko Ono's interview, they were conducted in England and New York in the fall of 1980, just a few weeks prior to John Lennon's death on December 8 of that year. Yoko was interviewed a few months after John was killed.

It always surprises me that people still ask why the Beatles ended. You'd think that with the surfeit of movies, books, and articles about the

Beatles' rise and demise, the question would have been well answered. Yet it lingers. People miss them, and in some way feel shortchanged. It was a fairy tale that had an unexpectedly unhappy ending. People feel a need to lay blame. Did Yoko Ono break up the Beatles? Was it Linda Eastman? Or Magic Alex, the Mordred of the Beatles' Camelot? Was it pushy Paul telling George how to play (it wasn't, although that didn't help), or Yoko sitting on George's amplifier, as Paul himself once joked about why the Beatles broke up? And why did they hate one another so much at the end? The interviews with the Beatles and their wives, friends, and business associates give insight, if not easy answers, to all the lingering questions, and no one can say which is more accurate. Reading the transcripts, it becomes clear that people who were part of the Beatles constellation each have their own truth. As Neil Aspinall, the Beatles' road manager and best friend from Liverpool, described it, "You think, 'I was there, and that's not the way it happened to me.'"

This is the way it happened to me.

In 1965, at Brian Epstein's behest, I moved from Liverpool to London to work with Brian and the Beatles. I was Brian's closest friend and confidant. We met when I was twenty years old, at a crowded birthday celebration given by one of my fellow students in the executive training program at Lewis's department store in Liverpool. Brian was only three years older than I, but he seemed worldly and sophisticated for his age. Perhaps that was because he had attended—and was thrown out of—at least six different schools, not including the Royal Academy of Dramatic Art.

Brian and I had a great deal in common, particularly because Brian was running the record department at NEMS (North End Music Stores), the family furniture and appliance store located squarely across the street from Lewis's, where I managed their record department. Before long, Brian invited me to work for him at NEMS, and eventually I managed the record departments in all three of the family-owned stores. The NEMS stores sold more records than any other in the North of England. Most everyone from the burgeoning Liverpool music scene came to NEMS to browse and listen to music in one of the record listening booths, including John, Paul, George, and Cilla Black.

Liverpool was once one of the most important ports in the British Empire. Tucked down the River Mersey, a safe berth from the stormy North Sea, it was the center of the country's cotton trade and shipbuilding industry. Its strategic value in World War II was essential to the war effort, and the Germans bombed the hell out of it. Much of the city was destroyed, but not its spirit, and in the 1950s, as the city struggled to revive, a vibrant music scene was born, and there were hundreds of nascent rock groups. The theory was that the merchant lines that made port in Liverpool hired many local boys when they graduated high school. These young men heard music in America, and when they came back to Liverpool, they brought with them the seeds of American rock and roll.

In late 1961, Brian took me out to dinner to ask if I would take over management of all three family-owned record stores. He wanted to direct all his attention to a new passion: a rock and roll group called the Beatles. I was to discover that Brian had many surprising passions, as consuming as they were fleeting. He first saw the Beatles in early November at the Cavern Club, a smoky cellar with barreled ceilings and sweaty brick walls. The legend that he was mesmerized by John Lennon in black leather trousers is true. Brian liked bad boys.

The Beatles were more impressed with Brian's gray Ford Zodiac than they were concerned about his lack of managerial experience. What really convinced them to sign a management contract with Brian was that he proposed to pay them a salary every week, so their earnings would be more reliable. (This went on to the end. Every Thursday, I sent forty pounds in an envelope to each Beatle.) The first time we heard "Love Me Do" played on the radio, it was October 5, 1962. It was a song that John and Paul had written five years before, as teenagers. I was with Brian in his car when the song came on Radio Luxembourg. We were so excited, Brian pulled over to the side of the road, and we got out of the car and pulled the antenna all the way up. There it was, fading in and out, distant and staticky, but you couldn't take it away from us. The Beatles were on the radio.

Brian and the Beatles soon moved to London, and I followed shortly after. Over the next five head-spinning years, I became director of NEMS, now the name of the Beatles management company; a board member of Beatles and Co., their business partnership; and I was the chief operating officer at Apple [Corps], their utopian business venture. We also managed a growing list of talent at NEMS, including Britain's superstar Cilla Black, the Moody Blues, Gerry and the Pacemakers, Billy J. Kramer, and the Modern Jazz Quartet.

Much of my time at NEMS was occupied with helping to make the Beatles' lives a little less chaotic, a twenty-four-hour-a-day job and a nearly impossible task. The Beatles always knew where to find me when they needed me, because there was a phone on my desk to which only they had the number. Keeping track of them was somewhat more difficult. I found the most effective way to ensure they were at least in Great Britain was to keep their passports locked in my desk drawer. Even this wasn't a discouragement; Paul called me from France one day, where he'd managed to talk his way past customs without a passport to shoot a scene for *Magical Mystery Tour*. It took some diplomacy to get him back home.

Of all the Beatles, John was everyone's favorite. He was a hooligan with a Beatles haircut. In middle school, he was sent to detention sixty times in one year, for transgressions including spitting on his desk and exposing himself. He enjoyed chafing people and being provocative. He was quick-witted and scathing. It's well told that when Brian Epstein asked what he should call his forthcoming memoir, John said, "*Queer Jew*," mortifying him.* The first year or so of the Beatles' success, it was fun for John to be a merry moptop, but

---

* The book was published under the title *A Cellarful of Noise*, in reference to the Cavern Club in Liverpool. John quickly redubbed the book *A Cellarful of Boys*.

eventually the real John would come out, and his behavior was not always compatible with being a Beatle.

In 1962, when John was still living in Liverpool, he confided to Brian that his girlfriend, Cynthia Powell, was pregnant. The couple had met at the Liverpool College of Art. Cynthia was soft-spoken and shy, from a relatively posh suburb of Liverpool called Hoylake.[†] Brian was concerned that if Beatles fans found out John had fathered a child out of wedlock, it would cause a scandal and hurt the group. He decided that Cynthia had to be kept secret. He arranged for Cynthia and John to get married quickly and quietly at the justice of the peace, followed by a small wedding lunch at a department store café.

When a reporter asked Ringo about the rumors John was married, Ringo responded, "If he is, we don't want to talk about it." On April 8, 1963, a son, Julian, was born without much fanfare. Ringo claims that he didn't even know John had a child until the boys were at their accountant's office and John started talking about having dependents to declare.

This denial of Cynthia and Julian's existence brings up the subject of Brian and John's vacation to Spain. The day after Cynthia gave birth to Julian, John dropped by the hospital to inform her that he was going on holiday for two weeks with Brian to a small fishing village in the south of Spain. John's reflection on his decision to go on vacation with Brian when he had a newborn son: "I was a bastard."

In today's world, the friendship between a gay and a straight man would hardly warrant a moment of consideration, but in the 1960s, it was quite a different matter. John and Brian had developed a loving platonic bond, and although Brian may have wished it otherwise, he was too shy and proper to ever make John feel uncomfortable. Their

---

[†] Yoko's assessment of Cynthia and John's attraction was this: "When he went to art school, I think she was like a different class of chick, you know rather elegant and graceful, and I think that's probably what impressed John. She was probably top of class, very intelligent as well. When he wasn't doing his homework, he probably had to get help from her, something like that." Please refer to Yoko's transcript for more.

relationship was more manipulative on John's part. The Beatle who could influence Brian controlled the group. Yet what might have started as strategy on John's part soon became real affection. The fact that Brian was gay made him more unique and fascinating than anybody John had ever come across in Liverpool. John was a voyager, curious about life, he didn't care what anybody thought, or so he said. As far as what transpired privately between John and Brian on that trip, one can probably guess, but we'll never know for sure. Brian never mentioned the matter, although it was greatly discussed within the Beatles' circle.

Back in Liverpool, John was at Paul's twenty-first birthday party when he was taunted about the trip by Bob Wooler, a local disc jockey, and John beat the hell out of him with a stick. "I must have been frightened of the fag in me to beat him up so bad," John later said in a 1971 interview that appeared in Peter McCabe and Robert D Schonfeld's book *John Lennon: For The Record*. Wooler sued John, who paid him £200 to settle the matter. "It's irrelevant," John told a reporter when questioned about his Spanish holiday. "Absolutely irrelevant."

A journalist once called Brian "deceptively genial," but he wasn't deceptive at all. His warmth was sincere, and he was without guile. It was more accurate to describe Brian as being "deceptively happy." It may be a cliché, but it's true; riches and fame can seem a bitter reward if there's no one to share them with. Brian found it impossible to form a personal relationship with someone who was appropriate. In England at that time, homosexuality was not only considered sick and shameful but also against the law. When Brian was discharged from the British Army on medical grounds, an officer told his mother, Queenie Epstein, that Brian was a "poor unfortunate man." I'm afraid Brian believed that too. Over the years, he had been depressed and suicidal, and he made one serious attempt that I thwarted before taking him to the hospital to have his stomach pumped.

When Brian moved to London, he became the patient of a physician who was amenable to overprescribing sleeping medications, uppers and downers, for his star patient. Ironically, the people who first introduced Brian to pills were the Beatles. The four boys began to use diet pills called Preludin—or Prellies—during their all-night stints in Hamburg. They continued to take them when they returned to Liverpool, and Brian started to take the Prellies, too, partly because of his desire to be one of the boys, and partly to keep himself awake on the long drives home from their appearances all over northern England. Brian's friends cared deeply for his welfare, and a few of us tried at various times to have a talk with him. The thing about Brian was that no matter how close you were to him, there was a point beyond which one felt it was inappropriate to go. If you went too far, the room would freeze with his iciness.

Brian's friend and New York attorney, Nat Weiss, had it out with Brian one night at the Waldorf Towers, as Nat remembers in his transcript. I tried to have a talk with Brian about his use of prescription drugs at his London home that ended with him shouting at me, "Leave me alone!" Eventually, in May of 1967, his body broke down and he was hospitalized at the Priory, an exclusive psychiatric clinic in Roehampton that specialized in detoxification, but when he was released, Brian went back to his regimen. We stood by helplessly and hoped the Beatles wouldn't desert him.

On the three-day bank holiday weekend of August 25, 1967, Brian planned to stay at Kingsley Hill, his country house in Sussex, along with Geoffrey Ellis, our colleague at NEMS. On Friday night, Brian got fidgety and unhappy, and although it was already late, drove to London. When I spoke to him the following afternoon, he was groggy from his sleeping medications and said he would take the train back to Sussex later that day. He never arrived. On Sunday afternoon, there was a desperate call from Brian's secretary, Joanne Newfield. Brian's bedroom door was locked, and no matter how loud they banged, they were unable to raise him. I remained on the line in Sussex, listening to the double oak doors splinter under the force of the butler and chauffeur. "He's just sleeping," I could hear Joanne repeating into the phone. "He's just sleeping."

His autopsy showed that his death was caused by an accumulation of a barbiturate called Carbitral that he had taken over a long period of time. It had built up in his system and eventually killed him. For a man who threatened to take his life before, it was bitter irony that his death was an accident. Most of all, I wanted it to be an accident for Queenie's sake, because she could never live with herself if she thought Brian had committed suicide.

One of the most endearing and illuminating moments I had with Paul was in January of 1968, when he and I attended the Marché International du Disque et de L'Édition Musicale, the international music industry convention held every year in Cannes. It was shortly after the critical debacle of *Magical Mystery Tour*, and a few weeks after Paul had announced his engagement to Jane Asher, a young actress. Paul suggested that we stop in Paris on our way to Cannes for a brief vacation. We checked into a two-bedroom suite at the Ritz Hotel, had a drink at the bar, and sat there trying to figure out what we should do next. It was Paris on a Saturday night. "What would you do if I wasn't here?" Paul asked.

I said that I would call an American friend who lived in Paris and ask if he was free for dinner.

"So, let's do that then," Paul agreed.

My American friend was delighted to hear from me and invited us over for drinks. I didn't want to say, *Oh, by the way, I'm bringing Paul McCartney*, so I decided to just let it happen. My friend greeted me at the door to his flat and shook Paul's hand without a blink of an eye. Paul and I were shown into the living room, where everyone realized it was Paul McCartney, and for a nanosecond the room froze. Then everything went back to normal, people chattering in French, smoking cigarettes and marijuana. I watched Paul deal with it all, easy, charming, relaxed. After dinner he asked if I was going back to the hotel. I told him that he could go back if he wanted, but I was going to a gay bar and hoped to meet someone. Paul said he would find his own fun and hailed a taxi.

In the wee hours of the morning, I was in bed with a handsome Parisian I'd met at the bar, when Paul returned to the hotel suite. He knocked on my bedroom door and entered without waiting for a response. He was totally nonchalant when he saw me in bed with my friend. He came over and sat down on the edge of the bed next to us. "How was the rest of your evening?" he asked. We chatted for a bit about travel plans the next day and he left. I loved Paul for the casual way he handled the moment. I'm sure my young Parisian friend told this story many times in his life, and no one believed him.

I have no idea where Paul went that night; I never asked. Four months later, I introduced him to his future wife, Linda Eastman. I knew Linda from my business trips to New York, where she ran with a smart crowd. She was twenty-five, pretty, blond, knowing. Her father was the attorney Lee Eastman, who represented some of the great creative artists of the twentieth century, including Willem de Kooning and Tennessee Williams. As you can read in Paul's transcript, in May of 1968, I introduced them at the Bag o' Nails, a popular music business hangout. They left the restaurant together that night. I also invited her to the launch party for *Sgt. Pepper* at Brian's house on May 19, and as soon as Linda arrived, she made her way to where Paul was sitting in an armchair, exhausted, a two days' growth on his chin, a dreamy look on his face. She literally sank to her knees by his side. There's a wonderful picture of her sitting on the floor in a bold striped jacket, gazing up at him like she's looking at a god. I remember thinking what a great couple they were.

In early March of 1969, Paul phoned me to say that he and Linda were starting a family. They were like lovebirds on a cloud, thrilled Linda was pregnant. They wanted to get married as soon as possible and asked if I would make the arrangements. The problem was that as soon as they posted banns to get married in Great Britain, it became public information. I was concerned that the ceremony at the

Marylebone Register Office was going to turn into a mob scene, with wailing young girls and a horde of paparazzi, but Paul and Linda were unperturbed about fans finding out. On March 12, 1969, the day of the wedding, the streets in front of the register were indeed mobbed with fans and had to be shut down by the police. We had to enter through a side door where the garbage bins were kept. Paul's brother, who was the best man, was half an hour late because the police had closed off all the surrounding streets.

One week and one day after Paul married Linda, I received a phone call from John. He and Yoko were at the Hôtel Plaza Athénée in Paris and wanted to get married, immediately. People believe that John's desire to get married so soon after Paul's marriage was a knee-jerk reaction. Perhaps it was psychologically about breaking up with Paul. When things were at their worst between them, John once said to Paul, "I want a divorce from you like I got from Cynthia."

At the time, many felt that Yoko Ono was a surprising and difficult addition to the Beatles' retinue. She was seven years older than John, a small, seemingly fragile yet persistent person, and more than a little kooky. "You know, we didn't like Yoko at first," Paul said in his interview. "People did call her ugly and stuff, and that must be hard for someone who loves someone and is so passionately in love with them." In the inner circle of Liverpudlians, we thought of Cynthia as family, and Yoko's ascension as First Lady of the Lennons was jarring. John's pal Magic Alex asks in his transcripts, "Why her? John could have had the most beautiful or intelligent woman in the world—why this odd little Japanese lady?" The reason, many people believed, was that more than a trophy wife, a model or an actress, John needed a chum. His love affair with Paul McCartney was ending. According to Yoko's interview, her relationship with John was platonic for a long time.

When John called and asked me to arrange for his wedding to Yoko, they were insistent that I tell not a soul, no one, not even the other Beatles. I arranged their wedding with the stealth of an MI5 agent. It was quite a task to pull off for one of the most famous couples in the world.

They insisted they wanted to be married in Great Britain, but once they posted banns, it would be in the press. The solution was to find a place in Great Britain where John and Yoko could walk in the door and get married with no residency requirements. Charles Levinson, the London lawyer who handled John's divorce from Cynthia, advised me that John and Yoko could tie the knot posthaste in Gibraltar, off the coast of Spain yet part of the British Isles. I called John and told him he and Yoko could get married immediately in Gibraltar, near Spain. My phone call to relate this information became the genesis of the lyric to the song "The Ballad of John and Yoko": *Peter Brown called to say, / "You can make it okay, / You can get married in Gibraltar, near Spain."*

I flew to Gibraltar the following morning just before John and Yoko arrived in a private jet. Both were dressed in white, like two virgins. They were signaling a fresh start. The couple were married in a brief ceremony by Justice Cecil Joseph Wheeler, to whom I paid 4 pounds, 14 shillings. Yoko wore oversized dark sunglasses with a big hat, and John smoked cigarettes during the brief ceremony. They were casual and seemingly unemotional, as if it were an obligation more than a celebration, although they hugged and cooed on the plane going back to Paris, but that was nothing unusual.

The newlyweds then took off to Amsterdam, where they held their famous bed-in for peace, yet again making international headlines, and perhaps seeming a bit foolish. I went to Amsterdam for a couple of days to make sure they were okay and to see if there was anything I could do. There wasn't. They were happily in bed, the room filled with press from all over the world reporting on their every word. John and Yoko had things in the palms of their hands, just the way they wanted it.

Clearly there was trouble in paradise. Just for the record, Yoko did not break up the Beatles; the Beatles were already in irretrievable disarray from the time Brian died and they lost their ballast. Yoko's constant presence was John's way of pouring salt on the wound. On December

31, 1970, the day Paul formally sued the other three to dissolve the partnership of Beatles Ltd., I handed in my resignation. It was a bittersweet goodbye. "I understood perfectly why you were leaving," Ringo said to me in his interview. "You said, 'There's no more I can do.' You didn't want to be a nursemaid anymore, and half the time the babies wouldn't listen to you anyway."

In February of 1971, I moved to New York City, where I became CEO of the Robert Stigwood Organisation in America. I oversaw all the company's divisions and artists' interest in the United States, including Andrew Lloyd Weber, Tim Rice, Eric Clapton, the Bee Gees, as well as theatrical projects like *Jesus Christ Superstar* and the movie *Saturday Night Fever*. John and Yoko moved to New York six months later, on August 13, 1971. John never went back to England. When he and Yoko first arrived, they rented a basement apartment in a town house in Greenwich Village, a relatively bohemian part of the city. But town houses in the Village are claustrophobic, without much more sunlight than living in a row house in Liverpool. I invited John and Yoko to lunch at my apartment on Central Park West, and when lunch was over, John went to the living room and stood gazing out of the tall windows of my apartment that overlooked Central Park, one of the most coveted views in the city. It was October, and the park was in its autumnal phase of deep reds and yellows—and in November, the Thanksgiving Day Parade goes by right under your nose. "This is so beautiful!" John said. "This is where I want to live."

When John left that day, he asked my doorman if there were any available apartments in the building. When there weren't, John went to the building next door, the Dakota, to ask the doorman if there were any apartments available there. Eventually, John and Yoko bought an apartment in the Dakota; then they bought the apartment next door, plus two smaller apartments on the eighth floor for their staff. Finally, Yoko bought an apartment on the ground floor for her office. The ceiling was blue painted with puffy white clouds. It was a pleasure having them for neighbors and running into them on the street.

A very short time after John was killed, Yoko asked me to meet her at the Tavern on the Green restaurant in Central Park. She didn't touch her food, or the tea she'd ordered. Her major worry was Sean. She said, "I don't know if I have natural maternal instincts." She'd failed with her daughter, Kyoko, and she feared she would fail with Sean too. She said that John had always looked after Sean, while she tended to business, and how could she ever be as good a mother to Sean as John was?

I felt terribly sad for her. "Just by telling me this proves you *do* have maternal instincts. You're full of love and caring, and I know you'll make a great mother." (Which she did.) I also said that I knew John sometimes bent the rules with Sean, and perhaps she shouldn't be so strict. One day in the park a year before, I had run into John and Sean eating ice cream cones. Ice cream was forbidden on their macrobiotic diets. John and Sean cheated by walking through the park all the way to Rumpelmayer's ice cream parlor on Central Park South so Yoko wouldn't catch them. When I told her that story, she smiled. "I will let him cheat too," she said.

I saw Yoko frequently over the years after John's death and enjoyed many dinners, but as time passed, she rarely went out. One day we were having tea at the Dakota, and I asked, "What ever happened to the present John commissioned Dalí to make for Ringo?" Yoko said she'd never heard of it. I explained that John was concerned because Ringo was feeling hurt and disrespected by the other three, and John wanted to give him something special for his birthday. He wanted to perhaps commission a work by an artist.

I made some inquiries and discovered that the artist Salvador Dalí was amenable to commissions, and that he was happy to make a gift for a Beatle. A few days later, I went to see Dalí at his home in Figueres. I explained that John wanted to give something special to Ringo because of their singular shared experience—four boys from nowhere to where they were today. I could see Dalí liked this idea and said he would think about it. I returned to New York, and a few weeks later, Dalí called to say that his "creation" was ready, and that I should come to Spain to pick it up. And not to forget his $5,000 fee, no checks, American dollars.

When Dalí presented me with the objet d'art he had made, I was a bit bewildered. It was like a coconut, or perhaps it *was* a coconut. He had cut it in half, and he lined it inside with some sort of natural sponge. Embedded in the sponge was a long curly black hair that he'd plucked from his mustache, he claimed, although I had my suspicions. When he added a few drops of water to the dry sponge, the hair unwound. I gave him $5,000 and took the coconut.

When I got back to London, I showed Dalí's creation to John and he was thrilled with it. He obviously had a penchant for surrealism. He loved Dalí's construction so much, he decided not to give it to Ringo and kept it for himself. He gave Ringo something else, I don't remember what. Yoko said she remembered once seeing something like a coconut, but alas, it was probably packed away in storage.

Just like Dalí's coconut, the invaluable transcripts in this book have been stored away in a bank vault for over forty years. They are a kaleidoscope of experiences and opinions. Yet everyone agrees on one thing: the story of the Beatles was meant to end when it did. "It was time for everybody," Ringo says in his transcript.

—*Peter Brown*
New York, 2023

Brian Epstein

This transcript is from a tape that was in the possession of Brian's American attorney Nat Weiss. It's a rare commentary recorded by Brian in 1966, the year of the Beatles' last tour. He has a beautiful, calm voice, his accent patrician without being stuffy.

BRIAN EPSTEIN: I don't think that you'll get any one of them or me to categorically state that they will never appear in public again. Not because of the financial aspect, but because it would be very difficult to progress from those sorts of tours. And in any case, this is my personal point of view, how creatively satisfactory for them are those tours, except in terms of finance. And they don't really think too much about that. They leave that to me anyway, but one understands it very well. So there's no reason why they shouldn't appear in public again, but I don't think that it will be in the concept that we've known previously. [Well, I think,] but one thing that, the thing that upset John most about that was that the interview, the initial interview, was done in his own home with Maureen Cleave, who we've known. We've known her in England, too, very well. We like her very much. We all like her very much. And you know, he said these things, and she was right to report them. But I think that what upset John more than anything else was that hundreds of people were hurt by that. And I think that John's a very sympathetic person. Incredibly sympathetic. And the last thing that he would want to do would be to hurt anybody's inner feelings, however much he may feel, feel sort of—but this is a basic thing with John not to go and hurt other people, not to go and smash other people out. Yes. And [Maureen Cleave] was upset herself. I could imagine. I mean, she was calling when I flew over here to see what, what was what, before they came, she was on the phone over a few seconds, saying, what could I do? And how can I have open songs, so forth?

But if the Beatles have taught me—and they've taught me many things—and one of the biggest hang-ups that I ever had personally was to categorize people, and they do not categorize people or things on music. You know, there, there's, there's nothing which has—there are some things which are trite and lousy, but one doesn't necessarily have to categorize them. I mean, the Monkees, who are enormous here, are enormous in England, good luck. Great. I think them, you know, I love their records and we met them in England and they're nice guys. So you don't categorize them as, as being, you know, when they first erupted in England, there was quite a lot of knocking in the press, which was, I suppose, to sort of say, well, here we are a great British people with our beautiful Beatles. Well, we are, you know, we do have our beautiful Beatles, but there's nothing the matter with the Monkees. And the Monkees are giving a great boost to the industry and the kids and everybody, and everyone's buying their records. And there's nothing the matter with that at all. No, I think.

Paul McCartney

Although the Beatles were nominally John's group, it was Paul who played the leading man. He was the backbone, a young man who wanted to succeed and continue to succeed. Whenever there was a pause, in conversation or in life, charming Paul would jump in. Boyishly handsome and effortlessly glamorous, he was the "cute" Beatle. He had beautiful hair, an adorable smile, and puppy dog eyes. He wanted to be considered cultured and erudite, not a working-class Scouse, something the media seemed to want to pin on the Beatles. His early life in London in the 1960s had all the trappings of a middle-class Englishman, not a rock star, including a relatively modest house in St. John's Wood, a classy but not showy neighborhood. He went to art exhibits, opening nights on the West End, and he befriended art dealers. He read. He had a sense of righteousness, justifiably in his business dealings. Although he was a true gentleman in the finest sense of the word, he was also quite a rake, and never lacking for female companionship, whether it was for a year or a few weeks, a day or an hour. The interview that follows is the last he gave before John was killed in December of 1980. There are candid revelations about the sense of loss of trust and friendship with John, his position on their business disputes, and his relationship with his now late wife, Linda.

PAUL McCARTNEY: Let's start.

STEVEN GAINES: Do you remember what your initial reaction to Brian Epstein was? Do you remember first meeting him?

PMcC: I just thought he was suave, sophisticated. You didn't get many people like that in Liverpool. He was classy.

SG: Were the guys put off by him at all?

PMcC: No, we liked that. We thought that was good for a manager. He looked like he'd make a great manager. We were impressed by his car, which was a Zodiac, which you could smell the richness just being in it. It was a big deal for us lads.

PETER BROWN: It's always been portrayed that the lads were really kind of urchins. But you weren't.

PMcC: I was thinking we were more working class. I think John was the nearest to [middle] class because his family at one time had owned something. And he had Aunt Harriet and Aunt Mimi. My father's family was old, from Everton,* a family of seven kids, and they were pretty poor. There were seven kids. So they were quite poor. But I never remember them saying they ever went without a meal or ever went hungry. Which probably means they might have once or twice. My family started off like that, and when my dad was fourteen, he became a cotton salesman. But the thing about my family, I think, that made it slightly not as working class as the others, was the aspirations of my mom, who was a nurse and always wanted us to talk nicely. I used to make fun of her, a fact that I regret to this day because she died when

---

* Everton was an inner-city neighborhood of Liverpool, generally considered to be the most deprived.

I was fourteen. And I know what she meant, but then being a little bit of a . . . My mom always especially wanted me to be a doctor.

Then George was sort of next, his dad was a bus driver. Mine was next, and I think John was sort of—but you're right, there was none of us from penniless families. You couldn't say that we were anything other than working class, except maybe me and John, but I'd say mine was on a lower level because it was a nurse and a cotton salesman. Brian Epstein drove a big car and his family owned stores. I mean, that was definitely the aristocracy.

SG: Were you aware that Brian was gay in the beginning?

PMcC: I think so. We used to hang out in nightclubs occasionally with him, and we realized it wasn't sort of our crowd. I remember not quite understanding the whole thing. Even if we knew, it wasn't something we ever talked about much, or we might have a little snicker about it as kids that age might do. We thought of Brian more as someone who would do us a lot of good. I was aware that, like, he was gay, and when you went round to his house there'd be boys rather than chicks. But Brian never made any kind of advance, which was like probably the big criteria— I suppose if he had, then we might have snickered more or whatever.

In Liverpool, people were wondering about John going on that Spanish holiday with Brian. And John kind of had a little covering of his tracks to do on that one because it was suspected quite widely that, "What was John doing?" And the other thing that was suspected, from us, was what was John doing manipulating this future manager of ours. Sucking up to him, going on holiday, becoming his special friend, so that when we all get managed by him, John will know him that little bit better than we do. We all suspected John of that. But that kind of blew over, and from that day to till Brian died, there was absolutely no kind of question of anything like that. And it was all just accepted, he knew that we knew. We never really talked to him about it at all. And it wasn't necessary then.

SG: You're portrayed as being the most demanding of Brian.

PMcC: I always was. I was inquisitive and ambitious. I realize now how ambitious I was. I did one or two things to [tease] ruin Brian, like I was saying before I mimicked my mom. One or two things that at the time, you think, well, it's the game, tough. This is the way we are, and if I think like that, you think like that. When my mom was saying I ruined it by making fun of her slightly higher-class accent that she was trying to put on us kids.

SG: What did you do to Brian?

PMcC: With Brian, I remember talking about [Allen] Klein—being in a lift in Hilly House, and saying, "We just heard that the Rolling Stones were getting sixpence royalty per record" or something like that, and we knew that we got four. We were bigger than them, and we didn't realize that they can give you a very artificially high royalty but take [everything else off you], which they probably did to the Stones. We didn't realize that. We just—anyone who got six was on a better deal than we were. I should think that Brian had taken care of other things with it and took a slightly lesser royalty. I'm sure his deal wasn't any worse or any better than the Stones. I remember saying to him in the lift, just between getting in the lift and getting out, "Well, you know the Stones . . ." That was one of the times that my ambitions sort of got the better of me. I was only trying to get us a better deal. But it ruined it a little bit there, I mean I'm sure not greatly, but he didn't like me too much after that for a week or two, you know, "Bastard. After all I've done for him, asking for twopence more, and implying I'm not as good as Klein, so you know, it was like you can have him."

SG: Do you remember the other incident? Was it the *Sgt. Pepper* cover, because he wrote about that?

PMcC: No, Brian didn't mind that. We were all sitting out at George's place and we played *Pepper* through, and Brian's remark was "Put it out in brown paper wrapper." That was his thing—he said because it's so good.

SG: Did you think that he was doing a good job, in the end? Did you realize that he was on too many pills?

PMcC: Well, you know, things echo . . . like when I started this business, one of the first things I said to everyone in this office was "Don't expect me to be in the office," and that was directly as a result of the situation with Brian. Because Brian was always evident in the office, and then he stopped being as evident and enjoying the luxury of success a little more, which made the office start to fuck up. Who's doing the watching up? It started to mess up a lot, and I remember people sort of sniding a bit, "Oh, Brian doesn't come in these days, we're lucky if he gets in here by two." Because it was beginning to happen more, which made me decide later that the first thing I would get straight with anyone I had working for me was "Don't expect me to be in" because I could see, if you set them up too much with a good deal . . . I think that's what Brian did. He set them up so perfectly, that when he wanted to go and enjoy his luxury—

SG: Is that what you thought he was doing, enjoying it? You weren't aware that he was incapacitated?

PMcC: Not really. He slurred a little bit, and that, but we were all— He was slurring from pills, and we— I've never been a big piller. Even in Hamburg, I remember them all saying to me, "What are you on?" 'Cause I was all [high-speed rambling]—"Nothing! It's great, though, isn't it?!" And I wasn't— Occasionally, I was up just because they were all up. They were all on pills, and I just didn't need to take anything.

So I wasn't particularly a pillie, Brian was doing that—I would be very laid-back on pot.

SG: Brian did feel towards the end that he was going to lose the group.

PMcC: Yeah, he was getting far out around acid, you know, because we were giving him all sorts of concepts—

SG: Do you think that's why?

PMcC: I thought, I thought, that he was—that we were asking possibly too much of him. I don't know.

SG: Do you resent the fact—I mean, looking back on it or when you realized—that he had written the 25 percent for him into the EMI contracts kind of surreptitiously, without letting you guys know?

PMcC: Well, I never knew the truth of that. I always used to say— One of the words that I've used ever since about Brian is that he was green—I never realized how green he was. To us, he was a sophisticated businessman, but ever since I've been in the London business scene and understood that when it becomes the norm, you realize that the sophisticated guy coming down isn't as sophisticated as you think he is. He was provincial, and so certainly his deals were pretty provincial—you can see that now. I never blamed him for it. I thought, actually, that it was amazing that he even did so well.

PB: There certainly were things that worried us, like the accountants got more out of *Hard Day's Night* than we did.

PMcC: We took a fee for *Hard Day's Night*, and the accountants were on a percentage. We caught that one. I don't understand—I could never quite work that out. But we always used to fall asleep at those sorts of meetings.

SG: But after he died, it turned out that even though he was dead and NEMS [Brian's management firm] didn't exist, that somebody was going to be getting 25 percent of you.

PMcC: That whole NEMS thing. That was sort of tough to find out all that stuff, but it may have just been naïveté. I never really put it down to him trying to screw us. Actually, if I think of it seriously now, I would pretty much say it was probably family business advice.

SG: I think that he was afraid that somehow, after you stopped touring, he was going to lose you, and that's why he had it written into the record contracts.

PMcC: But Brian was quite often trying to sell us, which was another thing that used to offend us mightily, because I remember one time, when we'd been touring, I think 364 days of the year, I know it was a pressurized period for us, because I remember once he came to *Thank Your Lucky Stars*, which was a record show that we used to do, and we were trying to tell him, "Look, we're really pressured, ya know? You've got us working too hard." I remember somewhere about that time he dropped the idea that he wanted to sell us to Lew Grade.* We were just appalled because it had been a much more personal thing, it hadn't been a business for us.

And we were like—well, it was some business thing, he was being given some kind of shove from somewhere, and we were gonna be sold to Lew Grade. And we said, "If you sell us to Lew Grade, the first and all the records that we will make from now on will be out-of-tune

---

* A famed British media impresario.

versions of 'God Save the Queen.' That's all we're gonna record from now on. You can sell us, but he's gonna get a bag of worms, Grade. You try to sell us, and that's all we're ever gonna do. We're just gonna lay down." And then he did it once again with Stigwood.

SG: With Robert Stigwood, were you guys aware that he had made an offer to buy NEMS for 51 percent?

PMcC: We could smell something was going on, it was obvious—again, we just dug our heels and said, "No, man. There's no point, we just don't want to be sold like cattle."

There were meetings with Stigwood before Brian died. It was put to us, "How do you like this man? Looks nice, doesn't he? How would you like him as your manager?" We were kind of saying, "Why don't you just continue?" and Brian said, "You know, there were all sorts of, well, business pressures, you know . . ." We said, "Get rid of some of your other acts or something," because that was another thing that I was always surprised at, was the fact that, it came down to his style, the fact that, like, he had a stable [of acts]. Which is, I suppose was, the way to do it in those days. But we always thought the Beatles was enough. Why do you want Billy J. Kramer, Cilla Black, Gerry and the Pacemakers, Tommy Quickly? You know, it was getting down the list there. We always just figured, well, you know it's all a headache. Get rid of all that, and just look after us or something.

SG: Do you think he killed himself, or was it accidental?

PMcC: I wouldn't know. He went out to the country, came back, didn't want companionship—came back up to town to try and—got pissed and—we understood it was barbiturates and booze. Well, I mean that was the stories, I don't know, that's what I got out of it all—obviously, there's going to be more sort of personal details.

Brian set up a ten-year contract, which we never realized. We signed just millions and millions and millions of documents. I remember Neil [Aspinall] coming round with it all, and all I asked him, "Is this all right to sign?" and Neil said, "Yeah." So, I signed them all. It turned out later, there was a ten-year Beatles contract amongst all those documents. In setting up the company, they thought they had to have some goodwill from these lads, so they tied us together for ten years. Apparently, the story I have it figured out, well, I'm real hazy about the sixties, you know, because it's just—

SG: Klein showed up on the scene, he got in touch with—

PMcC: Derek Taylor. He got in touch with Derek, I remember. Derek put him in touch with John and Yoko. He went around to see John and Yoko, talked them into it all evening, and John sent out a letter the next morning, to all the top businesspeople, "To whomever it may concern, my affairs are now in the hands of Allen Klein."

SG: Didn't John discuss it with you first?

PMcC: He said, "I'm going with Klein, what do you want to do about it?" and I kind of said, "I don't think I will, that's my roll." Then George and Ringo said, yeah, we'll go with John. Which was their roll. But that was pretty much how it always ended up, the three of them wanted to do stuff, and I was always the fly in the ointment, I was always the one dragging his heels. John used to accuse me of stalling. In fact, there was one classic little meeting when we were recording *Abbey Road*. It was a Friday evening session, and I was sitting there, and I'd heard a rumor from Neil or someone that there was something funny going around. So we got to the session, and Klein came in. To me, he was like a sort of demon that would always haunt my dreams. He got to me. Really, it was like I'd been dreaming of him as a dentist. He came round to the session, and he said, "I gotta have this thing signed, I gotta get you guys on a contract," and then so I said, "Wait a minute, c'mon, it's Friday night, what's the hurry? Give us the thing over the weekend, and we'll let ya know Monday?" Fair enough?

And everyone said, "Uh-huh, there he goes."

I said, "What do you mean, 'There he goes'? There is no one on the line over the weekend. It's gotta get checked out and deal with any rewrites and we're not in a hurry to go with this guy, so let's check it out."

John said, "Oh, fucking hell, here you go, stalling again."

I said, "I'm not stalling, I want it checked out. It's a big movement, going with a new manager, you know, and maybe we don't want to go with this guy. What's the hurry? Why can't he wait?"

"Oh, he's getting a plane tonight, and he's got a board meeting tomorrow morning." Saturday morning, right? Board meeting. Klein was the board, the table, and the legs. There wasn't anybody he had to go and check with. Which I sussed. I mean he's the ball game, Klein, so there can't be anybody he's got to check with. So I stuck my heels in, plus my bloody lawyer at the time was bloody Jewish, and he was after great bread on a Friday night, and he wouldn't deal. Anyway, so at this meeting, everyone said, "You're going to stall forever now, we know you, you don't even want to do it on Monday, you're going to stall on Monday, and that's for two more days." And I said, "Well, so what? It's not a big deal, it's our prerogative and it could wait a few more days." They said, "Oh no, typical of you, all that stalling and what. Got to do it now." I said, "Well, I'm not going to. I demand at least the weekend. I'll look at it, and on Monday. This is supposed to be a recording session, after all." I dug me heels in, and they said, right, well, we're going to vote it. I said, "No, you'll never get Ringo to."

I looked at Ringo, and he kind of gave me this sick look like, Yeah, I'm going with them. Then I said, "Well, this is like bloody Julius Caesar, and I'm being stabbed in the back!" It's the first time you realize in our whole relationship that whenever we voted, we never actually had come to that point before—three were going to vote one down.

That was the first time, and they all signed it, they didn't need my signature. So that was the first time I was sort of outvoted, and Klein went back to this supposed meeting. He didn't—he went home and he only went into the office on Monday morning. So it was fake. Which, I pretty much knew it was fake. But the others were just so keen, particularly John. I always had the impression that Klein had got them to go with him because he was the only one who was ever sympathetic to Yoko. Klein saw the Yoko connection and told Yoko that he would do a lot for her. Give Yoko a lot. And that was basically what John and Yoko wanted, recognition for Yoko. We found her sitting on our amps, and like a football team, an all-male thing, you really don't like to see a chick in the middle of the team. It's a disturbing thing, they think it throws them off the game or whatever it was, and these were the reasons that I thought, Well, this is crazy, we're gonna have Yoko in the group next.

SG: She was giving you advice in the studio?

PMcC: Well, she was definitely turning up. Looking at it now, I feel a bit sorry for her because, if only I had been able to understand what the situation was and think, wait a minute, here's a girl who's not had enough attention. I can now not make this into a major crisis and just sort of say, "Sure, what harm is she doing on the amps?" I know they would have really loved me. You know, we didn't like Yoko at first, and people did call her ugly and stuff, and that must be hard for someone who loves someone and is so passionately in love with them, but I still can't—I'm still trying to see his point of view. What was the point of all that?

SG: Were the other Beatles anti-Linda?

PMcC: Uh, yeah. I should think so. Like we were anti-Yoko. But you know John and Yoko, you can see it now, the way to get their friendship is to do everything the way they require it. To do anything else is how to not get their friendship. This is still how it is with John and Yoko. I know that if I absolutely lie down on the ground and just do everything like they say and laugh at all their jokes and don't expect my jokes to ever get laughed at, and don't expect any of my opinions ever to carry any weight *whatsoever*, if I'm willing to do all that, then we can be friends. But if I have an opinion that differs from theirs, then I'm a sort of an enemy. And naturally, paint myself a villain with a big mustache on, because to the ends of the earth, that's how they both see me. I feel like there's a lot of that—I mean, John said that business about where I turned up at his flat—that's the same thing, he's quite right, perfectly within his rights to do that, but it's just not done. I'm the kind of person that does turn up. I don't really mean— I like surprising people. I quite like doing that anyway. John got into his New York way of living, where you don't do that in New York. You always call, and I just didn't realize all that. And three or four times, I called up, talked to doorman, "Hello, it's Paul," give him a ring. I got in, whereas John actually turned away the Stones one night—the Stones weren't allowed in, they'd done the same thing, the Stones, and they got told they weren't allowed in.

SG: The major bone of contention was what?

PMcC: I think it was just that we were growing apart.

PB: You weren't writing together anymore either.

PMcC: We were hardly writing together. If we wrote together, it'd be two words here and just shuffling a few passages together.

SG: I read somewhere that John was angry because the Eastmans had advised you to buy more of Northern Songs, Ltd., stock, and you had done that without telling him.

PMcC: No, it had nothing to do with the Eastmans. The whole Northern Songs thing was always that John and I had always said to each other, if you're ever going to buy shares and stuff, you ought to always [invest in] something that you've really got total trust in, so you're not buying a pig in a poke. We always said the best shares to buy would be Northern Songs, because we believe in ourselves. So that was always our thing, and John and I until then never bought individually, but of course, we were always at liberty. I was always at liberty to go out and buy three shares if I wanted. No one could tell me no. What happened was that we were given the original issue—he was given, I was given—and I'd never actually bothered to add to my stock.

We'd always talked about it being a good share to buy and all that, and I remember one day I thought, someone must have been talking about investments, one of the accountants, because I was there, and instead of [investing in a] brush factory or something silly, like Ringo [invested] in Ricky Building—he got a mate out of the Ad Lib who was a builder, and he put money into that. I always thought that was wrong, and I thought, No, no, wait a minute. I've read [about] too many people in the music world [spending their money foolishly], and I thought that you had to be cautious and careful. I'd always been brought up to be that. My dad was canny with all that stuff, you know, never to be a borrower, he was all that stuff. My dad was always on to them, tolerance for other people's point of view, my dad would really drill them into [me]. So I was very careful about this, I'd just been brought up to naturally be quite careful.

One day, I thought, I need to spend a bit of money on something, invest in something, why don't I buy some of our [Northern] song shares? It didn't occur to me to ring up John and say, "Hey, old buddy, I would advise you to buy up some of our song shares. How about it?" Because I didn't think it was any of his affair anyway. But I didn't want it to get out, because you know, having read my papers, I thought, Well, if I'm buying shares, it'll do something to the stock market. They'll go down or something. Thought that was a bit funny. So I rang Peter, and I said, would you just buy me a few shares? Just you on your own there. Quietly.

The funny thing is, when Apple [started], everything was laid out on the table, it's like a Monopoly game. We saw who had what. I suddenly had more Northern Song shares than anybody, and it was like, oops, sorry. John was like, "You bastard, you've been buying behind my back." John saw everything like a Harold Robbins movie, you know, which it was. He's not incorrect. I couldn't get over the fact that we were really involved in all this. I think to this day, he'll not understand. I don't think he would accept right now, my naïveté in it. I think he still suspects me of trying to take over Apple. He still suspects that when I offered the Eastmans as [managers] instead of Allen Klein, he naturally assumed that I would be taken care of better than the others, and that the Eastmans could never be moral enough to be equal in their judgment and do the Beatles' thing rather than Paul's thing. I think they still suspect to this day.

They're very suspicious people [John and Yoko], and one of the things that hurt me out of the whole affair, was that we'd come all that way together, and out of either a fault in my character, or out of lack of understanding in their character, I'd still never managed to impress upon them that I wasn't trying to screw them. I don't think that I have to this day.

Once, I rang up Lee Eastman and I said, "Where's the Apple [lawsuits and negotiations] up to?" Like I might call today—because it's still going on. Exactly as complicated as it ever was. If I rang up today and said, "Where's the Apple thing up to?" and he would say that the problem is John's got this sort of—he can't do it, you three can't do the deal if John can't do it. He would want indemnity against any sort of bad things that occurred because of taxes. If he got nicked for tax, he doesn't want to be left holding the baby, so he wants you three to give him some kind of indemnity. Up until this time, he had had a million pounds cleared, [personal] debts that John was just doing all through Apple. We had just swallowed up the debt in the company, George,

Ringo, and I. Sure, we don't mind—if it has to be. But that was a million, and none of us had ever had a million cleared in debts.

I still don't want to screw him. I still do feel for the guy. I really like the guy, even though what I've gone through. I still see that he thinks he's the one who was hurt. I spoke to the Eastmans. I said, "If we all think he's not going to have a tax consequence, let's give [the indemnity] to him." 'Cause, you know, if all sides are that smart, let's all offer it. Break the deadlock.

I went to New York, feeling like the bringer of good news. I rang him up. "Hello, John, how are you? Hello, how's the kids? Oh, great. What's all this about publishing? Yeah, great"—laugh laugh laugh—"What about Apple?" Tense. You know, that was the unfortunate thing in the last ten years. The moment you mention the word Apple, all of us go, eeeeep! Dread and horror and shock goes through all our systems. I said, "Look, as I understand it, you need this indemnity."

John said, "Fucking indemnity. Fucking this, fucking that. You don't need to give me fucking indemnity, you fucking—" I think we ended up just sort of swearing at each other. I said, "Fuck you, ya big cunt," 'cause I just couldn't handle it. I couldn't be sweet and reasonable anymore. I was shaking for an hour after that.

Of course, the funniest thing was, I then meant to ring John Eastman and say to him, "No, no, it's not gonna work, this whole thing. I tried to do the indemnity, it's not gonna work." Of course, I got the phone numbers wrong. I rang John Lennon back instead. [When the phone was answered, I said,] "Hello, John? Yeah, listen, I just—oh—yeah well . . ."

But it was Yoko this time, and then I said, "Look, I didn't mean for it to get like that—but, shit, you know, it seems to have got . . ." The funny thing was, they knew I was trying to ring John Eastman immediately after, so that would have reinforced their little feelings about me—double-dealing. I've hardly talked to him since. I rang last Christmas, and I was smart enough not to mention Apple. We had a pleasant conversation. I was allowed to talk to his son, which was lovely. His son seemed very nice. And that was now the new formula for life, for the Beatles—to this day, I've not mentioned that word to them. If I talk to Ringo, we just don't talk about it.

The point I was trying to illustrate is that it wasn't so much John being a bastard as it was his being suspicious towards me, always being suspicious towards me. There was Northern Song shares. And I swear on any holy book you want, I know he won't believe it, but I know for sure that I didn't buy them with the view to— If I was really trying to do it, I could have bought an awful lot more. So it does hurt a little bit that there's someone who still thinks, like, I'm out to get them, or that I always was. That's one of the nice things about it— It's a pity [I never said to John, "Fuck off, I'm not trying to do it"—and never was]. But he knows I was kind of— We were behind the scenes, and we did a few little [things] that we had to do, and our ambitions, and it was never a kind of terrifying skeletons in the closet. It was always just normal—but, uh, they . . .

SG: They effectively blocked the release of *McCartney*, your first solo album?

PMcC: It came out that [the album] *Let It Be* was to be released. And I had been promised a release date. Things round about that time were so petty that they had a meeting and said, No, no, no, we'll hold Paul's and put *Let It Be* out. Then Paul can have June 26 or something. I was all geared to go. It was a little do-it-yourself operation: McCartney One. We'd done it all at home, we printed the role list, we had everything ready—in fact, we'd sent out all the envelopes [ourselves]. We didn't let anyone at Apple know what was going on, not out of spite or anything, more to create an exciting event—Linda and I worked it all out. We'd do all this. [Peter Asher] gave us a questionnaire, we filled it all in, like I've done with this Japanese jail bit [a self Q&A that Paul wrote for his book about being arrested for possession of marijuana in Japan], we had all of that done, so I was naturally all geared into this release date.

I thought they were just trying to do me in, and it became this thing. I said, no, I was there first, why should you be able to just change my release date and arbitrarily put yours in? No, I got it first.

I definitely planned all of mine with Neil and said we'll do it January 3 or whatever it was, and then they suddenly, they had a meeting about *Let It Be* and said, let's get it out and that I was in the way. So they voted me out again, they just swept me aside, and Ringo came to my house, and Ringo was the poor fucker just in the middle of it all. I doubt he meant to do anything, I think they sent him round just as a sort of scapegoat, and he didn't realize what he was telling me, really.

SG: What did you do?

PMcC: I just got annoyed with him. I'm not the beatdown type, but we shouted at each other, and the final sort of thing then was, "Get out!" I remember he was the only person I've ever told to get out of me house. That was the worst moment with Ringo, and I felt sorry for him because it really brought him down, you know.

I mean, it's only later you realize all of this is just really drama, you know. At the time, it was a clear-cut case of—they would again—just trying to do me in like they were trying to do me in with Klein, they were trying to do me in with— You know, they were just saying, it's only money, man. To me, it was like the only money I'd ever earned was all in Apple, all our Beatle success, it was all there. Also, it was a period of madness, as we talk about the *I Ching* and all that. And money was rather a dirty subject—it was Monopoly. John referred to it as "Monopoly money" and all that. But I was aware that this was it, this was my— And if that went down the drain, then everything I'd ever sort of meant, your capital to do anything else with or whatever, this was all the money I'd ever earned.

I suddenly started fighting for it, saying to Klein, "Wait a minute, have you paid the taxes?" Asking all sorts of questions which were most annoying to him. But the nice thing is, I feel very vindicated because on the Klein scene, you've got some gorgeous little things. Like we're sitting down and we're doing a good deal with Klein, always on the back of some envelope or something, and Klein will have 20 percent. I said 15 percent. For fuck's sake, it's a big act, man, it's the Beatles, it's a big group, you know. If he gets 3 percent of the Beatles, he's lucky! He wants 20 percent. And they think I'm trying to deal for me rather than the group. So Klein comes back, smiles as ever, and said 20 percent just on any increases I get. If I do a new deal with Capitol, and I make the royalty from thirty cents to fifty, that extra twenty, I'll get the 20 percent. Okay, I went for that bit. But when it came to court, and all the documents came in, this was a case that I really felt like it was touch and go, make or break. You know, I had to absolutely get this case won. Whereas if Klein beat me, it was going to be the end for me, 'cause I couldn't figure out how there could be any justice left if somebody like that won. I think that was a real mind-bender for me. I was growing this beard and going pretty crazy. I think we had to come back. Linda and I were in L.A., and our lawyers rang up, "We're having a meeting on Monday, can you come back?" Yeah, and we came back, whereas the others wouldn't. Klein was like, "Can you come in?" [The others were,] "Fuck off, you do it." So, we came back, Linda and I, flew back to London.

SG: This is the dissolution of the partnership, what you're talking about? The seventies one?

PMcC: Yeah, the big case. The funny thing was, when we actually got all their evidence—and theirs was very badly planned, and ours was really well looked into—we got all the best people. They got not-quite-so-good people, and they hadn't had time to sort of suss it out. Of course, in amongst our guys poring over it for weeks, trying to find the tiniest loophole, we found a check from Capitol where he had taken 20 percent on the whole thing, like $7 million had come in, and he'd taken 20 percent off that. And in fact, he should have taken it only on $2 million, his increase. He hadn't taken it on the increase, he'd taken it on the whole thing. Later, he offered—one of Klein's other classic tricks—he offered George to set up his own American publishing company for him. At the time, George didn't have an American song publishing company, and Klein offered to set one up for George. He ran around and set up Harry's Songs, Inc., New York [Harrisongs Music, Ltd.], which, of course, Klein owned 20 percent of it. I was vindicated, whatever I did, I certainly never got near any of that—what else had I done? The only thing I've actually done on the pure commercial basis, I now publish "P.S. I Love You" and "Love Me Do." [These first two songs were owned by EMI Music Publishing and up for sale. Paul bought them without telling the others.] Which is fine, it's quite allowed. And that's the nearest I'd come to . . . if I had been trying to screw people. Now the way things are, I could really get in there. But the way I see it, I never did. I know that, you know that, it's just that Klein and John really didn't. Yoko, I'm not sure that she still—

PB: The thing is, when John appointed Klein to be his manager, he knew exactly what he was doing. He knew Klein's reputation. Mick told him, "He really did screw me."

PMcC: And we said, let's get Mick around here, at Lady Hamilton's place, give Mick a ring.* "Hey, Mick, do you mind coming round?" He came round. We sat at that big, huge table in that huge room. Lady Hamilton's house. "We know you've been with him, what's the word, what's the score on Klein?" And he gave a kind of "Well, he's all right if you like that kind of thing. Depends on what you want." It was a lot of rather noncommittal answers, which led us to believe he's not bad. I just don't think Mick wanted to say, "He's a bastard." He didn't want

---

* Lady Emma Hamilton, the mistress of Admiral Horatio Nelson, once lived at 3 Savile Row.

to come out with it. Mick gave a very sort of noncommittal thing, he kind of said, "Well, you know . . ."

SG: [Mick] sued Klein eventually.

PMcC: But at the time, I don't know quite why, I suppose we put Mick right on the spot, "What do you think of him?" And he seemed to me, anyway, to give a noncommittal answer. "Well he's all right, if you want—"

PB: At the time, Klein was in the building as well.

PMcC: Ah. Well, that would color things. But [the conclusion] was a kind of, not bad, not bad, it wasn't a definite no, and it wasn't a definite yes. It was what Klein later called "a definite maybe."

SG: When you first moved to London, things kind of exploded, the way you guys became famous. You also became the leaders of a social circle of Swinging London. You had power. Were you aware of what was happening around you? Did you encourage that?

PMcC: We were just ambitious kids. You know what sums it up is John's own chant that he used to do. John would say to us—it was a joke, most of everything we did was pretty much a send-up—John would say "Where are we going, fellas?" and the three of us would echo, "To the top, Johnny." We always used to do that; it was like a little morale booster. It was just a pisser, just a take-off. "Where are we going, fellas?" "To the top, Johnny." It was like a footballer chant or something. That kind of sums it up. That's sort of what it was, you know, that's what we were trying to do all the time, get to the top. And now it's this model I've heard called "You oughta be careful what you dream, you just might get it." And that's us, we did. We weren't too careful what we dreamed, and we got it. Although, I've not got too many complaints. But I mean, it certainly came true. We believed in it, in ourselves so much, we knew the time was right, we knew we had a bit of showbiz training—we had a bit of time on the boards, you see, in Hamburg—which gave us an extra little bit of confidence. We'd always heard, like, people saying, "Oh, you young people use microphones, they didn't use microphones in my day you know, we had much more training than you on the music halls and the boards." So I remember we'd done Hamburg for a year or so, worked all these— We used to work eight hours a day in Hamburg. Which was a long time to be singing and playing, you know. So after we'd done it, put in our stint there, we pretty much knew that we had a little bit better grounding than most of the groups going around. We were really— We'd worked our way up from nothing to the guy saying, "Next show, next show." And we'd started to make a little show and were getting to know the hang of it. We pulled all that crowd in, moved to a bigger club, pulled that crowd in, moved to the Cavern, pulled that crowd in—everywhere we went, we got maximum capacity. So we were pretty comfortable.

SG: What about the American tours, did they shell-shock you?

PMcC: I think no—for me, it was almost all expected. We knew we were good. We had one or two worrying moments, which now just seem absolutely ludicrous. One time, we were worried that Gerry and the Pacemakers were going to be "the ones" to do it. In fact, John and I bought a lot of *Mersey Beat*s when there. Figured, well, we're allowed to. Because we wanted badly to win that poll. We felt it was, like, that would make the difference, whichever group "made it." But looking back on it, there was no way Gerry was ever going to be better than the Beatles, or bigger than us. He was always a little bit—he was one of our contemporaries—he was always just in the literary direction as John Lennon—or this whatever sort of ballad-y direction from me. We were always just a tiny step ahead of Gerry. Although he was the biggest competition, and the other big competition was Dave Clark Five. There were only the two moments I remember in the whole career where we just thought we might not make it. Those were the only two doubts ever for me, and I think even those doubts we knew we'd overcome.

SG: The story that I heard most often was that the last year you were on tour, the big American tour, because of John's Jesus statement and the Manila incident, touring was just too hideous in America—you threw up backstage because of a canceled concert when it was raining in Memphis or something.

PMcC: The only thing I remember about finishing touring was that it had been sort of said—but I thought it was too sacrilegious, too blasphemous to say—that the Beatles [would quit touring]. It just seemed like such a shock to me. I could almost see the headlines in the *Daily Mirror*, "Beatles Quit Touring." I couldn't really handle it, so if anybody talked about it, I never really would get into it or encourage it. And then there was one place where we played, I seem to think it was in Indianapolis, but I have no idea. We played under cover, and it was raining, it was in a big park, big baseball stadium, and we were just under cover, we worried that our amps were going to electrocute us, and it was the worst show ever. We all thought that no one had turned up, and apparently, they had sold out tickets, but by our standards it didn't look too good. A few people hadn't come, because of the rain or whatever, and I remember getting off the stage and getting into the back of a big meat wagon, big metal lines truck. We used to get into the back of these things, nothing in there but just metal, and we used to slide around with nothing to hold on to. And I remember John and George just bursting, saying, "Fuck this, we're not touring again," and I remember that was the first time I really agreed with them. I said, "Yeah, you're right."

SG: Were you serious?

PMcC: Yeah. I mean I think—

SG: The Cow Palace, '66?

PMcC: Somebody tells me that was the last one, yeah. I never thought, This is our last gig—definitely never. You just kind of feel it, and then you mainly try to hide it from people, because people would say, "Why haven't the Beatles toured for a while?" [I'd say,] "Well, we're just recording, that's what we're into now." Never once did we actually say, "Yeah, we've quit touring because it seemed too final, seemed a bit too—"

SG: Rock and roll bands had a reputation for being bad on the road, like tying groupies to bedposts and fucking them with a fish. But you guys were supposed to be celibate.

PMcC: You *are* kidding. No, not in the least bit celibate, we just didn't do with fish. That's all. I mean, tie 'em to the bed, we didn't feel the need to. There were many, many, many, many wild oats sewn from the word *go* to the word *finish*.

SG: How come I never met a girl in America who said, "I had a great time with the Beatles"?

PMcC: Well, I'm glad you didn't. I did. I met one when I was married. It was in CVS, in New York, and she was with John Hammond, blues player, gorgeous-looking blonde, kind of came in, "Hello, Paul," and it's like, "Hey, hey, met the wife? This is um . . . Tracy?" She said, "Don't you remember, you were such a great lay in L.A.?" Well, I did tell you. I had to tell her obviously. I was, we were all very much after the chicks all the time.

SG: But you couldn't walk out the door. You'd stick your head out—

PMcC: You could have it brought and things like that. British tours, we used to have a little routine we worked out with the tour managers. That, if there was someone getting particularly hot on the front row that you liked the look of, you know there'd be someone there with a little angora sweater on looking rather good—and that would be it. He'd go, "Do you wanna go backstage and see the boys?" and it'd be that kind of thing, and then they would come backstage to meet us, and then obviously then it was just social life.

SG: But on the American tours, where there were hundreds—

PMcC: American tours, no. L.A., for instance, it was a classic—the management people would arrange parties with lots of girls. And if ever we had dancers on our tours, that was the reason. Sometimes there were dancers on tours, and that was all atmosphere. We liked some nice dancers. They'd come out and do some quick kicks, and that was it. But then they were around for the tour, you know there was a lot of that. But it was pretty much red-blooded-youth type stuff. There was quite a lot of it. A fact for which I'm now quite glad, really. Because I don't anymore. Which is quite handy, because it's so bloody—I can't handle the pace, or the intrigue. I couldn't handle all that now, I couldn't handle someone turning up. I've pretty much had a fine time. I remember my dad saying to me once, he was rather envious of me. Because in his day, the big scare had been VD. We were no different from anyone else, except we could pause. It got to be a mighty fine line. But it was great fun. I had a great time.

SG: When did you first settle down, when you first wrote "Girlfriend," if I remember, in fan magazines—Marianne Faithfull's nanny.

PMcC: No, there wasn't—you're reading the wrong info here. Maggie— she was just a lady. Actually, I think of them pretty much all like that. They're very nice and I don't wish to be sexist here, but I must admit,

I was out— A fact which now, having teenage daughters, nervous, coming up—and, Christ, I'm the worst father now, because I know what I was after at fifteen or sixteen, and sixteen wasn't marriage. So that's what we were doing, we were just doing that.

SG: Except for Jane. Jane was a serious—

PMcC: No, I had a girlfriend while I was in Hamburg named Dot, Dorothy Roam, who was my first steady girlfriend, or serious and almost getting married— What are you laughing at? Ha ha.

PB: Really? Were you that serious?

PMcC: Yeah. It was actually sort of a big time in my life because I remember feeling very mature because I was going to leave all these rock and roll boys, all these young boys in leather jackets, and I was about to become a husband. And I did get a great sort of dignity from this. I used to sit around like I was older than everyone because I acted seriously. But it all didn't happen. But she was my sort of first girlfriend, and she eventually got married to a German in Canada. Seemed very nice.

SG: When did you meet Jane?

PMcC: And then Jane Asher was my second. And then, basically, Linda was my third. I've really only had three that-serious relationships.

SG: Jane was emceeing a TV show?

PMcC: Jane was sent by the BBC to cover our concerts for the *Radio Times*, which is the— She was sitting back there, and we were told to go and have a photo for her for the *Radio Times*. We had to in the middle of a concert when Billy J. Kramer was on—I think it was the middle of the concert, can't imagine how we got away with it with all the fans—it may have been at the end of the show. I seem to remember in the middle of the concert, all of us ran in, took a photo of us with Jane Asher, and that was it. I think later I managed to get in a word, "Would you like to come get coffee?" It was absolute normal social practice, that was how you did it. And I sort of somehow managed to get her to a hotel for a coffee afterwards. And they were nice enough to persuade everyone to go out and leave us alone, amongst much sniggering and everything. And that was, you know, it wasn't a sex scene at all. It was sort of like a beginning of a long time of relationship with her, and we kind of just went steady, and then I moved in her house—which I can hardly believe now, but did. Various reasons, which is all right. Crazy but all all right. And then we were going to get married. Jane and I were going to get married.

SG: You announced the engagement. It was in all the media.

PB: Christmas Day.

PMcC: I suppose we both felt it had been going on so long that we either ought to get married or . . . And then I just realized I didn't want to marry her, and she realized she didn't want to marry me.

SG: In the book *Apple to the Core*, they talk about Francie Schwartz. I don't know if you remember.

PMcC: Oh, I remember her. How could I forget?

SG: Well, the story was that Jane came home from an American tour, and Francie was there.

PMcC: Yeah, she came home from something and Francie was there, yeah. But we weren't going together anyway, pretty much. I obviously hadn't called it off quite definitely enough. Yeah, Francie was there— you know, these things get very hazy for me. These things aren't—

PB: Well, moving along.

PMcC: I think we had called it off, I think Jane was maybe sort of—

SG: She wrote a memoir, Francie Schwartz.

PMcC: She did, yeah.

PB: She made a career out of those three weeks.

PMcC: Ah yeah, that was a sort of funny one. She was— Trouble with me is like . . . You know I'm not—

PB: I think what went on was remarkably scandalous for very little.

PMcC: With me, yeah. I'm not exactly that scandalous. There's not an awful lot.

SG: Peter remembers that he introduced you to Linda.

PMcC: She showed you photos.

PB: That's right, and I gave Paul film, right.

PMcC: She was over to photograph the [Animals], some pictures, various.

PB: I invited her to be one of ten photographers for the *Sgt. Pepper* launch at Brian's house, where all the Beatles would be present. For some reason or another, Linda and I just hit it off immediately.

PMcC: She's a hustler too. Our Linda's smart, she can get into places. She still has that. She got into the Rolling Stones thing by accepting the invitation that was actually to *Town & Country*. She was actually the receptionist, Linda. She knew what she wanted to do like we did, and she wanted to photograph the Beatles, and wanted to photograph the Stones, and the rest of *Town & Country* didn't know who the Stones were, but to her it was like, eeeeepppp! She was a receptionist and an invitation came from the Rolling Stones for some photographer from *Town & Country* to be there, and she actually slipped the invitation into her desk, said no more, sat on it for a little while, someone found it in her desk, "Oh, what's all this? Oh, okay, if you're that keen, you might as well go, then," and she got to be the only photographer on the boat, 'cause they all saw this chick. And they kicked everyone off [the boat], and she got the exclusive photos.

PB: The other thing was when she came back for her portfolio, I said, "Listen, I have to be honest with you, I took one out," because I loved Brian Jones, I was very fond of him. Linda said, "Is it the one with Brian?" I said it was and asked her if I could keep it.

PMcC: Amazing how it all works. You've seen the Brian Jones pictures . . . ?

PB: The thing is, one night we had come from Abbey Road Studios after a recording session, it was quite early, and you said to me, "Let's go somewhere to eat." We went to the Bag o' Nails, and she was at the Bag o' Nails.

PMcC: That was the first night I actually said "hold up," you know.

PB: So, about how long ago was that after the *Sgt. Pepper* meeting?

PMcC: I'm not really sure, but I know we did—we went down—she was with Chas Chandler and the Animals crowd. We went down, Mal, you, and I—

PB: No, it was just the two of us.

PMcC: Just you and me? We went down to the Bag, and we kinda just . . .

PB: Linda came over to me.

PMcC: And said hello you, and then went back to her sort of thing. I was kind of doing the looks and all that stuff, and then she passed [our table], and I said, "Do you want to come to another club? How about going to the Speak?" Yeah, all right, and so I pulled her around to the Speakeasy, and that was the start of our whole relationship.

PB: That's how I remembered it.

PMcC: Yup, Bag o' Nails, down at the Bag o' Nails.

SG: Did you feel like you were encouraging the drug revolution?

PMcC: No. You're sort of part of it, really.

SG: In one article, you admitted taking hallucinogens, and you said the reason you said it publicly was because you wanted to be honest when you were asked that question.

PMcC: The LSD thing? Oh yeah, absolutely—at the time, the whole sort of thing about acid, as anyone from then will remember, was that it was a sort of honest thing. You couldn't fail to be pretty honest on it. It was like the only thing you could handle was honesty. And so it was a very sort of— In fact, I think the word was almost coined rather back then. And I remember just somebody came round, and during some interviews, "Oh, well, have you ever taken LSD?" And I said, "Well, you know, I'm not kind of sure you want to hear the real answer to that. 'Cause, like, you know, if I tell you, I'm not sure how you'll feel about printing it, 'cause I feel like you might be doing worse by printing it." They said, well, you know, the press or anybody—so he said, "So have you?" and I kind of said, "Yeah, about four times" or whatever, and he asked me about it, and I pretty much told him what it was about. Don't know how I felt about it. And then later, people said, no, you shouldn't feel responsible, you should have said no then. But I felt, actually, I wasn't the one who spread it around. I was the person asked for the answer to a question. I gave the answer to the question. In fact, it was really their responsibility to print it or not. If they had felt it was going to encourage some kind of drug revolution, they could say, well, just lose that question from the article, we have plenty of other photos of his house, but you know the press and the scoop and a plot story— He was never going to kill that story, was he?

SG: Can you think of anything else, Paul? I think you've been terrific.

PMcC: Oh, thanks . . . I often find that I talk, and I feel totally free and fine, and I see something in print, and I'd rather see than have somebody else see it. Particularly what I've said about John. There was a recent interview in *Newsweek*, where the chicks doing it took one of my quotes and slightly led it on—"Is it true what Paul said about that you've done everything except be yourself?" Which wasn't what I said at all. I said, "John has never had a family. He had a family, a son and a wife, and never got to see them. And now, I think he realizes that he's gotta look at it. And he's enjoying it, and he's totally got into a nice— That's why I think he's doing everything that he's doing." And of course, John's reply was like, "He doesn't know zilch about what I'm doing, man. He's just as curious as all the rest." And I just don't need— [tape ends abruptly]

Alistair Taylor

Alistair had an unusual position at NEMS, the Beatles' management company. "My official title was general manager," he said. "In fact, it would be closer to the truth to say administrator-troubleshooter. Brian once flattered me, telling someone that I could do the impossible in twenty-four hours but that miracles took me a bit longer." Alistair could not only make jet planes appear out of the sky or produce a work visa on a Sunday, but he was involved in some of the Beatles' more far-fetched ventures, like buying island getaways for them in Greece. Alistair grew up in Liverpool, where he was Brian Epstein's personal assistant in the record shop in Whitechapel, and he had the historic honor of accompanying Brian to the Cavern Club the first time he saw the Beatles on November 9, 1961. Not long after, Alistair relocated with his wife to London, where he became general manager of NEMS.

STEVEN GAINES: How well did you get to know the Beatles?

ALISTAIR TAYLOR: Astonishingly well. Obviously, looking back now, I sometimes wonder whether I knew them at all. Well, I mean, I never really thought of them as employers, to be honest. They employed me, but they were great friends. Particularly Paul, because Paul used to come home with me sometimes, and he'd ring me up and say, "Look, come on up to Cavendish Avenue, you know, I'm fed up." We went on holiday where I used to go up to the farm [in Scotland] with him and Jane in those days. And I went to holiday in Greece with them. I saw the beginnings of a real rift [between the Beatles]. There had always been the odd moment. I mean, we lost George now and again, didn't we? Not [just] stormed out, but he disappeared, said he was fed up with it. You know, he wasn't having anymore. He was fed up with being a goldfish in a bowl. I can remember two, at least two occasions when that happened. Pressure, really. I mean, bear in my mind, these boys couldn't even step out the door. Not being able to do your own shopping. I mean, the times I'd gone with them, they'd be lying on the bottom of a car and climbing over dustbins. Those things stick to my mind. Crazy, crazy.

SG: You mentioned that Paul used to come over when he got fed up with his house in St. John's Wood. Was this while he was living with Jane Asher?

AT: Yes, it was a nice walk from his place to mine. He'd often just walk home with me and come in and have coffee. Then for a while after the Jane scene, he was with [twenty-three-year-old] Francie Schwartz.* Everyone remembers Francie. She was the first one after Jane Asher of any permanence.

SG: She wasn't very permanent, though.

AT: No, she wasn't, but she was longer than the usual at that time. I never found out from that day to this why he broke up with Jane, and that's the gospel truth. I was away when it happened. To be honest,

---

* Alistair is mistaken. The gorgeous brunette Francie Schwartz didn't happen after Jane Asher; she happened during Jane Asher and ended her relationship with Paul. Francie Schwartz sold her story to *Rolling Stone* and later wrote a memoir called *Body Count*.

I adore Jane to this day. She's a super girl. It might sound strange, but I felt too close to both of them. It was just one of those things. Paul never talked about it, and I didn't feel that I could ask him why.

I have one favorite story, but I never told it before. Paul and I, and Jane, went up to the farm in Scotland. We flew up in a private plane. Paul was very weird, he sent Jane out back to look for something and said to me, "Can you get down to the chemist? I've got crabs. For Christ's sake, get me something. Jane mustn't know. Tell the chemist it's for you."

So I went, "Oh Christ." Jane came back in, and I thought, What the bloody hell do I do now? So I called a taxi. I went to town to see Bob Graham, our solicitor, who handled everything for us in Scotland. I said, "Bob, I've got—I've got a dose of VD."

"Christ," he said, and he just grinned. I said, "I must get something for it." So he said, "Leave it with me." He said, "Go and have a drink and come back in about half an hour." When I came back, he had this bottle of clear liquid. He said, "Here's the bill." It said: *For Sheep Dip, three pounds fifteen*. I just thought it was lovely, you know, the sheep dip.

Another time, Friday afternoon, Paul phones. On a Friday afternoon. We're in the studio, he rang me from Abbey Road, and he says, "Alistair, I want to go to the sun this weekend and come back Monday." So, I said, "Where do you want to go?" He said, "No idea, you choose. Get the jet. I want a private jet. Pick me up from Abbey Road, midnight tonight." This is three in the afternoon. This was after Jane. He said he'd found this bird who was a waitress in some bloody club down in Chelsea, and would I find her for him and tell her she was going on a private jet with Paul McCartney? He had a rough idea of where she lived. I knew the club and went there and asked, "Do you know her address?" And, I mean, she didn't know who the hell I was. I just said, "Right, I'll pick you up at, sort of ten o'clock tonight, in the car." You know, "Get yourself packed." I get the jet, find the girl, and we piled on the plane and flew off. Champagne, and magazines, and we landed in the Bahamas at about four in the morning. This private jet comes down in a two-bit airfield. All in the dark. There's a funny little customs man wiping sleep out of his eyes. While I went to look for Paul's car, we walked into what had obviously been the bar. It was all in darkness, a little cafeteria thing. About ten past four in the morning.

Suddenly the lights go on, and out walks this guy in an immaculate white jacket. "Would you like a drink?" Four o'clock in the morning, and they didn't know who was arriving. I thought, This is continental service. This is fantastic.

Paul said to me, "Oh, come back and pick us up." Of course, they got involved in the great crowd over there with Aga Khan, you know, he built this great holiday village, the other side of the island, and I gather they had a monumental time there.

SG: I don't understand how Paul could have bothered to pick up a waitress in Soho, though. With so many women after him . . .

AT: Another classic occasion, the one person that never, ever bothered me was Ritchie [Ringo]. He was always apologetic, and he never bothered me. I'd find he'd done something. And I used to say to him, "Look, why on earth didn't you ask me to fix that for you?" "Oh, no. I don't want to bother you." Anyway, he'd gone off to . . . Sardinia, on holiday. And I got a frantic phone call from him. And he said, "Look," he says, "it's bloody awful. You know, I've got to get out of here. I'm coming back home." He had Maureen, the nanny, and Zak. Bang to the luggage, and mother-in-law. He said, "Well, I'm booked out on a flight to Paris, but I can't get from Paris to London."

So I said, "Don't worry, I'll see you in Paris." I got on the phone to my people in the airport, and they said the jet was available. I rushed out to Luton Airport—no jet! It hadn't been put up on the service porter. I haven't got a plane, and Ringo and his family are landing in Paris. I got an old prop plane, finally took off. We landed in Orly about five minutes after his plane. I went tearing up this blasted corridor. No sign of Ritchie. Not a sign of anybody. So I tramped all around the lounges, the bars. No sign. I shot into the VIP lounge and got a couple of Air

France people, and I said, "Right, come on. We've got to find Ringo Starr, he's somewhere on this airport."

Well, you wouldn't credit you could lose Ringo, but we lost him for about two hours. We searched every bar, restaurant, VIP room, and we couldn't find him. I said, "This is ludicrous." You know, "If he was on the flight . . ." "Yes, he was on the flight." "And he landed?" "Yes, he landed." "He's not flown to London?" "No, he's not flown to London." And suddenly, I looked up and there's Maureen, walking through the lounge. And he was sitting, totally unnoticed, and we'd all walked past him. He'd been there for two hours, sitting, surrounded by luggage, and nobody took the slightest bit of notice of him. And he never forgave me for that. He never forgave me. I mean, we joked about it, but he used to say, "Oh yeah, great. The only time I ring you—" I was sick as a pig over it, because it was one of the rare occasions he ever asked me to do anything for him.

SG: Was George a very distant kind of person?

AT: Well, no. I mean, it's very strange. Whenever I was with George—I used to go out to George's now and again—it was always super. I always enjoyed it. We'd sit and philosophize, just sit by the pool if it was nice, and talk about mainly Indian and Eastern bits. Then I've had lots of fun times with John, and Mal Evans. Somebody once asked Mal, who was his favorite Beatle? And he thought for a minute, and he said, "The one I was last with." I thought it was a fabulous answer, it's what I wish I had thought of. But I was closest to Paul.

Queenie Epstein

"Before we begin, I want you to understand that Brian loved the truth," said his mother, Queenie Epstein. "Therefore, I want this to be the truth. So go ahead. Ask me what you want to know." To understand Brian Epstein, you first must appreciate the remarkable Queenie Epstein, a combination of Bette Davis and Golda Meir. Her first name, Queenie, was the English translation of her name in Yiddish, Malka, or "queen." She was the daughter of wealthy Lancashire merchants who attended the finest boarding schools in England for Jewish students. Queenie was straight backed and rigid in her ideals and ethics. Brian got his unerring sense of right from her. They had a special bond that many gay sons have with their mothers. Some saw her as overbearing, but she felt it was her responsibility to protect Brian from people who would hurt him. She wanted him to be with people who understood that he was different. The interview took place late one October afternoon in 1980, in the living room of her home in Liverpool. During the interview, the phone rang. She answered and said, "Oh no, wait . . ." Her psychiatrist had died.

STEVEN GAINES: When were you in therapy? Is that after Brian died?

QUEENIE EPSTEIN: No, and I started actually—my worst time . . . [Queenie singles out a decades-old article.] The [writer wrote] how dreadfully

[Brian] upset his parents. Which was so *untrue*. Yes. I mean—we were sad for him. Except for the dress-designing bit, we went along with him. But that was my worst time. You see, we couldn't understand Brian. And even I couldn't understand. I suppose it was his sense of drama. He liked to dramatize his unhappy childhood. Oh, but it wasn't all bad.

SG: Maybe it was more unhappy to him?

QE: Do you think so? But he was a very, very happy— I mean, he certainly had terrific moods. Particularly when he was young, he was very happy. He was sixteen years old, sixteen attending Wrekin, and he wrote to us that he didn't think he was going to be academic. He'd got this idea of dress designing. His letter said, "I can imagine you will be horrified by this." But when he came home, we said we weren't annoyed or horrified in any way. I suppose, really, we could have got him to Paris to apprentice him to the designers, but I thought it was all very far away from our way of life.

SG: Instead of becoming a dress designer, he went into the family business?

QE: Yes. At seventeen. It was very hard on Brian when he went into the family business. Brian was a very honest person, and he hated to have to sell anything to anybody that he didn't approve of. But he had great ideas about window dressing. There was a bit of friction with his grandfather. Contemporary furniture was the thing. Brian must have been the first person ever to display furniture with the backs in the window.

SG: Brian went to a lot of different schools.

QE: It was because of the war, really. You see, Brian was five, and the war broke out in '39, didn't it? You know, Brian had an eye operation during the Blitz. Did you know Brian had the most dreadful squint? Oh, a terrible squint. Harry and I were very distressed about this squint, and bombs were falling and everybody asked, "Why are you worried about this squint?" But I couldn't stand it. I went to the hospital with him. Oh! Do you know, they wouldn't even provide me with a bed. They had to send a chair down for me to sit on. And we had to go down to the air raid shelter because the Blitz hadn't started. I used to go down and cry every night in the shelter.

SG: Years later, Brian was drafted to the National Service.

QE: You know, he got us to move heaven and earth to get him to a station in the smart barracks. We bought Brian a grand car, and one night he drove through the gates in his grand car, in a bowler hat, the way officers dressed in those days, and the guards on the gate saluted him. When they realized they were saluting a private, he was confined to barracks.

SG: Why was he discharged as psychologically unfit?

QE: Well, I suppose he was himself. It was very wrong of the army. But, in those days, you didn't talk about those things. The army rang up. I said, "Well, what is wrong with my son?" I was the only one in the house when they called. They said, "This unfortunate man." A few months later, Brian told us. I don't ask for self-pity, but it was a pretty difficult situation. I mean, we were middle-class Jewish people. It was very difficult for my husband to understand. I've had a terrific guilt complex myself, because I had the feeling that it must have been something else. But anyway, we got over it. And from then on, I felt that whatever Brian wanted to do, he must do.

PETER BROWN: Did Clive [Brian's brother] know about Brian's problem?

QB: Yes. He told us all.

[Brian was blackmailed by a man after a sexual encounter in a public toilet. Brian cooperated in setting a trap, and the man was arrested and went to trial. Brian was named only as Mr. X during the trial, as per English law. When it was all over and the blackmailer was remanded to jail, Brian was close to psychological collapse, and went to Spain to recover.]

QE: He'd been away for about five weeks in Spain on holiday. And when he came back, I was worried about him. I could see it coming. I always knew, I sensed when he was getting tired of something. It was a terrible winter, if you remember . . . the winter of '62–'63.

SG: Did Brian see a psychiatrist? There's certainly no shame in that.

QE: We were very suspicious of psychiatry in England. He hated it.

SG: Did he go to the psychiatrist because he was homosexual? Or was it because he was beaten up and blackmailed? That must have been terribly damaging to him, and traumatic.

QE: Yes. How do you know about that? He must have been about, about twenty-three.

SG: Queenie, were you aware that Brian was taking so many pills?

QE: Well, I knew he was taking sleeping pills. And I knew he was taking Dexedrine. Oh, you'll want to know about that—those last ten days? Harry [Brian's father] had a coronary. After Harry died, Brian did everything he could to make me very happy. I know this'll sound stupid, but he did say he really liked to live with me. And I said, "Well, Brian, you've left home and you're happy." It was the only thing Harry and I wanted to know. Brian was very anxious. But then Brian took a flat for me in London. The last ten days . . . it was quite true . . . all that cocoa. Hot chocolate. He brought it back. I'd take him out for dinner every night.

SG: Do you think the fact that he discovered the Beatles, and became an international celebrity, so widely admired, absolved him of some of the bad feelings he had of himself?

QE: Oh yes! Don't you think so?

SG: The weekend that he died, he was expecting company at his house in Surrey and the company canceled. He was disgruntled that the company canceled. Do you think that could have set him off on a depression?

QE: Yes. I do. And then he went back, came back [to London], and I think—almost certainly—I think that I should have stayed the last day. Brian would leave notes out for me . . . when he first got involved with the Beatles: *Please do not disturb*.

SG: Do you think it was suicide, or do you think it was accidental?

QE: I'll never know.

PB: I don't have any doubt that particular occasion was a mistake.

SG: Freud says there are no mistakes.

QE: Well, there's calls for help. My psychiatrist told me . . . but I just didn't realize. I always felt I failed Brian. But he was an absolutely marvelous man. The night his father died—it was terribly sudden, I woke up and found his body dead—the night his father died, Brian came to me and said, "I need you far more than you need me." But I always felt I failed him. Well, I like to do as much as I can because I still have the feeling that . . . I don't know. Although people tell me that Brian was well loved, I want everything good to come out of it.

Nat Weiss

Nat Weiss was the head of NEMS in America (where its name was Nemperor). He was one of Brian's few close friends as well as a wise advisor. Weiss was one of the top attorneys in the music business, known for his integrity and skill. He was also a fixer. As a former successful divorce attorney, he was a man who knew how to negotiate delicate situations, including the blackmail attempt Brian endured in 1966, during the Beatles' final tour. He'd met Brian Epstein two years earlier, through a mutual friend at a small cocktail party at the Plaza Hotel.

NAT WEISS: Brian was talking to me, but he wasn't paying any attention. His eyes were focused on a boy across the room. But he never made a move. Brian was the worst cruiser in the world. He could never pick up anyone. People used to ask me about his gayness, I would say, "He was the worst homosexual in the world." I mean, he really was the least predatory homosexual I have ever met. I didn't see Brian again for another month or two. He was staying at the Plaza and asked me over for breakfast. We chatted for a while, and then Brian asked if I could help him with a problem. A boy named John [Dizz] Gillespie had ripped him off a few months earlier. Gillespie had held a knife to Brian's throat and taken his money. Gillespie was American, but Brian met him in England. He would come to England, have this affair with Brian, rip him off, go to California, come back, and make up. Brian was very forgiving because he liked him so much. Brian believed he and Gillespie had a serious relationship. I spent my adult years encountering all kinds of hustlers—but this Gillespie was an expert. I'm listening to Brian talking about this con artist that he was worried about because he was coming to America this summer, when the Beatles were on tour. Brian said, "Look, I don't want to see him," because the Beatles tour was coming up. The first big tour of the Shea Stadium, '65 tour. Brian said, "What I want you to do is get him out of my way. I don't want him to show up on tour." So I met this boy Gillespie. He was cute. Dark and handsome. I'd say he was about twenty, twenty-one at the time. His first protestations were "You know, I love Brian" and "I don't want anything from Brian." Then he said, "Well, if I had a car, because after all, he's got plenty of money and I just want a car." He was a conniving thing. You see, Brian was a very believing, you know, person, and I just saw this kid as, you know, something straight out of Fifty-fourth Street that just had a good score. I discussed this with Brian, and Brian gave me $3,000, which I gave to Gillespie. When Brian and the Beatles were in New York, we put Gillespie up in the Warwick Hotel and I kept him under lock and key until Brian left town.

The night after Shea Stadium, Brian stayed up all night at my apartment and did something that I'll never forget. He left my number at the Waldorf Towers to refer all his phone calls to my home phone. If you listened to the radio, you'd know that Brian Epstein was staying at the Towers. Well, the phone never stopped ringing. And Brian was sitting there, really amused by all the callers coming in, because I picked up and it was some fan calling from New Jersey, who wants to give a Cadillac to the Beatles, and Brian said, "Oh, make sure it's gold." It was like, Brian was saying all these offhand comments, you know. Meanwhile, it was a nightmare. Brian was, like, saying, you know, um, "Find some tricks to take to Shea Stadium." I'm in a juxtaposition of finding tricks, the nightmare of Shea Stadium, the phone calls [laughing]. All of this was going on at once. The amazing thing about Brian is he would be out giggling and laughing all night long, and then suddenly you'd see a whole formal Brian, someone with his affect who, you've never met him before. It was like a curtain went down and then it went up again.

Dizz Gillespie disappeared until he resurfaced in August of 1966. The Beatles were on an American tour, and Brian and I were staying at the Beverly Hills Hotel. Lo and behold, who shows up but John Gillespie. Instead of being fearful, Brian loves the whole idea. Brian said to me, "I know he really loves me and that's why he's here." Brian was the sort of person who—you didn't want to say to him, "He doesn't love you." You always wanted to indulge Brian's fantasy because it would depress him terribly if you told him no.

Brian's sensitivities were like mercury in the sense, like, the wrong word, and his spirits would plummet in a second. He would sink. The wrong word would set Brian off immediately, so if you doubted his own instincts, he'd say either "You're wrong" or "You're angry," and he'd get depressed. It prevented you from being really truthful about certain things, because you didn't want to disillusion him.

But this thing with Gillespie was very serious. The Beatles had rented a house in Beverly Hills, an enormous house, and Gillespie and I and Brian spent the day at this house while the Beatles had gone to San Francisco to play that last gig, the end of August. That afternoon, Brian said, "I have an announcement to make. Tonight is the last time the Beatles will ever play." He said this to just Gillespie and me in the house that day.

SG: Why didn't Brian go to the last concert?

NW: He wasn't up to it. He didn't even go to Dodger Stadium. He just didn't want to go. There was no need for him to go. When we went back to the Beverly Hills Hotel the next morning, Brian and I realized our briefcases were missing. In addition to $20,000 cash, Brian had bottles of Seconals and Valium in his briefcase, and a few [painkillers], which he was just beginning to get interested in. Gillespie also stole some early Beatles memorabilia; Brian always carried a telegram or their acceptance letter with him. Brian always kept these things with him in his briefcase. I had nothing in my suitcase. I had some papers in there, which amounted to twelve dollars.

Brian was very upset that Gillespie misled him and stole from him again. When he got back to London, he went into a severe depression right after the last tour. He really sank into an extreme depression at that time. He didn't want any scandal or any publicity about the whole thing. But then, lo and behold, three days later, I get a ransom note to give Dizz $10,000, and in return for Brian's briefcase and its contents. It would be dropped off at the bus station in L.A. But it was not Gillespie who showed up at the bus station; it was another kid that we caught. He led us to the suitcase and an empty bottle of Seconals, but there was only $12,000 left. Apparently, Gillespie took $8,000 and bought a car [laughing].

Alistair Taylor on Brian's Death

STEVEN GAINES: Did Brian Epstein's death take you by surprise?

ALISTAIR TAYLOR: I certainly didn't see it coming. Once or twice, he threatened. I wasn't as close to Brian in that respect as probably Peter [Brown] and other people. But I know a couple of times . . . I mean, once he did ring and say that he was—he's had enough and he's going . . . I remember I went tearing around, and he was sitting there. And he said, "What the hell are you coming around for? You twit."

Brian's death was very strange because we had a tremendous row the week before. Robert Stigwood [Brian's putative partner in NEMS] was with us then. He managed the group Cream, and they were playing the Fillmore in San Francisco and they were due to fly out on Sunday morning. On Friday, I said to their road manager, "You got your A-2s, okay? You know, working visas?" They hadn't got anything. So I said, "Christ almighty. You know, you won't get through the airport." It ended up with me going over to the American embassy to get it fixed. I actually got them to open the American embassy on a Sunday morning. Robert Stigwood said, "I think you better go with the band." I said, "No way without Brian's permission." About five o'clock the next day, there's a telegram under the door, and I've still got it at home. It said, Under no circumstances will you leave for America. Epstein. I blew my bloody lid. I grabbed the phone. I was so angry. "After all those years," I said to Brian. "As if I had been trying to con a trip to America!" He apologized. I said, "Now, am I going to San Francisco or not?" He said, "No, definitely not. I need you here." I said, "Fine. Are we friends again? Yes? Cheers."

Two o'clock in the morning, the phone rings. "Alistair, this is Brian. Wouldn't you just love to be in San Francisco tomorrow?" I said, "Oh gosh, Brian, you're joking." He said, "I'd love for you to go. You'd really enjoy it. Stay out there a few days. I'd feel happy. Bye-bye." Typical Brian. I was at the airport later that morning having coffee, and in through the door walks Brian! "I've come to see you off and wish you luck," he said. He sat and we chatted. He apologized again for the row, and that he didn't mean it. I've puzzled on this from, from that day.

I got home the following Sunday morning. Brian's secretary rang me. They had found Brian dead, and she couldn't find Peter Brown or Geoffrey Ellis, because they were out of town, so I was sort of next in line. Brian was just lying there. Enormous double bed, and Brian was sort of curled up there, and he'd obviously been going through some mail. There was a plate with some chocolate biscuits, and a half bottle of bitter orange, some bottles of tablets, with tablets in them, and he was just asleep.

The doctor came and called the coroner's office, and within literally ten minutes, the doorbell rings. It was a reporter. A reporter, within ten to fifteen minutes, was ringing the doorbell. Who was the first one? I have a feeling it was someone from the *[Daily] Express*. Obviously, someone in the coroner's office got fifteen quid. I mean, this is nothing unusual. I wasn't surprised, quite frankly. And then there were a couple more. Then the reporters started coming immediately. I answered the door, and they were saying they heard Brian was ill. "No," I said. "He's just gone out for a breath of fresh air."

The great panic was trying to get a hold of Brian's brother, Clive Epstein, particularly, so he could break it to Queenie. Because we were terrified when we realized that if the press were onto it and something came over the radio, and Queenie heard it—it was awful. Brian's brother, Clive, was up in Liverpool. I'll never forget that call until my dying day. It was frightening. Oh, when I think back, it sounded—I didn't know what to say, to be honest. Clive answered the phone, and I just said, "Brian's been in a dreadful accident." He asked, "What's the matter? Is he all right?" And I just said, "He's dead." Clive let out one scream, which I can, I can still hear. I said, "The press are here." It was horrendous, that phone call.

Peter Brown on Brian's Death

The day after Brian's burial, Paul insisted that we have a meeting. Too soon, I thought. But we each handled grief in our own way, and Paul's was to shoulder on. I think he had some concern that the group would fall apart without Brian if they didn't keep busy. I didn't want the media to see us all arriving at the office to have a huddle the day after Brian was buried, so we met in Ringo's London flat.

Only the original Liverpudlians were in attendance: John, Paul, George, Ringo, Neil Aspinall, Mal Evans, and me. Paul's pitch was that we could not let Brian's death stop the momentum, or mar the achievement of *Sgt. Pepper*, and we had to decide right away what to do next and not appear to flounder. Paul already had been entertaining an idea for a TV show about a bus filled with an oddball collection of characters, Ken Kesey meets Roald Dahl. But only Paul was for it, and after the discussion heated up a bit, I suggested we take a coffee break.

I walked to a window and stared blankly at the street when I felt someone wrap their arms around me from behind and hug me. It was John. He asked, "Are you all right?"

"No, I'm not," I said.

"Nor am I, Peter. Nor am I."

Allan Williams

Allan Williams was a Liverpool club owner and promoter who booked rock and roll groups into local clubs. It was Williams who was responsible for booking the Beatles at clubs in Hamburg, Germany, in the city's sleazy redlight district. Williams is also the first person to try to manage the Beatles. It didn't work. He claims they didn't pay him commissions. He's famous for advising Brian Epstein, "Don't touch them with a ten-foot barge pole." Williams wrote a memoir called The Man Who Gave the Beatles Away.

ALLAN WILLIAMS: Uh, I think the sixties is the most magical decade of this century. The twenties was for the rich, you know, the gay, the Roaring Twenties, and the thirties were for depression. But the sixties were for everybody. There was no class or race barrier, the flower people, for instance. It was millionaires involved in it. And it, it affected everybody. Since then, I would say the seventies was a flopper, and the eighties doesn't look all that much exciting.

STEVEN GAINES: The book you wrote, *The Man Who Gave the Beatles Away*, portrays the Beatles as being real rip-off artists. Were they that?

AW: Yes, especially John, who was a bit ruthless. He was a sort of a cynical guy in those days. I believe he's okay now, he's quite mellow now.

PETER BROWN: Not too much.

AW: Isn't he? Well, you know, of all the people, he comes through a lot of stick. Or a lot of people think he comes through a lot of stick in my book. But that's the way John behaved. He behaved really outrageously. And Paul used to pour the oil on the troubled waters, as it were. But of all the people, only John, out of all the Beatles, have said that my book is the only book that gives a true insight to what it was to be an early Beatle. I admire him for that.

SG: You wrote about a transvestite that you met in Hamburg, who you say had sex with some of the Beatles?

AW: In actual fact, she fucking said that she had John Lennon, but you know, I didn't wanna go as far as that, because the Beatles were notorious liars. But, you see, part of the fun in the sixties, when any new group came over to Hamburg, these transvestites were so beautiful . . . they didn't know. And, of course, they had tits. And they didn't have any beard. There was one in particular who looked like Veronica Lake. Everybody used to be sent up by her. If you get the lads a bit pissed coming from Liverpool, they had never ever seen anything like it.

Hamburg was the vice center of the whole of Europe. And, of course, the Beatles were thrown in at the deep end. A lot of people in America think the boys were all clean-cut, dressed in suits, but they witnessed every degradation possible in Hamburg. Hamburg was their education. They were introduced to booze, pills, and everything else in Hamburg. They were on amphetamines. It was all speed, and even cannabis wasn't all that . . . it wasn't all that popular then. That came later. Towards '64 or so.

SG: Although, Cilla Black said that she remembered them smoking pot in the Cavern Club.

AW: They were trapped into it, in Hamburg, as I was telling you. They'd get boozed up and the tits used to be flopping, and of course the transvestites always had this Marlene Dietrich type of voice. They would say to the boys, "Oh, you're handsome. Would you like to come to bed now?" And, of course, they thought it was their birthday, until they got into bed, and then usually they . . . And then we'd, we'd all be outside [laughs], waiting for the roar of anger. Sometimes it didn't happen, they stayed [laughs].

SG: But the Veronica Lake transvestite told you she had John?

AW: Yeah. She said she'd had John.

SG: Were, were the boys ladies' men in Liverpool?

AW: Yeah, I would say so. They were very promiscuous. Very promiscuous.

SG: You warned Brian not to manage them. They wouldn't pay you commission, is that what had happened?

AW: What happened, Steven, was that the first time they went to Hamburg they were playing at a club called the Kaiserkeller for a nasty individual, Bruno Koschmider. Koschmider's club was sort of a typical sort of showbiz type, a décor of rowboats, and a bar made out of the bulk of a ship. And the stage was some sort of a bit of a boat. Which they smashed one day because it was so awful.

SG: The Beatles?

AW: Yeah. Hamburg played an important part in molding their career. They served their apprenticeship in Hamburg. They were a shit group, to be honest, in Liverpool. They hardly ever had a consistent drummer. And you've only got to listen, really, to the Hamburg tapes, to realize how bad they could play.

SG: But you said that they really got their education in Hamburg.

AW: Life education. They met rough people. I'm not saying that they didn't have nights. Most groups came back from Hamburg with a little "green blood" [laughs]. I got some stick off Mrs. Best, you know, Pete Best's mother? She had some interesting comments. She eventually had a solicitor write to me because she assumed that I was alleging that the Beatles caught a dose. And I said no. I said it was just a generalization. I never said the Beatles. But she was very, very annoyed about it and tried to get the book stopped.

Bob Wooler

Wooler is a Liverpool disc jockey, compere, and café owner. He knew the boys when they were one of hundreds of bands striving to get noticed in Liverpool. He is also infamous as the man John Lennon beat up because he cast aspersions on John and Brian's trip to Spain. His interview that follows is a brief portrait of a man who is besieged by the press for some tidbit about the Beatles. He mentions deserving a "fat check" in the interview.

BOB WOOLER: Is there anything new to tell? Well, there are new things to tell, because nobody's told the full story. It's rather like *Citizen Kane*. You view this entity from different angles, and this is why it's so fascinating.

STEVEN GAINES: When did you start as a disc jockey?

BW: I was a railway clerk, frustrated. Aren't we all? Dying to be a songwriter, the skiffle thing happens, we're in '56. Some lads in the office form this skiffle group. I encouraged them, got some booking, and gradually moved them onto the "jive hall circuit." The Beatles were the harbingers in every respect, we had about 350 other groups in

Liverpool, and they all formed part of this assortment called Merseybeat. I felt that these groups are going onstage and nobody knows who they are. It seemed a shame that the promoter doesn't at least get on the microphone and introduce them, so I introduced myself in that role. And from that moment on, I got to work more and more, and finally abandoned the railway in December '60. I eventually get a job at the Cavern. I also met the, the Beatles, who coincidentally, were in a similar boat to myself, because they had been deported from Hamburg.

SG: Why were they deported?

BW: It was alleged they set fire to a cinema. I met the Beatles kicking their heels in the Jacaranda, which was a Liverpool coffee club that Allan Williams owned. I got them a much-chronicled booking at Liverpool Town Hall. I asked for eight pounds, and we settled for six. So that was a pound a man, because there were five Beatles—Neil Aspinall, the driver, you see, so it was a quid a man. That was the sort of money we were paid in those days. Um, well, that night at Liverpool Town Hall was a turning point. We didn't use that term *Beatlemania*—that was to come in '63, via the press, they coined that—but really it was the start of big things, nothing like that particular hysteria and fever pitch had been achieved. So from that moment on, they, they developed even more. I brought them into the Cavern, and they played there 292 times. That's a factual number. I was asked many, many times, uh, "How many times did the Beatles play here?" So, I decided, well, I'll look through all the diaries and, uh, add up the, uh, number of times, 292 is the correct. I also did shows at other venues, so all in all, I figure I did about 450 shows with the Beatles during those three years, their apprenticeship years in Liverpool. People don't think, Who was in that band room with them at the Cavern? for instance. They were in that band room. Picture a lunchtime session there. I'm on the turntable, we only had one record player then, and I'm on a microphone.

SG: Tell me about this famous incident where John Lennon punched you in the nose.

BW: Now, I've been asked many, many times, and the answer has always been no, so I'm going to have to disappoint you on this. I'm not going to talk about it.

SG: Can I tell you what I've heard?

BW: Oh, well, no, I don't wish to know really, because I'm only interested in my account, okay? Now, you're doing this rather provocatively. Pity you.

SG: I am going to write about it, and I would prefer if you could make it factual and set the record straight. I don't want it to be incorrect.

BW: You're writing about it, are you? Do you feel it's important?

SG: It's not of crucial importance, but as long as it happened and there was a settlement—

BW: There was a settlement? Is this what your book is all about? Some people feel that they can get extra mileage out of this from a money point of view, but at the same time, they open themselves to litigation. You know, I'm wondering how the Beatles are going to view this finished book. Peter, do you think you will still be friends with the Beatles?

PETER BROWN: I don't know. I might be.

Dick James

Dick James was one of the first people in the record business with whom Brian and the Beatles came into personal contact. Picture Dick James, né Reginald Leon Isaac Vapnick, the 1950s Hollywood version of a music publisher—balding, short, thick black eyeglass frames, a cigar between his teeth. A former singer for dance bands, he wrote and sang on one hit, the theme song for *Robin Hood*, which was produced by a young and green in-house producer at Parlophone Records, George Martin. Dick James had recently gone into music publishing. He was a very lucky man to have met Brian in 1963, when Brian was desperate to find a music publisher. His transcript captures what the burgeoning music publishing industry was like in the 1960s, and how it was being transformed by new technology.

Dick James formed a company with John Lennon and Paul McCartney called Northern Songs Ltd., of which he owned 50 percent. At the time, it was 50 percent of mostly nothing, but still a mistake on Brian Epstein's part to agree to give James half of what would become one of the greatest songwriting partnerships in history, with a catalog that would be worth billions. On Brian's behalf, the modern music business was then inventing itself, and there weren't many guidelines or precedents for him to follow. Still, when the Beatles signed with him, instead of typically advancing a new act some of their royalties, he loaned them the money "at a good rate," he protested, so they *could buy new clothes. Seven years later, when James smelled trouble brewing between the Beatles, he sold them out, and the Beatles lost control of their publishing rights. The transcript below is what Dick James promised would be the very last time he'll tell the story.*

DICK JAMES: I met Brian about November '62. I had written a song, and [music producer] George Martin said, "I'm experimenting with a group from Liverpool. I'll send your song up to them." I went up to his office to listen to this song of mine, recorded by the Beatles, and George Martin said, "What do you think?" I said, "It's awful. Murder."

He said, "If you like, I'll make it the B-side." Then he played "Love Me Do," and I said, "Well, it's all right, but I don't think much of a song. There's no melody to it. It's nothing that's going to last, you know. It's just a riff." They also did "P.S. I Love You," which he made the B-side.

Now we spin forward to late June, and "Love Me Do" went out. It didn't shake the world. I think we got to about number 19. It was around about November when I had a call. George Martin said, "Dick, the Beatles came down yesterday, and they've written some new things, and they are quite good. I'd like you to meet the Beatles' manager, Brian Epstein, because he's looking for a publisher to work on their next record." Record companies turned him down. Most publishers didn't have the opportunity to hear the material. Then he put this tape on, and I heard "Please Please Me." I said, "Who wrote this?" And George Martin said, "John Lennon and Paul McCartney, who are two of the boys in the group." I said, "Are these the same writers as 'Love Me Do'? It's a totally different song. This is fantastic. This is number one. If we get the breaks, it must be number one."

Brian signed the publishing contract himself, because he had power of attorney to do so for a single song. But when it came to signing John Lennon and Paul McCartney publishing, to be called Northern Songs, Paul was under twenty-one. Jim McCartney, his father, objected to him being published by a London publisher. He said to Brian, "Why can't he publish with a Liverpool publisher?" Brian said, "Well, for the simple reason that there aren't any. You know that. And there aren't any in Manchester, and there aren't any in Birmingham. The publishers are all in London."

Jim dug his heels in and refused to sign. I remember John saying to Paul, "Come on, sign the bloody thing." Brian said, "No, not, not until he's twenty-one. That's the way it's done." Paul asked, "Will you have patience? I'm twenty-one in June. And the day I'm twenty-one, I'll sign the contract."

Everything after "Please Please Me" and "Ask Me Why" went into Northern Songs, owned 50 percent by Dick James Music. The other 50 percent was split up 20 percent to John Lennon, 20 percent to Paul McCartney, and 10 percent to NEMS. Which really reflected Brian's 25 percent interest in the Beatles.*

SG: Why didn't you give the Beatles an advance?

DJ: With a hack songwriter who would hawk a song round from publisher to publisher, the advance was usually five pounds, or ten pounds. You know, you could buy a meal for five pounds, or buy a suit of clothes for ten pounds, which you can't very well do today. There was no sort of thousands of pounds advance. When they started to be very successful, after about four months, and it was taking several months for the money to come through the pipeline, from the record company to the publisher, and then to accounting, Brian said, "The boys would like to buy some new clothes, and they want to buy some material things. Can you rustle up some money for me?"

I said, "Well, I haven't got it yet either. But what I will do is [lend] it." And let's face it. Lending money wasn't expected then, either. They

---

* The way Dick James accounted the Beatles, he would take a dollar royalty in the United States and pay them 50 percent. But he wholly owned a New York corporation that had a sub-publishing deal with his own company in England. All those corporations were owned by Dick James and the Dick James Organization. He would keep fifty cents here, remit fifty cents, and pay the Beatles 50 percent of what he received in England (50 percent of 50 percent).

borrowed the money from Dick James Music. We managed to rustle up, with a reasonable amount of interest, £10,000. Ten thousand pounds was a lot of money. It's like, one might almost say, like £100,000 today. A bank wouldn't do it. No security. Catalogs weren't security, in those days. And it was only a matter of a week.

PETER BROWN: It was a month.

SG: Do you think the fact that the Beatles never received an advance, or that you charged interest on the "loan," or that you owned 50 percent of their publishing, caused some animosity between them and you?

DJ: No. That was not the basis of what later, unfortunately, brought a certain amount of animosity. There'd been a stock flotation. We were left with—I think it was 36 percent. I was intent on building up Northern Songs, and I often talked to Brian about it, but Brian was always too busy. I think by this time, the pressure on him was so great several months before he died. I'm not making excuses for how he died, or why he died. You know, he died, and it was very tragic and I know it was an accident—[despite] whatever anybody thought. In fact, I was one of the first people that Brian's secretary, Joanne, called. I sort of got in touch with the family, et cetera, et cetera. I was one of the first to know. *[Not true.]*

It was just unbelievable that it happened. But here is the man with the Beatles and Gerry and the Pacemakers and Billy J. Kramer and Cilla Black, running an organization that was almost impossible to control. You could understand how the pressure on a man, uh, builds up and up and up, and he just couldn't get away from the pressure.

Geoffrey Ellis

Geoffrey Ellis was "the man in the suit" who ran the business side of the Beatles for NEMS. There is no one associated with the Beatles who had more of an overview of their business deals and finances. He was the one who signed the checks and minded the shop. By watching another man's pocketbook, you get to know them quite well. Ellis was born in Liverpool, where he first met Brian Epstein. He was an Oxford-educated barrister who spent a decade in the insurance industry in London and New York before Brian offered him a job at NEMS. When Ellis joined the company he learned that Brian had made a costly mistake on the Beatles' behalf.

In 1964, offers for endorsements and products came in every day, for lunch boxes, bobbleheads, Beatle wigs, and baby bibs. Merchandising and endorsements were a whole new commerce in the music business. Brian sought advice from attorney David Jacobs, who represented Judy Garland and Liberace, among others. Jacobs advised Brian to set up a company just to handle licensing in the United States, and recommended a former nightclub owner of his acquaintance, Nicky Byrne, to run it. They called the company Seltaeb, Beatles spelled backwards. Byrne would do all the work, from sales to shipping, and, without lifting a finger, the Beatles would get 10 percent of the profits. The offer sounded fair to Brian; in the record business, a 10 percent royalty would be handsome. The first check Brian received was for $9,700, which quite pleased *him until Brian realized Seltaeb had made $97,000. The cut should have been reversed, with the Beatles getting 90 percent of sales. Brian had given away tens of millions, perhaps hundreds of millions in merchandising. He dreaded telling the Beatles about his mistake for months. When he finally explained it at a meeting, eyes downcast, John said to him, "It's not a big deal, Brian."*

GEOFFREY ELLIS: When I ran into Brian in Liverpool and he told me he was starting up this crazy group—that must have been about 1962—like everybody, I thought it was crazy. I remember his mother saying, "You've got to get it out of your system." Brian said he was moving his company, NEMS, from Liverpool to London and he didn't like business administration. He was surrounded by people who wanted to come and work for him, but whom he didn't trust. There were a lot of people out to make a fast buck [off the Beatles]. Whereas Brian, his life *was* the Beatles. He asked if I would come and work with him, and I said, "You're crazy." Eventually he made it sufficiently interesting, but only partly monetarily, because this was the height of Beatlemania, and it was madness. As far as the business—the office and administration were concerned—he created a sort of nightmare. It all needed to be controlled. Hiring and firing, accounts, payments in and payments out, all of it had to be administered and controlled.

STEVEN GAINES: Was Brian's talent more as a showman and not as a business administrator?

GE: He had considerable talents as a businessman, as a negotiator, but he didn't have the inclination to sit down and do all those administrative chores. I mean, he would come into the office and say, "What's that check you're signing?" And then he'd look into the whole background. He knew what he was up to.

SG: Yet Seltaeb, the merchandising deal in the US, was a big mistake. Tens of millions of dollars were lost. How did that come about?

GE: The same merchandising rights had been granted, probably inadvertently, to more than one area. This was the sort of situation: rights might have been granted to an English company for worldwide merchandising in watches. Then when Seltaeb granted exclusive rights to North America to another company for categories of merchandising, they were also granted rights to jewelry, and then they subcontracted to a firm in Chicago to make Beatles jewelry. The firm in Chicago made watches, exported them, sold them in Britain and the United States. Nobody actually sat down in an office and fraudulently said, "You can have the exclusive right to watches throughout the world." There were misunderstandings, lack of communication. When the Chicago factory found out that somebody was selling watches in Britain, and they believed they had worldwide rights, they were naturally upset about it and went to Seltaeb. Then, when a chap in Britain found Chicago was selling watches in the United States, an unholy row brewed up about it because there was a lot of money to be made out of merchandising. This type of situation happened half a dozen times in different variations. Apart from these technicalities, the Seltaeb people in the United States [whom Brian went into business with] appeared to be taking advantage of the situation by taking very large advances, which should have been accounted to the grantor of the rights. They appeared to spend all the money on high living and on themselves. And the commission percentage that was negotiated was not very satisfactory to the Beatles, and it certainly wouldn't be countenanced today.

SG: But the problem was, the partners in Seltaeb then turned around and started to sue NEMS. And nothing was done about it, and they got a judgment against NEMS.

GE: Yes, they sued NEMS, for having granted the same rights which they thought they had elsewhere. And I'm inclined to say that the reason why they got a judgment in default was entirely the fault of the American attorney who was handling it. At that stage, Brian and I did in fact fly to the States.

SG: Brian hired Louis Nizer.

PETER BROWN: The point of the NEMS story was the fact that Brian didn't charge the Beatles for the legal fees. It was charged against NEMS out of his commission.

GE: Well, you know, I don't recall that through his company Brian paid rather than the Beatles.

SG: Also, the royalty rate from EMI was especially low in the beginning. How did that happen? Another bad deal?

GE: When the original contract was entered into, and it was before my association with Brian, he had had a hard time getting a contract for the Beatles, which is history. Eventually he was very pleased on their behalf to accept a contract in what were then normal terms for new artists. They were low by today's standards, but they were normal terms at the time. I think that's a penny a record, a very standard royalty and virtually impossible to get anything larger than that. Brian, in fact, got a great deal of satisfaction when the contract came up for renegotiation; he was driving up in a chauffeured Rolls-Royce and going into the boardroom and dealing with the chairman, Sir Joseph Lockwood, and demanding things which made me cringe in horror. "Oh, they will never do this," I told him. But EMI was living off the Beatles at that time. Brian was arrogant in negotiations. I always cringed at what he would ask for, not only in record deals but in appearances. For American concert tours, he would demand vast guarantees. I said to him, "I really don't know how you think you can get away with this." He said it was perfectly simple. "If Elvis got a guarantee of half a million dollars, I must get three-quarters because they're the Beatles." Sir Joseph gave him almost everything he fought over, and he did fight, all the way. He took a very, very long time. Negotiations lasted many,

many months indeed. And eventually Brian got virtually everything he wanted to get.

The business owes so much to what he did in those days, really, because Brian used the strength of the artists in a way that nobody had done until then. Also, he changed the nature of certain aspects of the business, particularly of the record producer. Nowadays, a record producer waltzes into the company and can demand 2 percent, 3 percent, even 4 percent royalty.

Uh, at that time, there were no independent producers. George Martin wanted an increase in his £3,000-a-year salary from EMI because they were making a fortune out of what he was producing. They made him a derisory offer. He decided he would go it alone, and he went to Brian and he said, "I'm going to leave EMI, but will the Beatles stay with me?" And Brian said, "Yes, they will."

George was able to resign and say to EMI, "I'm leaving you. But the Beatles will only be produced by me, so you've got to pay me to produce them independently," which they did. So far as I know, this was the first time certainly in the pop field that a producer had become independent of a record company instead of just being an employee. And so, there were various people, really, who owe their livings today to Brian and the Beatles backing George in doing this.

SG: Did Brian spend lavishly?

GE: He lived a very well-ordered life, on the surface. He liked to have servants and a certain elegance. And a bit of rough trade to boot. The reason he wanted success was to lead an elegant life. And indeed, he certainly had a reputation in London. In the pop business, he was way above the crowd because he had a pretty house and a butler and big cars and style.

SG: When did Brian's personal life start to fall apart?

GE: The falling apart of his personal life, in my view, was considerably aligned to the falling apart of his professional life. I thought about this quite a lot through the years, since the last year of his life he was extremely insecure. He was always a little bit insecure with the Beatles, although they were much more dependent on him than he probably ultimately realized. But with their contracts coming to an end, which I don't think is generally known even now, that by the time that he died . . . their contract had expired. And I think he was extremely insecure about what would happen in the future, because the Beatles had started Apple already and they indicated they wanted to do a lot more of their own thing. I feel fairly confident that had Brian lived, he would have maintained an association with them, probably not as strong an association with them as he had. And I think this probably did contribute to his falling apart.*

And I think his personal life, the tricking more and the more sordid areas of his life were increased at that time. I don't think he was of very strong character, despite all I've said about his arrogance and his apparent strength in dealings. Underneath, he was really quite soft. I always found him, with rare exceptions, to be very charming. Incidentally, I think quite a lot of my value in my employment is the air of respectability. I think he needed all sorts of props at the end, which possibly we all didn't give him.

SG: Didn't Brian secretly have the NEMS management contract written into the EMI contract? Wasn't that something that they didn't know about? Wasn't it out of the ordinary to have the management contract written into the contract with the record company? To have EMI pay

---

* Sir Joseph Lockwood's version: The structure of the contract was that the management contract was terminating in September 1967. But the EMI contract, which had been signed earlier that year, was for nine years. All monies would be payable to NEMS, and NEMS would then deduct 25 percent and pass on the remaining 75 percent. It has been suggested that Brian acted totally honorably by giving NEMS income for another eight years after the management contract had actually expired.

25 percent directly to NEMS for nine more years, even if NEMS no longer managed them? Was that a devious act on Brian's part? Certain people have said that it was slightly underhanded, the fact that the record contract was not geared in time into the management contract means that it was a devious act.

PB: Well, it was a frightened act, not a devious one.

GE: I would agree with you, that it was probably more of an act of insecurity rather than deviousness.

SG: Did anybody try to stop him from taking pills?

PB: Absolutely.

GE: Brian had suicidal tendencies, undoubtedly. But I'm convinced his death was an accident because it wasn't the right moment. If people are committing suicide, I think that they probably plan it sensibly. The medical verdict was that it was a low drug intoxication. He'd just gone over the edge. If it had been deliberate, surely he would have done it more effectively.

Peter Brown on Manila

The experience of the Beatles in Manila the summer of 1966 is of special significance because it greatly contributed to their decision to stop touring. It was also terrifying. I was there, and I know. As usual, there are contrasting accounts of why and how it happened. I encourage readers to refer to George Harrison's, Neil Aspinall's, and Ringo's transcripts for their versions of events.

On our last day in Tokyo on the 1966 tour, Brian Epstein and I were having lunch in the hotel's restaurant when Jacinto C. Borja, the ambassador to Japan from the Philippines, was ushered to our table by the restaurant's maître d'. The ambassador wanted to confirm that Brian had received an invitation from Madam Imelda Marcos, the wife of the president of the Philippines, Ferdinand Marcos. In honor of the Beatles appearances in Manila, Mrs. Marcos had invited two hundred children to Malacañang, the presidential palace, to meet the Beatles. The Beatles and two hundred kids. The Beatles and two hundred kids was a recipe for mayhem.

Brian said, "It's very kind of Mrs. Marcos to invite us, but we do not make public appearances or go to parties while on tour." At the moment Brian declined the invitation, he had little knowledge of the intemperate Imelda Marcos, or her dictator husband, who had come to power just a year before, partly by murdering or imprisoning his rivals. The only thing we knew about Manila was that we were being welcomed with open arms by an audience of possibly a hundred thousand fans over two shows, with a $1 million box office guarantee, most likely the highest-grossing stop of the 1966 tour.

When our plane landed in Manila, the door opened, a staircase was rolled up, and a man in uniform came aboard and demanded the Beatles get off, with Neil Aspinall scurrying after them. They were surrounded by the Ejército Filipino, the Philippine ground army, carrying rifles. The boys were told to leave their handbags on the tarmac and to get into one of the waiting cars, separating them from the rest of us. No one spoke English and could explain what was happening. The hand luggage the Beatles left behind on the tarmac contained some grass and uppers, and Neil quickly gathered them up and jumped into a second limousine. When the driver asked him where he wanted to go, Neil shouted, "Wherever they're taking the Beatles!"

Brian was horrified to be separated from the Beatles, as they were from us. Inside their limousine, they kept asking the driver, "Where are we going? Where are we going?" It was the only time they could remember being separated from Brian and Mal and Neil, with no support at all. They were vulnerable and helpless, like children suddenly separated from their parents. Meantime, back at the airport, Brian was apoplectic with the authorities, who either didn't understand the words, *Where are the Beatles?* or were intentionally ignoring us. It was maddening.

The boys were being driven to a ramshackle cluster of buildings on Manila Bay, where there was a scrum of reporters waiting for them, shouting the same dumb questions at them about their hair, or Ringo's name, all of which the boys answered with good grace. Still no Brian or Neil or Mal. It was even more unnerving for them when they were hustled onto a boat called the *Marima*, which belonged to a man named Don Manolo Elizalde, a founder of the Manila Broadcasting

Company. Elizalde was also a pal of the Filipino concert promoter who, in turn, had been dealing with NEMS's in-house booking agent, Vic Lewis.

It would turn out that Vic Lewis had promised all sorts of favors behind our back, and the people he made deals with also made deals behind his back. Manila was entirely corrupt, and we had blindly stepped into a terrible situation. Lewis had arranged with the promoter for the Beatles to stay overnight on the *Marima* instead of a suite in the Manila Hotel, a reservation Lewis had quietly canceled. Not coincidentally, that day was the birthday of Don Manolo Elizalde's twenty-four-year-old son, Fredrick, who had invited a dozen friends on the boat, including the reigning Miss Philippines, to party with the Beatles.

Brian was shaking with fury by the time we were driven to the navy yard. When we didn't see the Beatles anywhere, somebody pointed out at the bay, where in the distance was the *Mirama*. Brian was so upset by this point, I thought he would have a stroke. We were taken to the *Mirama* on a skiff, and although the boys seemed okay and had just sat down to dinner, Brian decided it was best not to allow this abduction to go on any longer. He insisted the Beatles disembark immediately, and we were taken back to the dock and finally driven to our hotel, only to discover Vic Lewis had canceled our reservations. Fortunately the suites were still available.

The following day, the day of the two concerts, military officers pounded on the door of Brian's suite, demanding to know what time the Beatles would appear at the presidential palace. Brian told the officials the Beatles would not be able to attend the party and sent regrets. Not more than a half hour later, the diplomatic attaché from Great Britain to the Philippines, Leslie Minford, rang Brian's suite, but Brian stuck to his guns. The Beatles had two shows later that day, and they wanted to sleep late.

We soon found out what it was like to be subjected to Mrs. Marcos's petty vengeance. The concerts went well, but by the time we got back to the hotel, it was all over TV that the Beatles had snubbed hundreds of orphans by not showing up at Mrs. Marcos's event. Brian offered to go on Manila TV and apologize for the misunderstanding and take the blame, but somehow the broadcast was disrupted, and he couldn't be heard. It turned out the station was owned by Don Manolo Elizalde, on whose boat the Beatles had been hijacked.

The morning of our departure, it was newspaper headlines. The Beatles had insulted the people of the Philippines and their hosts who had greeted them so warmly and treated them like dignitaries. Suddenly hotel room service didn't come, or when they did come, the cereal was served with sour milk, and Neil was afraid they had spit in the food, and he wouldn't eat it.

We were told that our commercial KLM plane was waiting at the airport and it would take off on time with or without us. In the transit lounge, before boarding, men dressed in short-sleeve white shirts were shoving and shouting at us, "Regular passengers! Regular passengers!" Some of the men had sticks, not batons, and although they didn't hit us, they were anxious to. It was honestly terrifying. We were bullied and shoved from one side of the room to another.

Above us was a balcony filled with angry people shaking their fists, shouting "Beatles go home!" and spitting on us. We didn't say anything, we were so terrified. Since Mal Evans was the biggest, the goons took him on first. He was pushed forward by one of them, while another tripped him. Another thug tried to hit Neil, who put his hands up in defense.

When they finally let us on the plane, Brian was sitting in a window seat, perspiring heavily. "I'll never forgive myself," he said to me. "I put the boys in danger." As we taxied down the runway, I could see Brian was losing his composure. Vic Lewis came down the aisle to demand to know from Brian if he got the cash the promoter was supposed to pay us, but after the Marcos incident, the Filipino promoter refused to hand over our share of the concert takings. There was already $500,000 that had been wired to us as a deposit, and we expected to leave with an equal sum, most of it in cash. Treasury officials threatened not to let us leave the country unless Brian paid a hefty cash sum in tax. The cash was never paid by the promoter.

Vic Lewis, who was worried about his personal cut, stood in the aisle and badgered Brian, "Did you get the money? Did you get the money?" Brian was near hysterical, and Vic Lewis leaned over me and tried to slap Brian in the face. I grabbed his arm and forced him away down the aisle.

Vic Lewis

Fussy, officious, annoying, Vic Lewis never quite fit in the NEMS picture, yet he played a pivotal role in that he booked all the Beatles tours worldwide, in particular their tour to Japan and Manila. Before he became a booking agent, Lewis was a former bandleader and singer whose one hit was the novelty song "Robin Hood." His booking agency, the Vic Lewis Organisation, had a client list that included Shirley Bassey and rock star Donovan, plus all the NEMS acts, which included Britain's superstar Cilla Black, the Moody Blues, Gerry and the Pacemakers, Billy J. Kramer, and the Cyrkle. In 1965, Brian Epstein bought Lewis's company outright and gave him a seat on the board of NEMS, plus a salary and commissions.

VIC LEWIS: Brian and I used to fight like cats and dogs. I would never see face-to-face with him. And he wouldn't see face-to-face with me. He ended up, I must say, very well, but he didn't at the beginning. Brian was no businessman at all. Contrary to what a lot of things have been written about him. And on many things, when he called me in, when he used my abilities as an agent, he would argue against the point of asking me. I said, "Look, if you don't want me to tell you what you asked me, why ask me? Make your own decisions."

STEVEN GAINES: You set up the famous Japanese and Manila tours. Can you tell me anything about the Japanese tour? Was there a group of kamikaze Japanese students who wanted to kill the Beatles?

VL: When we arrived there, they were threatening. Imagine the reason was it was the hall that we were playing, which was called the Budokan, that had never been used for anything other than the actual fighting of war heroes, a special dance. And to them, the Budokan was the holy of holies. This group of young people said to play in a shrine was an insult. And they vowed that the Beatles would never leave Japan. Thousands of them raided the town with sticks, and they went on strike. And we had a situation whereby we took over the top five floors at the Hilton Hotel. The Beatles were not allowed out at all the whole five days we were there. Every day at showtime they went down in the elevator and we got into three cars, and we would go eighty and we wouldn't stop until we got to the stage door. There were men with rifles throughout the hall, the roads, bridges, everywhere, armed guards all the way.

There were major problems in the Philippines. They wouldn't go to the garden party given by the president's wife for children. I was sleeping in bed when two generals came to my bedroom door and said, "What time are you coming to the party?" I said, "What party?" I went down to Brian's suite in my pajamas and said, "Brian, you better get out of bed. We're in trouble. We've got to go to this garden party." Brian said, "Don't think about it. I've not received an invitation. I've never heard anything about that." I said, "Brian, get real, it's the Philippines." These generals kept on coming back to me, but the Beatles didn't go. Brian didn't even tell them about it.

SG: Do you remember the name of the promoter in Manila?

VL: I hope he's dead. He found me. He came here. He came here. It was through Don Blake. He'd come to book Matt Monroe, who was tremendous in Spanish-speaking countries, and he came to book the Ariana stadium, which is the biggest in the Philippines. They put up the money to get hotels booked. I went over with Monroe and it's fine, everything was 100 percent, right. So I had no compunction of saying to Brian, the biggest box office we could get was to go down there for one day. This guy has got to have the money in the bank.

SG: How much money was in the brown paper bag?

VL: Oh, it was a fortune. It was like $400,000 per show. And there were two shows in one day, we were talking about a million dollars. We did sixty-five thousand [attendance], twice.

SG: And was that the money in the brown paper bag?

VL: No, the legit.

PETER BROWN: The legit money, you had to leave behind? You never got that money?

VL: We got the 50 percent deposit. I always put on any contract about anything that had to be paid out before we even leave for the airport. It must have been the brown paper and the remaining part of whatever. I wouldn't worry too much about brown paper. Not that I actually feel sorry for them. Not very sorry for me, you know?

PB: No, but I mean, we did lose a lot of money on that gig on the Philippines.

VL: I still maintain, and I should make it very clear . . . I say it was Brian's fault. He had no right to make that decision. I mean, the boys were quite prepared. I would've made the odds to that, but we could have all been killed. No doubt about, I mean, we were in that much of being, being absolutely hacked to pieces. I planned everything . . . And we drove back to the gates and as we got there men with a motorcade came along and they'd locked it. And there were all these thousands of people coming down at the car, oh, we must go now, we've gotta or be blown up or killed or something like, you know, and, and Brian was still adamant about it, you know, about what he wanted to do. Oh fuck. He was a very stupid man. I mean, he could have come outta there. I mean, he could have gone [to the party] and most probably given him a piece, but you don't . . . I think the promoter was something Rome or so. I don't remember, Rome Romero, Romero . . . But that was a very interesting story. There were so many odd things that happened.

George Harrison

George Harrison remained an enigma to many people, even those who were close to him. For a man who lectured passionately about karma and the meaning of existence, he seemed self-protective and closed off. Witty when called upon, there were also moments when he could be quite boorish. Perhaps it was because he was only twenty years old when the Beatles became a global sensation. That might not seem particularly young in today's world of social media fame, but at the time, it was uncharted territory for the kind of adulation he was experiencing. It was also difficult living in the shadow of Paul and John. In the beginning, they were openly dismissive of him. Paul said he always thought of George as a little brother. At first, John pretended not to knows his name and sardonically referred to him as "that kid." Ironically, one of George's compositions, "Something," became the most covered song in the Beatles catalog. This interview was conducted at George Harrison's palatial home, Friar Park, in Henley-on-Thames, on November 5, 1980. George was gracious but cool. He made a pot of tea in the drafty, vast kitchen of his 120-room estate, and spent two hours lecturing about Transcendental Meditation and the details of a limited edition of his autobiography, I Me Mine, which is certainly how he must have felt getting out on his own.

In 2000, George was diagnosed with oropharyngeal cancer. After treatment failed in Great Britain and New York, he was secretly moved to Los Angeles in a house on Heather Road in Beverly Hills that belonged to Paul.* Paul went to visit George and sat quietly next to his bed and held his hand lightly. George died on November 29, 2001, in the company of his wife, Olivia; his son, Dhani; musician Ravi Shankar; and Hare Krishna devotees who chanted verses from the Bhagavad Gita. He was fifty-eight years old and left nearly $100 million in his will.

As George says in his interview, "Krishna says death is inevitable. There never was a time when you weren't and there'll never be a time when you cease to be. The only thing that changes is bodily condition. It's the same soul leaving the body at death as it was in the body at birth." George told Olivia that he didn't want to be remembered for being a Beatle, he wanted to be remembered for being a good gardener.

STEVEN GAINES: Manila looms large in the horror stories about touring with the Beatles.

GEORGE HARRISON: Manila is one of the nastiest times I've ever had. They took us right off the plane, these gorillas—huge guys in white shirts with short sleeves—and immediately confiscated our diplomatic bags—personal hand baggage from which we've never been parted, and which could never have been searched—Beatles privilege—and [these men] took just the four of us—John, Paul, Ringo, and me—without Brian or Neil or Mal.

SG: Is that true that you were able to carry drugs? You didn't have diplomatic immunity.

GH: Well, because in those days, there were never any guerrillas and hijacking and stuff like that.

---

* Reportedly, Paul McCartney refused to sell the house on Heather Road, afraid it would become a tourist attraction, and because it was where George's soul departed.

GH: They removed us to a boat in Manila Bay, surrounded by a ring of cops with guns everywhere. There was this terrible tropical heat. Straightaway, we thought we were busted because we always carried our hand luggage with us, with our shaving gear, cigarettes, and various other things. Cannabis, nothing nasty there, but . . . We thought they'd go right through them and find all the dope in our bags, and there we were on this boat, in this one cabin, surrounded by cops, very depressing. Brian came and rescued us, took us back to land. But originally, it was just the four of us on the boat. I remember going mad, demanding they let us off, and finally they did, someone put us in our hotel. We don't know why they took our bags, we don't know why they took us off the plane or why they put us on the boat. No one would explain anything.

It should be stated that for the Beatles, one essential safeguard was the presence of a small, experienced, and subtle retinue of people. In case of any public exposure, Brian Epstein was always available [to take charge], or perhaps a press representative might be the maximum on most occasions, and very often Neil [Aspinall] and Mal [Evans] would suffice. Somebody had to be around to take care of business and keep away a crowd of people, many of whom were mad as hatters. It's also worth saying that the reasons in general the Beatles security was minimal and restrained was that each of the four had a distaste for the concept of servants. Second reason, these were the 1960s, before the growth of terrorism, kidnapping, et cetera. The other reason was that pop music had not become rock, with all its swagger and presumption, poses and teams of retainers. We only ever had a roadie or two roadies, to look after our equipment and our baggage. I mean, can you imagine that now people are like—truckloads of equipment. Anyway, I don't know if any of that explains, but that's why it was.

SG: Were you aware of the influence you wielded as a Beatle? People copied the way you dressed, became interested in Transcendental Meditation, or took LSD because of you.

GH: LSD was just such a violent big experience, it seemed to have speeded up the process of perception. Normally something which might take a number of years of experience in order to result in some sort of knowledge—happened after ten hours of LSD. I mean that's how it affected me personally. Before it, I was totally ignorant, and afterward, I knew I was totally ignorant, and I was now on my way to having some sort of knowledge. I didn't have to go through any debates about the idea of God—just the whole word, God, I couldn't come to terms with it. I related it to childhood experience of Catholicism and going to church on a Sunday and seeing all that phony baloney. Whereas the moment I'd taken LSD, it just made me laugh because I understood it inside—just in a flash. I understood what the whole concept of God or religion was just by seeing it. I could see it in the grass in the trees, and the energy in between everything. It was just a realization. Those sorts of realizations didn't contain any sort of question or answer. It was just there. It was there. It was an absolute truth; it was like a light going *ching*. You didn't have to question whether it was, or it wasn't, it just was. And that's the sort of realization I had on the first acid trip. That from that moment on, I was perfectly satisfied with the fact that creation is, got supreme consciousness controlling it. Don't ask me why, to explain it, because it was a transcendental experience that was beyond the mind.

Before acid, we'd always tended to be a bit against whatever was the norm. We'd already been living for several years as the antiestablishment type of thing. When acid came along, for me, it just showed that love is a power that is binding everything together or repulsing everything away from each other, but it is an incredible power. And it enables us to feel things much deeper and see things much deeper. It was difficult to understand because after the first acid I ever had, it took me at least six months to try and scramble my brain back together again. What it did was blow away all those thought patterns that you programmed from birth, thinking that you had a set path, how you'd assume these thought patterns, and it just wiped all that away.

While it was fantastic in one respect, in order to come back down like the spaceman who goes to the moon and then he must come back down with that knowledge that he's gained—how to still walk around on this planet amongst the mundane, through the ignorance that abounds and how to come to terms with it without going bonkers. And that was the hardest thing about it. After a couple of LSD trips, it left me with a feeling of how it affects the brain.

SG: Did you take a lot of LSD?

GH: Not really—I took three very powerful trips—big, very important—and then it left me a bit unsure because I had to try and figure something out. I kept trying to. I kept thinking I could figure out the answers to it all, but the answer went round and round back to where you started. It was like the trap—like Memphis blues again to be stuck inside. And that was the frustration.

And I didn't take acid after the third time—by that time, I had gotten into Indian music and spent time in India—because one of the other things that came out of acid—or acid was like the key that opened the door, and when the door opened, Indian music, it just made total sense to me. India, when I went there, there was so much about it that felt like home to me. Not the surface that you see—all this poverty and the flies and the shit everywhere—went beyond all that. Smells in the atmosphere and the people's attitude and the music, the food, the religion—everything about it seemed like a home in a home. Home.

SG: That must have been the end of all drugs. Did you stop?

GH: No. Because then it also opened this other question which in my mind I needed to know—this thing kept coming into my conscious, or subconscious, which was this desire to know about the yogis in the Himalayas. Part of my trip to India was to go and try and check them out and find out [what] absolute was the cause of this other thing called the relative, and the Memphis blues again, stuck inside the physical relative world where everything is day/night, yes/no, up/down, good/bad, this/that . . .

Everything is dramedy. So if you accept gain, you set yourself up for loss. By embracing the day, you automatically have the night. You can't escape it. The only way you're not influenced by such things, if you're very successful, is not to think that it's wonderful because you can deal with it. You automatically inherit failure if you take on success.

Then came Maharishi, who in his way explained it much more simply by having the flowers and saying the petal is made out of sap—you see the petal leaf and the stem and all the different pieces of the flower, but the petal is made out of sap. The leaf is made from sap. The stem is made of sap. It's all sap. The sap is the cause, the effect is petal, leaf, and stem. See? So, you've got this cause and effect. The effect is relative—the leaf is relative to the petal and all these bits. But the absolute cause of it all is the sap. So, likewise in consciousness, you have an absolute state of consciousness which is pure, and it isn't this or that, good or bad, yes or no. That's why when they say we are all—that God lives inside all of us—that an atom is the same whether it's a piece of metal or a piece of wood or whatever—you can reduce all atoms or all matter down into energy and it's that energy that's within every atom which is the God or whatever you want to call it. Which is the absolute cause of the relative manifestation of relativity.

So after again realizing that, I also read somebody said, "Look fear in the face and it won't bother you anymore." 'Cause I knew I had to do acid again, just to not have it in the back of my mind as a fear of it. So then I did a lot of acid until in the end, I just threw it down the toilet because all it did was give me a pain in the back of the neck. Literally. Just you know, ughhhh. Then I could drive a Ferrari through the peak-hour traffic round Hyde Park corner on acid, and I learned how it was me controlling the body but it also had a negative thing because you could no longer go through the *Alice in Wonderland* bit where the carpet would fly and the room—

I'm not sure which year, but I went through the acid and the whole India bit, and then I took more acid to get over—so I no longer needed to think about it anymore. And then I just continued—

SG: Did the maharishi disappoint you?

GH: No. Not at all. The only thing that wasn't positive about that—I know exactly now what happened—it took me years to figure it out, but now I know—I don't want to mention it on your tape because then what I'm doing is setting up another character [Magic Alex] in your wonderful sixties plot, who actually is a turkey and who through his wonderful plotting and scheming, because of jealousies and various other worldly passions, set up Maharishi into our eyes as not being honorable. But Maharishi is and always was 100 percent honorable, as far as I'm concerned. He never did anything to let me down. All we did was let ourselves down and let ourselves be influenced by an idiot. Maharishi got harmed, we harmed ourselves, and ultimately in the karma of it all—

PETER BROWN: Have you ever spoken to Maharishi again?

GH: Maharishi? No, I've never— This is what I was going to get to later, is that although the sixties disappeared and seemingly all the love potential just went out the window, too, and everybody turned into ugly monsters again, there is actually—the sixties created a good solid base, and there's a load of people into meditation, yoga, and Zen or whatever, and they've all progressed on over ten years, and so there are a lot of good people but they're just low profile, because the more subtle tends to get not seen amongst the gross—

SG: When did it dawn on you how influential the Beatles had become?

GH: We didn't realize. You know, I think it just went in stages. We kept realizing we were getting bigger and bigger until we all realized we couldn't go anywhere—you couldn't pick up a paper or turn on a radio or TV without seeing yourself. I mean, it became too much. We became trapped, and that's why it had to end, is what I think. Because again, as it says in my book, you have to have space. We were like monkeys in a cage.

I think it was helped a bit by the fact that it was four of us, who shared the experience. I mean, there was more than four of us, there was Peter Brown and Brian Epstein, but there was only four of us who were actually the Fab Four—whereas Elvis had an entourage and maybe fifteen guys, friends of his, but there was only one man having that experience of what it was like to be Elvis Presley. I think that was far lonelier than being one of the Fab Four because at least we could keep each other laughing or crying or whatever we did to each other. It was definitely an asset being in a group.

SG: Tell me about the legendary Ad Lib [nightclub] scene.

GH: We used to go to the Ad Lib, but the thing was, we were probably so conceited and so in awe of ourselves. We used to hang out with people like Mick Jagger and the Rolling Stones quite a lot, and I suppose maybe Chrissie Shrimpton, who was with Mick and David Bailey. I knew them a little bit only because I married a model [Pattie Boyd]—whom you'll no doubt interview—and she was always hanging out with them and carrying bags full of shoes. I touched on the model world mainly because I was married to one. People didn't really look like they looked in magazines, because they had David Bailey taking the photos and they were all made up. We were also hanging out with Brian Jones.

SG: What was Brian Jones like?

GH: I liked Brian a lot, and later on, I realized it was probably because we were both Pisces. We both had similar natures. He was also similar in that he had a Keith and a Mick, whereas I had a John and a Paul. We both had that problem of two mighty egos to deal with in order just to try and survive. It was like a constant competition, which again rather than having just naturally, by being, you were allowed to have your space, you still had to prove and fight. I liked Brian [Jones] a lot—he used to get into a lot of trouble because it was the nature of Pisces—I didn't invent this, I read it and lived it, and I tend to agree with it—is that [Pisces] have a tendency to be quite spiritual on one hand but the other extremes like the two going in opposite directions. The other side is very prone to being drugged, and that you know I've had that problem in my life for a long time—I was very susceptible to dope, and Brian [Jones] was even more susceptible. He'd come [to my house], and I'd just hear his voice wailing at like five in the morning: "George, Geeooorrggeeee." So I'd wake up, see what was going on, and I'd look out the window, and he'd be all white and just shattered walking around the garden—just looking for somewhere to be. I would always meet him at that time of day and just try to calm him down. And I saw him a lot before he died in that sort of circumstance. The last time I saw him, I think was when I'd been in hospital to have my tonsils out and he came to see me in hospital and the next week he was gone.

He was like all of them who kicked the bucket—it was sad because there were too many pressures, really. Not just the pressure of being famous and having the press hounding you day and night and young fans hounding you day and night. Plus the drugs hounding you day and night. But they keep hounding you day and night. He had a lot of pressures.

PB: He left the Rolling Stones.

GH: Well, yeah, that's disputable. There are different schools of thought on whether he left or whether they were giving him the boot. In order to save face to say he was leaving to form his own band. But I don't know, it's not my business. But you know Mick had a very cross attitude on that.

SG: A philosophical question: When did the sixties end?

GH: I don't know if they ever began, really. I think we were still living in the fifties, is what we were trying to do. We were still in the fifties 'cause that's when it was starting all our influences in popular music and clothes. We started out just trying to get enough money so that we could buy James Dean jeans. We were just fulfilling our dream to be just like our heroes from the fifties. The sixties are only handy as a thing to call it. It's like subdividing the day into hours.

SG: The energy didn't dissipate at some point?

GH: Well, the energy dissipated as much as our brains. The energy dissipated because we grew and we fulfilled the certain desires that we must have had. Like I said, the fifties could be the "heroes of rock and roll" sort of thing. Just to be up there with guitars. Those desires that were probably to make a lot of money must have been in the mix. I remember being a kid of about twelve, dreaming of big motorboats and tropical islands and things which had nothing to do with Liverpool, which was dark and cold. I remember going to see Cliff Richard and thinking, Fuck it—I could do better than that.

I didn't know why I liked Indian music or any of that. Now I do. It's the karma thing, ya know—the only answer is to get to the spiritual side. And that is hard to explain. It's easier to tell everybody to go out and buy the autobiography of the yogi and a bag of [pot].

As Krishna says, it was inevitable. There never was a time when you weren't, and there'll never be a time when you cease to be. The only thing that changes is bodily condition. As you can see when a baby's born, and it goes through childhood into a young man like we all are, and we're getting it being a man, an old man, and then we die. And it's the same soul leaving the body at death as it was in the body at birth. The only thing that changed really is the bodily condition. And that is still only a few minutes out of the twenty-four hours of life span, and so to understand it fully is to say, when we die it's like, you know, having whatever credit and debit in your bank account counting as a kind of karma reaction, and when you get into your next body, you pick up whatever credit and debit you had. You know karma is such that it must be worked out.

You have to work your way back up it again. If you get a copy of my book, I describe it like you're born, it's like saying you've got a bit of string with all these knots in it, and what you've got to try and do before you die is undo all the knots. As you try to undo one knot, you tie another twenty. And so, it's karma—why I was born at that specific time to those parents in that house in that part of England in that year. This idea is what I think is the basic difference between Western and Eastern thought. That is like you know if you have a coin or all those [fortune-telling] sticks—and this is from the Western point of view—you throw them about, and that coin landed there with its head up, and that coin landed with tails up, is purely coincidental. But from an Eastern point of view, everything in creation at that precise moment had an influence on why that coin landed heads up or tails up. It's tails or heads because it's a whole other set of influences operating that. So it becomes diverse, you know. All the attributing circumstances as to why I was born in that house and why wasn't I born in John Lennon's house. Because he was born there. You know tonight why somebody was born in Vietnam or why is one person in Hiroshima when the bomb falls. You know it's a very difficult thing to understand, even to understand it enough to be able to get yourself off the mental hook, because we had this in India, because when we first went to India. When we first went to India, we'd been to Japan and the Philippines. Then we went to India. And we had all these Nikon cameras they'd given us, and this old Cadillac took us out of Delhi, and we went for a drive out to these villages, and that was our first real experience of what it was really like in India. Just on the street level. This little village full of people with no clothes, all dirty. Crowds of little kids who, if you pulled out a coin to give it to somebody, just to get rid of them, all these kids come with flies crawling all over them. I realized the Nikon camera I had was probably worth more money than everyone in that entire village had ever earned in their entire lives. So, how do you deal with that? With the contrasts that's happening in the world? You know I live in this gigantic mansion when other people have got no home.

I went into India and saw people with leprosy. You'd see a guy with no arms and legs, and the bit that he did have was all scaly and awful, and he's sitting on a little wooden box with roller skate wheels and he's being pulled along the street by his granddaughter. Or sometimes you'd see somebody with no legs on one of these things just scooting himself along the street by his arms. All the people who are in an impoverished country like India, there's a lot of diseases, and people are just made into cripples in order to make a living begging. That's when I began realizing, shit, I'm relatively good-looking, healthy, rich, and this person here is just, you know . . . How do you come to terms with that? You don't necessarily. Although it does help, you can't help people by giving something. If everyone who had something gave a little bit of what they had, it wouldn't be any problem. It's like something on TV the other day about asking people would you be willing to give up one meal a day in order to feed the rest of the people in the world. You know that kind of thing. It would be quite easy to give up one meal a day, but personally I don't think you have to do that. I think there's enough food on the planet for everybody.

You know, most people wouldn't even have to work if it was properly organized in the production of it, but then it means things like unselfishness, of which there is not much on the planet. Everyone's so into grabbing what they can for themselves. And there's enough food to give to people, but instead they burn it and tip it into the ocean in order to keep the prices high. You know, you wouldn't even have to go without a meal. Just a proper distribution, a humane outlook on the management of the world's resources. Everything would be okay. The way I came to terms with it was by understanding the law of karma, which is every action has an opposite but equal reaction. Like Jesus said, "God is not mocked for reap what you sow."

Then you realize that past karma is why I was born in that house in this body at that time and why I wasn't born on the banks of Calcutta. And then you start realizing is what we are now is the result of past actions and what we're going to be in the future is the result of our present actions. So, though it still doesn't help the guy with the hump on his back, at least you've only your own—we can only deal with our own actions, and maybe we've done some good actions in order just to be whole.

SG: I'm going to interview John when I return to New York.

GH: You'll probably think [John] is a piece of shit, you know? He's so negative about everything.

SG: Why is there so much tension after all this time?

GH: I don't know, because after five years of him being at home—for me, I thought I'd feel really good. Any bad feelings over things that might have happened in the past have been long since forgotten. And John, after five years, I would have thought it'd be great, and [then] he comes out in the paper, and it's not what I feel so much as what everyone else is saying. What's wrong with John, he's become so nasty. It sounds like he hasn't moved an inch from where he was five or six years ago.

SG: Well, maybe he has bad influences around him.

GH: Well, that was one thing [about] John Lennon that hit me too. Long time ago. At the time of this interview, George was about to publish his own book, titled *I Me Mine*.

SG: Why is the new book you wrote, *I Me Mine,* so expensive?

GH: Because I didn't particularly want to write a book. The publisher only does limited-edition expensive books. The amount of money I've made from it I've spent back buying copies of it to give to friends. It's just a lovely thing, look at it.

PB: Incidentally, Paul's done a book. It's called *Japanese Jailbird*. He's written down the entire recollection of his Japanese bust, from the moment he got off the plane to the moment he was released. He said he did it because prison was such a horrifying situation that he wanted to remember it, because he didn't want it to be lost in his memory and pretend it wasn't as bad as it was.

GH: I sent Ringo, John, and Paul all a copy of my book. I got a call from Paul. He called me up just to say how much he liked it. I shouldn't have called it *I Me Mine*, because that title was a bit much. I sent a copy to John. I'm wondering if he's actually received it, if he's received it, he probably doesn't like it or something offends him about it.

Alexis Mardas

Alexis Mardas was also known as Magic Alex, a name John bestowed on him because he was so taken with Alex's inventions. Alex was handsome, charming, and a charlatan. (He sued the Times in Britain for calling him a charlatan and settled out of court. He's dead now.) He was a snake oil salesman with a pushcart of whimsical inventions, like an artificial sun that could hang in the night sky and light up the streets, color-changing paint, a composing typewriter that sings as the songwriter types the music, and a light machine that turned music and words into colors, so that the deaf can hear through seeing.

Although John was usually suspicious of outsiders, he was somehow taken in by Alex's dazzle. Yet Alex wasn't just another talented hustler trying to make some bucks off a gullible rock star. He fed on John Lennon's fame. He was smitten with John-the-Beatle, and jealously guarded his role as John's best friend and whisperer. It was Alex who talked the boys into almost buying four Greek islands, and it was Alex who poisoned the Beatles against Maharishi, claiming he was molesting young acolytes. Alex also had an uncanny knack for avoiding trouble, like the night his apartment was raided for drugs, and he was in Paris for the night, but Jenny Boyd, who had rebuffed his advances, was arrested, and Alex got to play hero and bail her out.

It was also Alex whom John sent to Italy, where Cynthia was on vacation, with an ultimatum that that John was going to sue her for adultery, naming Magic Alex as the correspondent, and Alex was going to cooperate. It was true. Cynthia admitted that Alex had seduced her one night with wine and candles. Cynthia and John wisely both withdrew their threats and were granted an uncontested divorce, a decree nisi, which became final in May of 1969. John gave Alex a black £6,000 Italian Rivolta automobile for his trouble.

Interviewing Alex was cloak-and-dagger. He sent a chauffeur and a limousine with dark windows. His office was at a huge industrial plant on the outskirts of London. There was an armed security guard at the front double doors, forms to sign at the front desk, and personal identification checked before being issued an identification badge. Both Alex's suit and his office looked very expensive. He said he was in the "personal arms" business, and that he was designing bulletproof equipment, including cars. Alex's version of events follows:

STEVEN GAINES: How did you meet the Beatles?

ALEXIS MARDAS: I met the Beatles through John Dunbar, who was a partner in a gallery called Indica. I made a light machine that he sold to the Rolling Stones. John Dunbar knew John Lennon. John Dunbar approached John Lennon to buy a stroboscope. I don't know if you remember the famous stroboscope. A big strobe light, basically. I met John at John Dunbar's house the first time. I didn't realize that John was a Beatle. When John appeared, he didn't look like a Beatle. I was fascinated by his intelligence and his spirit. John was a person with a great sense of humor. We talked for something like four hours. John asked me to go to dinner. He had a big Rolls-Royce.

I think what happened to the Beatles is difficult to describe. Whenever we used to go out, thousands of girls [were available]. And very pretty girls. I was scared to death that they would kill me, when I was sitting next to the Beatles and [the girls] overran us. They would tear your clothes apart because they love you. Every time the Beatles, they want to screw a girl, it was the easiest thing in the world. Walk out into a disco or to walk into a restaurant, point to the girls, and say that we liked this one. And this one we like.

Personally, I believe that this is reason John is with Yoko today. And perhaps, this is the reason Paul was with Linda at the time. I'm sure they're madly in love. As far as I'm concerned, and this is not a great compliment for Yoko and Linda, but both of those girls, they're not the most feminine girls I've seen in my life. I mean, a Beatle could have, uh, the most beautiful girl in the world. They had everything. I mean, the money, glory, anything you can imagine. Knowing John so well, I believe that the only reason he picked Yoko was [he wanted] a negative reaction. I mean, it was purely a negative reaction because he couldn't take any more girls in the world, actually. I mean, he knew that he could have any girl. And the girls, that were nice-looking—he couldn't stand them. I mean, from morning to night, there were girls not boys—actually, running after them. We used to go to his house and think that we are in peace. Suddenly a girl with a broken leg is jumping over John's fence to, to get an autograph. It was a pain in the neck. John wanted to be with a woman. But he needed as well very, very much a friend. He needed a male friend. And my opinion is that Yoko, he managed somehow to combine both. He had a fear for pretty women running after him. Yoko was not very pretty, uh, at all, and he replaced a male in his life plus a female.

SG: Did the other Beatles dislike Linda as much as they disliked Yoko?

AM: Yes, they did. They did. Perhaps they disliked her more than they disliked Yoko. Not perhaps. Indeed, they disliked her more than they dislike Yoko for, uh, several reasons. Eh, one of the reasons is that they dislike Yoko. But nobody ever thought really at the time that this story of John and Yoko would last. Yoko was a very peculiar animal altogether. Um, but the general idea is that it's one of, uh, John's eccentricities. But how long will it last? The case with Linda was not the same. What's common between Linda and Yoko was that Yoko was pussy with John. Linda was pussy with Paul. But we never thought that Yoko would be in some art house somewhere one day. She has no chance. This was with Linda as well.

The other thing is that, uh . . . I mean, at a certain point, I thought they would commit suicide or something. The change was too fast for them. They started with nothing in Liverpool. Too fast they had everything in the world. The Beatles are going too fast. Everything. They made all the money. George Harrison was the youngest millionaire ever made. I know other millionaires. But, uh, they have the money from their fathers. George made his money. They had all the money in the world. More than they could spend. They had all the publicity in the world. They had all the glory they wanted. I mean, their own Queen in their own country made them MBEs. If the Queen of England was in a car going down Oxford Street, perhaps a dozen people in the street will turn to see the Royal car and applaud. But if a car with a Beatle inside was going down a street, there was a guaranteed traffic jam. And, uh, the Beatle had to run to save his life, jump out of the car and start running the other way.

We went to once the cinema. And, uh, they wanted to go to a movie. They wanted so much to go to a movie. It was . . . They couldn't dare to go to a movie. So we managed one night. We went to the movies. The conclusion is that I thought that we would get killed at the end of the movie. Somebody saw a Beatle. I don't remember with whom I went. One of the Beatles. Most likely John, actually. Uh, somebody recognized, in the middle of the film that there was a Beatle and screamed. Screamed, "A Beatle!" So, people they walk up from their seats, and they start running to approach the Beatle like, uh, rats. They want to see him. So the projection stopped, the lights went on, and we had to escape from there. It was like a cinema on fire.

We reached a point where quite often, the Beatles were longing to have privacy. Even Ringo at the time was saying that he would give anything in his life to go to a local pub, which is a tradition in England, to stay around to have a drink. He couldn't. So he had to build the pub in his house because Ringo had a full pub inside his house. But it's not the same thing, because he missed the pub. That, that depressed them very much. I mean, they had everything from the one side, and from the other point of view that they lost completely their freedom. And for me, this is the reason they moved out of the stage completely. They didn't want this publicity.

SG: That's what George said today. He said it was too much. It was horrible.

AM: So they made a mistake. They thought that by moving out of the stage and sitting home and going to the studio to make recordings, people will forget, and they will leave them alone because they're just recording artist. It was the same. Didn't make any difference. They were equally famous. And it was a tremendous stress for them and tension daily. I mean, they, they hardly moved ever out of the houses, because they couldn't live in town. They used to live isolated in the house without friends, without anything. So you can go mad like this because you have everything, and you can't use it.

PETER BROWN: *In February of 1968, the Beatles decided they would all go to Maharishi Mahesh Yogi's spartan ashram in Rishikesh, India, for a three-month course in Transcendental Meditation. When word got out where they were going, what was supposed to be a holy retreat became more like summer camp for young celebrities. The glamorous gang of petitioners at the maharishi's ashram included John and Cynthia, George and Pattie, her sister Jenny, Ringo and Maureen, Paul and Jane Asher, jazz musician Paul Horn, Mia Farrow and her sister Prudence (whom George longed for so much he wrote the song "Dear Prudence" for her), and singer Donovan (then dating Jenny*

Boyd.) *The journey proceeded by plane, taxi, jeep, donkey, and ox-drawn cart, over a rope bridge, to where lay the maharishi's ashram. It was not Shangri-La, although Ringo compared it to a Butlin's holiday camp.*

SG: What happened in Rishikesh that caused the fallout with the maharishi?

AM: I can tell you exactly what happened in Rishikesh. It was a misunderstanding, to start with, between the Beatles and myself. Although it's not nice to say, I believe that at the time I had a certain influence over the Beatles. I will tell you what happened in Rishikesh, but let me say something first. Again, it is immodest to say this, but I believe that at the time I had a certain influence over the Beatles, specifically over John, and John was in his own way, leaving the group. I was extremely close with him, and [he gave me] the name Magic Alex. John and I had fairly intelligent conversations together. John got [influenced], I believe now, from all the pressure I was applying to him, that there is another way [instead of drugs] and it's worth trying this other way, and if it doesn't work, go back to drugs if you like. Go back to drugs or go and do anything you like. So they went to meet Maharishi to see what else is around [instead of drugs].

And it was supported by George automatically, and I knew that George was going to support this. So they went to India anyway after this. I suggest to John to introduce him to Maharishi, and I knew that Maharishi was coming in England and I want them, I wanted to introduce them personally to Maharishi. And I believe that Maharishi can help, uh, not practically, purely by diversifying John's mind from drugs into something else. Not that Maharishi had any, uh, abilities, magic abilities.

At a certain point, they left for Rishikesh. I refused to go there, although they insisted so much, for many reasons, because they left for Rishikesh as a group, I mean as a friendly group, together. I was fascinated by India because I knew India and they wanted me to go there because they were going to Maharishi and I was involved with Maharishi before. But I refused because I felt that I put so much work in electronics and for six, seven months, absolutely nothing had happened because I was splitting my life into two. As well, the team of people I had in the electronics were not people to carry on their own. When the Beatles arrived in Rishikesh, I was receiving nonstop letters to come to Rishikesh and I still have those letters. Letters that were insisting. One of the Beatles came back fairly early. Ringo came back earliest. I saw Ringo and he said that I must go to Rishikesh. As well, I received a very warm letter from Donovan. I [received] another letter from Jenny [Boyd]. She was in Rishikesh as well. Jenny, at the time, was my housemate in London. She was living with me in the same place because the police raided her flat. When they raided her flat, I was in Paris for two days. I arrived back in the middle of the night, and I thought there were burglars in the house. When I arrived, the house was totally apart. The police got in and took the house apart, completely. They cut the mattresses with knives. They lifted carpets. They ripped everything. And they broke things as well. Plus, they arrested Jenny. In Jenny's room, they found a pipe that belonging to Mick Jagger. Mick, I think, gave it to Jenny. And Mick had smoked on a couple of occasions on this pipe. When the police got Jenny, they asked her if she smokes [marijuana] or used any drugs, and Jenny said, "Yes. I do." I had to act as a guarantor, to sign a piece of paper to, to get her out [of jail].

Jenny sent me a very warm letter from Rishikesh, saying it was great there and they needed me and they were all together. John sent me a letter, and I got a message through Ringo, and Donovan sent me another letter, and then people from the Apple office in London would start pushing me because they were receiving messages from the Beatles that I must go there.*

---

* There were no cell phones in those days, so the messages to Alex must have been sent by carrier pigeon.

The pressure went so high, I went. When I got there, I didn't believe it. I had said to them that Maharishi can do miracles, but this was a plot. I never believed, personally, that Maharishi can do miracles. I never believed that Maharishi was a holy man altogether. I thought that Maharishi is phony on his own. I mean, he is a traveling yogi who walks around, who makes money, and he tries to teach. There was nothing wrong with his teaching, as far as I was concerned. I knew Maharishi because Maharishi came to Athens to give some lectures, so I was present in the lectures and had a good long talk with Maharishi.

SG: Why didn't you tell the Beatles before they went to Rishikesh that Maharishi was a phony?

AM: This is a good [question].* I didn't . . . No. I want to say I had several problems with the Beatles, which again, it's better if I don't go there, but the problem was . . . Personally, I wasn't touching drugs at all. I mean, not because I had something against the drugs, but I was all the time high on my own, and what was the point to go botanicals? John was doing his best to put me into drugs because he was enjoying himself. He felt that we are friends and I had to share the enjoyment, to try it at least once, and I was trying to persuade John that there was no need. I don't need it. The day I need it, I will try.

It was an adventure to [travel] to Rishikesh, partway by donkey, part by plane, part by jeep. But when I arrived at the ashram, I thought, This is a joke. I mean, [I wanted to] take them away the next morning, if possible. Rishikesh was not an ashram. I spent a considerable amount of time in all sort of ashrams, I mean tantric ashrams, Hindu ashrams, Krishnaveni ashrams. Rishikesh was a luxury hotel with full service. Maharishi was preparing a swimming pool. It's the first one I've seen in an ashram. Also houses with several facilities, and meals. It was totally organized, like a private community belonging to Maharishi. He

---

* A question he never answers.

had an accountant, who I met on the very first day. I've never seen a holy man with an accountant. I mean, they are ways to run communal monies, use committee who does this but not a qualified accountant keeping books, or the bookkeeper, they're running the place.

And because the Beatles didn't know anything about ashrams and they haven't seen anything before because they went for Maharishi, not for the ashram. Maharishi didn't allow men to stay with their wives. John was delighted with the idea. He loved it, actually. I think it made Cynthia very unhappy. She wanted to stay with John, everybody had his own problems. My great interest was with John. I was very happy because I found John much healthier. The color in his face was different and he was happier and he took the whole thing very seriously, and he was trying hard and he was so excited when I arrived because perhaps I was part of the reason he was there.

Uh—but, uh, for the Beatles was, uh, they couldn't see what I could see there. Uh, not that they would like it very much without, uh, George, perhaps yes, but John, not necessarily. All those, without all those comforts around. I mean, I don't think that John was prepared to make his bed and cook his food. Perhaps he would have been prepared after the first week, if you like, or ten days in the ashram, because John acclimatized fairly fast in situations. But arriving there and having no services, I don't think that he would like it very much, although John was simple in the way he was living at home.

I went to see Maharishi. Those talks, they turned into business proposals at the end of the day. I never thought that Maharishi was a holy man, but I never thought that Maharishi was a businessman as well. I mean, making money off of the thing. Then there was a question of the Beatles and all the other people in his place that they had to pay to Maharishi a specific part from their annual income. The agreement there was that the Maharishi followers, they had to pay to Maharishi personally. They had to pay Maharishi, depending on the category of people, not in their financial state but anything between 10 percent and 25 percent—in some cases, 35 percent—of their annual income to support his movement. He asked everybody for this. The third day, I had enough.

SG: What was it that you told the Beatles to get them to leave?

AM: It was a matter of presenting evidence to the Beatles. My decision was not to take the Beatles, because the Beatles don't belong to me. I decided to postpone this decision for a long period of time because I felt that the good was done to the Beatles, in this place, after London, the lack of drugs. The fact that John Lennon himself was going through a difficult period in England, and he was getting detoxicated. Not from drugs, from the period. So I decide that I'm going to leave them there for as long as possible because the surrounding does them good.

The other problem with Maharishi is that Maharishi was a clever man. He was trying to use me. He was trying to use me in the following way: when he realized that he had a potential enemy, he tried to flatter me. He knew my interest in electronics, and he was starting to discuss with me a big project to put up in the Himalayan hills. It would be one of the strongest radio stations to broadcast his message around the world.

SG: The straw that broke the camel's back with the maharishi was that he was fooling around with an American girl?

AM: That's correct. This is absolutely correct. Not only with one American girl, but he was also fooling around with several American girls. The story is appalling. The Maharishi was making all of us eat vegetarian food and badly cooked, in a sense, very poorly cooked, but hielf, he was eating chicken. Exclusively chicken, nothing else. No alcohol was allowed in the camp. I had to smuggle alcohol in because Cynthia wanted to drink. Cynthia was very depressed. John was receiving letters from Yoko Ono. Yoko was planning to win John. She was writing very poetic and very romantic letters. I remember those letters because John was coming to me with the letters, and Yoko was saying to John that, "I'm a cloud in the sky, and, when you read this letter, turn your head and look in the sky, and if you see a small cloud, this is Yoko. Away from you but watching you." It was very romantic if you like.

Poor Cynthia was prepared to do absolutely everything to win John. She was not even allowed to visit the house where John was staying. Cynthia thought that she would spend her twenty-four hours a day with John. But Cynthia was not prepared to meditate and to be influenced by Maharishi's teachings. She was longing for a drink. And a lot of other people that were longing for a drink. Now, drinks, they were strictly prohibited in the ashram, but when it was discovered that Maharishi had a drink, and I said, "Just a second, at least equal" [laughs].

SG: How'd you find out about Maharishi and the girls?

AM: I found out about the girls because Maharishi used to isolate people who had problems with meditation. Maharishi was promising that if you sit under the tree, you close your eyes, and you repeat your mantra as much as you can, you will meditate. People would sit down under the tree, they'd repeat their mantra twenty-five thousand times. If somebody was walking behind them, they would open their eyes and turn their head. So Maharishi was forcing everybody to meditate, and a lot of people, they were saying to him that, "Doesn't work for me. I can't meditate. That's that."

After dinner means eleven o'clock at night to see him privately. He was living in a luxury villa. It was a kind of fortress, isolated from the rest of the houses in the community, on the other end. He never invited any of the old ladies. He was talking to the old ladies during the lecture about their problems, and then he was speaking to girl twenty-one years old and suddenly he's, "And you have a problem and that you should concentrate and we should meditate together and come to see me."

But although Maharishi had a lot of free time during the day because we had periods of free hours during the day. We had to meditate, all of us. Maharishi wasn't meditating with us. He was at home, working on his [inaudible]. He never suggested to anybody, "Come see me during the day [inaudible]." He was suggesting come after the dinner. After dinner—

SG: Did any of the girls tell you that he came on to them?

AM: Listen. Not only she told me, we went there watching [through the] maharishi's windows. Because for me, it became kind of a personal battle between Maharishi and me, a mental battle, if you like.

Peter Brown on Maharishi

It turned out that although the Beatles were finished with the maharishi, he wasn't finished with them. I got a call at the office from an executive at ABC-TV in New York who wanted to double-check that the Beatles were on board for the maharishi's one-hour television special. I said the Beatles were not on board at all, and that we had never heard of a TV special, let alone committed to it. Later that day, I got another call from ABC, saying that the maharishi insisted it was true. I called the maharishi where he was staying in a hotel in Falsterbo, a seaside resort in southern Sweden near Malmö, and told him to stop using the Beatles' name, but either he couldn't understand what I was telling him or he was faking. I decided the best way to put an end to it was to go to Sweden and see Maharishi myself. In early October of 1967, I met with him in Falsterbo, and as forcefully as possible, I told him the Beatles were not in his TV special and that he must stop using the Beatles' name. He smiled beatifically and nodded, but by the time I arrived back in London, ABC-TV was on the phone again, saying that the maharishi was still insisting he could deliver the Beatles. Now I asked George and Paul for their help, and on the fourteenth of October 1967, we three flew to Sweden, where George and Paul told him sternly (as sternly as they could get) that they were absolutely 100 percent not going to be on his TV show. That was the last we heard from him.

Pattie Boyd Harrison Clapton and Jenny Boyd Fleetwood

In retrospect, Swinging London didn't do justice to the excitement of creativity in London in the 1960s. It was a silly description made up by Time *magazine to try to explain the excitement and creativity of what was happening, but it's hard to capture lightning in a bottle. It was exhilarating to get up in the morning in London. We were at a confluence of history. England was reviving from the horrors of war in the 1940s; we saw the end of the grim, gray conservatism of the 1950s and politics so riddled with scandals that it took the rigid class system with it. There was a new aristocracy in London, not of lineage but of accomplishment: people in their twenties, trailblazers in music, art, photography, and fashion. Ironically, Swinging London was classist in its own ways, the way a high school cafeteria might be. The nucleus was small, perhaps only thirty people, and it had its own social elite and royalty. They had their Olympus, the Ad Lib Club, improbably on the fourth floor of a building, above a cinema. It was where Ringo proposed to Maureen. At the pinnacle of the new elite were four young lads who had somehow amassed much more influence over the public than mere mortals from any walk of life before them. Perhaps at the very top were model Pattie Boyd and Beatle George Harrison, the couple who personified Swinging London to the hoi polloi. Born in Somerset, Pattie had spent part of her childhood in Nairobi. A product of convent schools, she was working at a magazine in London when she was discovered as a model.*

Pattie was a rare agent of inspiration, the muse incarnate. It's an indescribable effect, and the best evidence of her gift is in the songs that were written for her. Her first husband, George Harrison, wrote "I Need You," "If I Needed Someone," "For You Blue," and "Something," one of the most covered love songs in recording history. Her second husband, Eric Clapton, wrote "Bell Bottom Blues" and "Wonderful Tonight" for her, as well as one of the greatest passionate love songs, "Layla."

Jenny Fleetwood, Pattie's sister and wife of Mick Fleetwood, is now a PhD, author, and drug counselor.

STEVEN GAINES: You were a photographic model when you met George. Did you want to become an actress?

PATTIE BOYD: No, I just did some commercials. My agent sent me for what I thought was another commercial [but turned out to be the movie *A Hard Day's Night*].

SG: You met George in the scene that takes place in a railway car?

PBOYD: That's right. That was the first day of shooting. I was nineteen years old. George was shy. Towards the end of the day, Tuesday, he asked me to come out with him. I declined. Because I was seeing someone. We had to go back the next day for a bit more shooting. And by that time, I didn't think he . . . He was very handsome. Yes. Very handsome. We had to do more shooting and he asked me out again and I said yes. I was with George for two years before we got married. It was a small wedding, just our families and Brian. It was real quiet. No big publicity. We moved to a house in Esher, not far away.

SG: What happened to your modeling career? You became one of the top three or four models in Europe, didn't you?

PBOYD: I was working an awful lot before I met George. Once we were married, I could be more selective about what I did.

SG: How did the Beatles first become interested in Maharishi?

PBOYD: I saw on a poster that the maharishi was going to be lecturing in Wales. He was appearing there at the Hilton Hotel in London. I saw this in a newspaper on the Wednesday before and told everyone. The four Beatles went to the lecture, and they were in the audience. Everybody was watching enrapt, a pretty big audience, about fifteen hundred people. After they took a picture of Maharishi sitting in a chair and smiling, with the Beatles literally at his feet, they looked totally magical, you know? I think it was just the most perfect timing because everybody was a little bit lost. We didn't admit it to each other, but I think everybody was.

SG: When the maharishi came along, did the drinking and drugging stop?

PBOYD: At that point, everybody had a lot of LSD. Everybody was very out of it almost. They lost touch with reality. So Maharishi was actually the other end of the scale.

SG: You went to see Maharishi at Normal College, in Bangor, North Wales, where he was speaking. All these amazing people went to Wales. There were the four Beatles, Paul with Jane, and Mick Jagger.

PBOYD: When we went to Wales, that was when we heard the news of Brian's death, which was such a shock, he was so positive and so strong, so good to everybody. It was such a shock.

SG: John told the press that meditation gave them the ability to withstand that kind of shock. Was everybody aware that Brian was so deeply troubled?

PBOYD: No. No. He kept it a good secret. I didn't realize that at all. I'd see him occasionally. We were at his house in London, you know, we'd all be pretty [high], and Brian would be really fine. Do things like cut up newspapers and stuff like that. It was just sort of funny, but I suppose it was, you know, in fact he wasn't.

SG: Why was he cutting up newspapers?

PBOYD: Well, 'cause he was so high, I suppose. It was just something to do. Just, being silly. I mean, everybody being high at the same time there was no one to . . . say there was that firm route . . .

SG: You and George were the last people to leave India, why did everybody else leave? But somebody came back right away saying the ashram was really disgusting. Think Ringo had already left because Maureen had a phobia about flies. Why did John leave?

PBOYD: 'Cause somebody, whether they made up a rumor or it was true about Maharishi, that he tried to have sex with one of the girls, sort of shocked us, in particular John, who wanted a reason to get out anyway. That's why he left. He was in love with Yoko, was all this time. Yoko was in. And I think she would write to John in India.

SG: How does Magic Alex come into all this?

PBOYD: Magic Alex had a very close relationship with John, and he didn't like the idea of John and the maharishi, he wanted his own guru.

I know there was a little gossip about Mia Farrow and Maharishi.* Then there was this other girl that was quite high up in the Transcendental Meditation people. She was Indian, but American. Alex immediately befriended her. I think his reason was to make mischief. For the first few days, I felt very—lots of animosity towards Maharishi. I didn't quite get into it. I remember thinking, Everybody else is thinking he's okay, so it must be me. I remember George came to me and said, "Listen, you're responsible for this," because I had seen the poster.

JENNY BOYD: Pattie had a dream. She said that the maharishi was playing around with a chick. Pattie said, because she and George were responsible for me, they weren't going to let me stay there. "You are going to come with us. We're leaving." Then I remember that after breakfast [one morning], they obviously talked about it, and everybody walked to the gate. There was the maharishi with the boys, standing under the umbrella. When we left, he called out, "No, come back, come back, come back." There were cars of schoolkids waving.

We drove for miles, miles, hundreds of miles. I remember at one point all the cars stopped and suddenly John screamed! Suddenly just screamed. He was desperate to leave. I don't know why. But see, he believed in the maharishi, absolutely believed. The whole thing was, you'd spend as long in meditation as you could, which would mean you'd go down supposedly and get rid of whatever the core grievance was within everybody. So John would have a terrible time, and then he'd come up and say, "I was trying to meditate but I can't do it." He was trying to get into it. And I think it affected him the worst. Because he was suspicious originally, then he started to believe. I think he got the spiritual belief cut off, which is far more dangerous than any other belief [to lose]. I remember us stopping in the cars

---

* Many years later Mia Farrow confirmed that when she was alone with Maharishi, "Suddenly I became aware of two surprisingly male, hairy arms going around me." She left the ashram immediately.

that were driving us away, and the question was, "What do we say?" Obviously, whatever the Beatles said at that time was very important. Do we dare tell the world? It was a very big issue—"He's a shit; no, he's not." There were a couple of other people at the ashram who were Maharishi addicts who probably had been with the maharishi for seven years.

SG: All these years later, do you think the maharishi was up to no good?

PBOYD: To this day, nobody knows. Nobody really knows. Alex's main thing was to prove to John that this man wasn't anything he was cracked up to be. Alex was a very proud person, and he gained John's confidence and friendship, which was very important to him.

JBOYD: I rented a room in Alex's house. I was sort of dating Donovan at the time. Alex, who was a very naïve, intelligent person, heard Donovan was going to India, and I said I would meet Donovan there because I was going with my sister and George. Donovan said he wanted to take me away. Alex was always playing a sort of thing with Donovan. For me. Alex didn't really want me. It was almost because Donovan was so . . . John Lennon came around that house also. And that's where they tried to bust him. The police were obviously waiting outside. They knew John [Lennon] came around, too, and they tried to bust him. They were waiting there for a month. The day the police actually went for it, we all left for India.

SG: Did Magic Alex get busted?

JBOYD: No. *I* got busted, because I didn't know until after I came back from India, they had found drugs in the apartment. By English laws, the person who rents the apartment, which was Alex, should have been busted. Not me, but because his father is like a high hierarchy in the

Greek army, they said, 'If you touch him, there's gonna be so many unhappy English people in Greece. So then the rap was on me.*

SG: What did Alex look like?

PBOYD: A star. Handsome. He also had the most amazing things in his mind. It was fantastic. A wall of speakers in the wallpaper. I think so. But they were still very naïve that time. There were also so many people ready to jump in. You knew they were sort of hustlers.

PETER BROWN: I must say, I'm very intrigued about Magic Alex. I never saw any wrongdoing from Alex that I can put a finger on. It's just that in retrospect, he always seemed to be there when something wrong was going on. I do remember this quite clearly that it was Alex who came back from Italy and told John that Cynthia had been messing around with somebody.

PBOYD: I think Alex offered to go to Italy. I think he asked John, "Should I go and check on Cynthia?" I think Alex wanted to be a very loyal friend to John. He wanted John's attention. There were enough men that wanted his attention at that time. It wasn't physical, it was mental. They were almost desperate, the heterosexual ones. Alex had seen Cynthia in Italy with Roberto Bassanini, who she eventually married.

SG: When did you and George break up? Do you remember what year? You were still with George when Eric was in love with you for a long time. Because George had a fight with Eric over you at that point.

---

* Alex was luckily in Paris the night of the bust. No matter what he told everyone, although his father was an army officer, he did not have the power to protect him from the police in London, let alone threatening to make English people unhappy.

PBOYD: Well, I told George. I just wanted to die. He did have a fight.

SG: But I remember reading that you went to a big party, and you and Eric were on a path off in the forest or something, walking hand in hand, and then George drove up and his car headlights picked you out from the forest.

PBOYD: Well, actually, no, we went outside to talk. By this time, it was sort of getting light mist on the ground.

SG: I remember hearing that you were faithful to him and you were faithful to George, and that's when Eric wrote "Layla."

PBOYD: 'Cause he wanted me to go and live with him. I couldn't.

SG: Why did you finally break up with George?

PBOYD: Because we were going in different directions.

SG: It wasn't that George announced he was in love with Maureen, Ringo's wife?

PBOYD: No, we were just sort of, you know, we were moving in different directions.

SG: Marriages in the rock and roll business don't last long. Some women are always involved with musicians. For instance, a girl who marries a tailor—whose first husband is a tailor—almost never winds up with another tailor.

PBOYD: I guess if you're into music, you want, you know, don't want to live with somebody, go out with somebody who goes to bed at ten o'clock at night and has to teach school the next day.

SG: Was George very frustrated that he couldn't get his music on the albums? Was that a matter of great contention to George?

PBOYD: Well, it was, yes. Paul was particularly choosy on, on songs that he'd written himself.

SG: What was it that pulled them apart finally?

PBOYD: I think they disagree with each other a bit too much.

SG: What caused the animosity?

PBOYD: Maybe four people were becoming individuals, you know, before they hadn't fulfilled their individual needs, they were branching out. 'Cause they had the time and the money to branch out and they became individual personalities? But very much so.

SG: Do you think that Yoko and Linda helped polarize the situation?

PBOYD: Yes. Strong women. Definitely.

SG: I mean, I think also to some extent John had been taking a back seat over for a while. George had been feeling his own as a musician, and Paul had taken over. George probably felt stronger than he had before. And that led to conflict with Paul. They were all feeling assertive at the same time. How could George go along with Allen Klein?

PBOYD: Klein was very clever. He could turn on his charm if he wanted to. You see, at the time, it seems like it was a choice between the Eastmans and Klein. I think George didn't get on at all with John.

On the trip to Haight-Ashbury

PBOYD: That whole hippie movement, which by the way, the Beatles found disgusting. I think the hippie movement . . . I went to Haight-Ashbury with George.* There was really no grace. It was summer and we understood that it was a beautiful and nice, a charming place to go to. I don't remember why, but the limo driver refused to take us all the way. He wanted to park in a narrow little road up a hill. He told us we can walk down to Haight-Ashbury and he'd wait for us. We walked down and went into one shop, and people started recognizing George, they were walking towards us, recognizing him and me. By this time, it was quite frightening. And then I remember just telling the people to stop following us. Somebody said, "Let's go into the park. Let's go to hurry up." And we tried to keep walking, but then we had to stop because there were so many people behind us, and we tried to carry on walking and then we said, "Okay, we'll stop here." Suddenly, out of nowhere, this guitar appeared and was forced into George's hands. They kept insisting he play for them, and there was suddenly an incredible realization that all these people had dropped out, decided that they were hippies or whatever their attitude was, it was their interpretation, and it goes all wrong. George gave the guitar back, and they allowed us to go up the street to the car. Sure enough, because George didn't accept some drugs that they were trying to give him, they started rocking the car. *Bang.* It turned into a horror show, which was rather frightening.

---

* Pattie forgot they were all on LSD that day.

Neil Aspinall

Neil Aspinall was the true and only fifth Beatle. To give any other person that appellation is specious. He was a Liverpudlian mate from their days in the Cavern Club, and just as much a part of the Beatles as any of the others. While it's true he carried their instruments and helped load and unload equipment, he also went with them everywhere on all their adventures. He was part of meetings, his opinions weighed with equal respect with any of them. He was an outspoken guy with a northern trait: He spoke the plain truth. He saw everything and knew everything. He was trusted. He never gave interviews, and the one that follows is only because Peter Brown asked him. After the Beatles dissolved, Neil took over running the moribund Apple company and editing a film that would eventually be released as Let It Be. *It was the outtakes of this moment that were used to make the brilliant six-hour Peter Jackson documentary,* Get Back. *Neil was also assembling a massive book project, to which all the Beatles contributed, called* The Beatles Anthology. *For Neil, it was like tending a graveyard. Neil was diagnosed with lung cancer in 2007. Paul went to visit him at Memorial Sloane Kettering Cancer Center in New York, where he was moved from London as a last-ditch effort for a treatment. When Neil died in New York, on March 24, 2008, Paul offered to pay for all his medical bills.*

STEVEN GAINES: Pattie told us a story about a rude awakening you had when you and George and Pattie and her sister Jenny went to Haight-Ashbury in 1967, the summer of peace, flowers, and LSD.

NEIL ASPINALL: I was there. What I really don't like talking about is . . . You know, you can ask Pattie, right? You get her point of view. Okay? From what she was seeing, right? And when you tell me what she said, I think, *That's not what happened to me.* Mind you, we were all smashed on that trip to San Francisco. We were on acid, for a start. We got in this private jet [somewhere in the United States], and I remember going to San Francisco, and taking George and Pattie and Jenny. We went to Big Sur. I remember Pattie and Jenny dancing on the beach. I had one of those little concertina things. When we went to San Francisco, we got out of the car and we were walking down the street and suddenly we realized there were hundreds of people following them. They were getting a bit worried, and they wanted to make it back to the, to the limo. And these people just surrounded them and said, "Well, you know, give us some blessing or give us some . . . lay something on us."

SG: The story you just told is exactly parallel to what she remembers. She said you went to San Francisco. You were on acid. You walked around Haight-Ashbury and people started following you. They wanted George to bless them, or lay hands on them. They went to this big park, and they demanded that George play guitar. Pattie said George realized that he was like a "thing" to them, and that wasn't what it was about, his music, or anything spiritual. The crowd turned hostile?

NA: The thing that really pissed me off about it was just walking down the sidewalk in Haight-Ashbury, there were these big Hells Angels guys who would just break you in two. You know, just [the wrong look and] they would kill you, right? That's what it looked like. Maybe that's not what they were, but it looked like that. In leather with studs in the back. Big, big Harley-Davidsons—and you'd be walking down the thing, right, and two of them would be arguing, and then everything's all "Peace and cool. Really, man, I'm not really angry." It was all so phony. That's the, the thing that really—

SG: How did Hells Angels get invited to that Christmas party at Apple?

NA: You've got to ask George that. I don't know. I just know they ate the turkey—by the time it had gone from the kitchen through the door, it had disappeared.

PETER BROWN: But don't you know that there was a fight? They kept demanding to know when the food was going to come.

NA: George had invited them. Derek Taylor asked them, "Look, can you please leave?" And Frisco Pete said, "Well, it's not up to you, man. George invited us. If he wants us to leave, we'd leave." Derek [Taylor] told George, "These guys have been here for a long time now, can you do something about it?" And George said to Frisco Pete, "Hey, listen, you know, uh . . ." He did one of those like ying-yangs [laughs]. You know when it's like, you know, ying-yang, in-out, up-down. "I invited you. I'm asking you to leave." And the guy said, "That's cool." And they all left.

SG: George was brave.

NA: Not really. He invited them.

PB: But they were looking for a fight.

NA: Not with George, no.

On Brian Epstein

NA: When Brian was going to be the Beatles' manager, my sister called me and said she heard he was gay, which was like a big scene. I said, "No, I didn't know that." She said, "Well, he is, so careful." I told the Beatles, "Hey, do you know that Brian's queer? But don't tell Brian, because I don't want to have any problems." You know what Lennon's like. The first thing, he goes to Brian. He and Brian drove off into the fucking [night in Brian's car] pilled out of their brains. And John said to him, "Hey, Neil says you're a queer, man. Is that true?"

I don't know what the end of that conversation was. All that I know is that when I went to some ballroom in Manchester, while the boys were onstage, Brian said to me, "I've got a bone to pick with you" [laughs]. I said, "Oh, have you? Well, what is it?" He says, "Well, you've told the boys something that's not true." I said, "Have I? What's that?" He said, "You know what it is." And I said, "Well, so do you. What's the big deal anyway?" But he kept trying to tell me he wasn't. I said, "Yes, you are." He said, "No, I'm not!" I said, "Well, you are." And he said, "No, I'm not. I'm not." I said, "Well, what do you want me to do, mate? This is crazy." That was the day that Brian and I established some sort of relationship. After that, he was always okay. We certainly didn't care. Everybody has their own life.

SG: Did the Beatles know that Brian was being blackmailed the final night of touring at the Cow Palace in San Francisco? Did they know then that's why he wasn't at the last concert?

NA: Well, why would Brian be there? He had his own things to do, and at the time the concert was over, it was not the last concert. I'll tell you what happened. I don't know what the sequence of events were, but I remember [we were coming home from Japan and Manila], being in, uh, I think it was the InterContinental Hotel [Taj Mahal] in Bombay. And we're all sitting there and Brian's there. I think Brian might have said something about the '67 tour or something. I remember George saying to Brian, "Hey, listen, this fucking tour in America every year, like, it's not an annual event because I don't feel like doing it anymore." And the others all think, Yeah, that's a good idea. We don't feel like doing it anymore either. There was no pre-planned thing that we knew Candlestick Park was the last gig. That's not true. We never planned anything up front. That was the last gig we did in America, but it was months later that they would say, "Hey, are we going back to America next year?" No, no thank you. But it wasn't pre-planned. Nothing they ever did was pre-planned. No pre-planning. Like I was saying to you before, when you were talking about Candlestick Park, you know, we were all supposed to know that that was our last gig in America, right?

Neil on Manila

SG: Can you set me straight on what happened in Manila on the tour of 1966? Were you roughed up at the airport?

NA: No. We got off this plane in this crazy place. Hot and horrible. And we all carried drugs, right? Well, they did. [The Beatles were told by armed policemen to leave their handbags on the tarmac, to get into one of the waiting cars, and were driven away, leaving Neil behind.] That leaves me with a bunch of loonies. Nobody speaks English. The only thing I'm interested in is that those four cases over there aren't going anywhere. They're going to go with me. But there's so much confusion that I end up in some car with these briefcases saying, "Take me to the Beatles!" This guy drives off, and I end up at the end of some pier, with all these guys minding this pier with submachine guns. They've all got submachine guns, right? And for the first time in my life, I was confronted with this fucking submachine culture that you don't get in England. I ended up on the end of this pier. I asked, "Where are the Beatles?" They pointed to this little pink light disappearing over the horizon, and they said, "There they are." I said, "What do you mean 'There they are'? Where's the hotel?" They're on this fucking boat. Apparently, they'd been taken from the airport straight to this boat. The boat takes off, and they're like, "What the hell are we doing here? Where's the hotel? What's going on?" It was total confusion, a situation that we'd never been in before. Manila was lunacy.

So the boat comes back, we go to the hotel, wake up the next day, and we're all waiting for the room service to come. The Beatles are all in bed looking at the TV, seeing this commentator at the president's palace saying, "The Beatles will be arriving any minute now." You're in bed waiting for your breakfast to arrive, and some television commentator is saying you're gonna be, you know, eighteen miles away at the reception for Imelda Marcos. The Beatles are lying in bed waiting for their breakfast, just getting up. The whole trip to Manila was very confusing. Like ordering food. The food would come up on some big trolley, a big silver tray with one of those rolltop things. We'd say, "Oh God," and roll it back again, you know. We didn't eat for three days because it was almost like they were sending us putrid shit. You know, and even the corn flakes you got at breakfast, you're like, "Corn flakes, we can't go wrong with that." Right? Except the milk was undrinkable. I didn't eat for the whole time I was in Manila.

They were playing to one hundred thousand people in two concerts that day, and then we were going to leave in the morning. The next day, I went to the airport with Mal and put all the equipment into some van, and at the airport, there was like a roundabout, like at any airport, but there's a traffic controller telling us to keep going round and round in circles. I said, "Stop!" I said to Mal, "You stay with the van. I'm getting out and find out what's happening." I got out of the van and I went into the airport, and the people who were at the desk were gone.

The terminal was empty. It was like it was designed, almost, to give us a bad time. So I just jumped in front of the van and said, "Stop!" And just as we got the equipment out, the elevator broke down. Because you have to take all the stuff up in the elevator. So we had to lug everything up by hand to wherever the terminal was. Then we get there and we're all going to New Delhi, thank you very much, why are they putting tags for Copenhagen on our stuff? Because they were sending them anywhere in the world. They weren't going to send them to where we wanted to go. I ended up [jumping] over the counter where the, the bags are going down the [conveyor belt] and taking all the tags off and getting the new tags saying New Delhi on them. Then we got through to the departure lounge. And I mean, it was fine, no hassles, nothing. It was just me and Mal. You know, we're all there. And next minute, there's all these guys walking down the corridor with short-sleeved Hawaiian T-shirts on, like, hustling and pushing and punching, just creating this whole fucking scene. It was amazing.

SG: Were there any tough moments after John said, "We're bigger than Jesus"? There was supposed to be snipers at concerts.

NA: Nah, there was no tough moments. A banger went off in Memphis, I think, and everybody ducked for ten seconds.

PB: But wasn't George and the boys a bit more worried about it than anyone else? Because Paul was besotted by the Kennedy assassination.

SG: It was reported that there was a rainstorm and where they're supposed to play isn't covered, and they were afraid they were going to get electrocuted. Brian said, "We've got to cancel this. I'm not going to send them out there to, you know, to get electrocuted in the rainstorm."

NA: I remember it raining somewhere, and the promoter said, "Just don't touch the mic with your lips and you'll be all right."

PB: Do you remember when we went to that party at Brian's house in the country? There were two occasions when everyone was there. It was the housewarming party, which was crazy. Everyone was on acid. And then there was the other party . . . Brian wanted to talk to them about the renewal of their management contract.

NA: I remember a party when we were all going to plan what we're going to do in the future, but nobody talked about it. We were all going to meet at Brian's house in the country to plan what we're going to do in the future. It was an impossibility because we'd never done that before in our lives. When we all got to Brian's house, nobody had anything to say. The only thing I remember is Brian saying to me, "You've got a nice profile." And I thought, What's he talking about? [Laughing.] It was just one of those silly days. It was a nice day, but we never talked about anything.

SG: I think the reason that he asked them down there to plan about the future was really to talk about them renewing the management contract. Brian had a lot of fears about whether they were going to leave him. Did they know that he was incapacitated on pills and sleeping all day and was missing meetings?

NA: No, I didn't know. I know he'd been through one trip where, uh . . . he tried to commit suicide, so the paper said, but really, he'd just had too many pills. I think it was a much looser situation than anybody ever gives it credit for. We didn't care. It's like me now. I'm looking after Apple, and I don't think that Lennon, McCartney, Harrison, and Starr give a shit whether I get up at two o'clock in the morning and take care of business from two in the morning till ten o'clock the next day. They don't give a shit as long as business is being taken care of. Who cares whether it's taken care of between nine in the morning and five in the evening, or ten in the morning till six? Who cares? As long as business is taken care of. As far as we were concerned, our business was being taken of. And don't forget, we'd stay in bed till three o'clock in the afternoon, get up, go over to EMI by five o'clock, and work until five o'clock in the morning. Then go down to some club or get a meal wherever we could find one, then go home and go to bed. If our lifestyle is that bizarre, how could you complain about someone else's life?

SG: After Brian passed away, the next thing that happens was *Magical Mystery Tour*. Was it a fiasco because Brian wasn't around, or was it just a fiasco?

NA: It was a bit of both, and a bit of something else at the same time. The need to keep on trucking despite everything. Don't know what we're doing, but we're gonna keep on trucking.

SG: Were they surprised when *Magical Mystery Tour* got slagged off by the press?

NA: No. They were pissed off. I mean, if you make a Technicolor movie, where you've got a dream sequence in which cows are changing color, and it's shown on black-and-white television [laughing], so you've got half an hour of nothing but clouds, black-and-white clouds, I mean, you'd expect to get slagged off. You don't put a colored product on black-and-white TV.

SG: One of the people I'm curious about is Magic Alex.

NA: Magic Alex kept bringing me fucking apples with a radio in it. That's all I remember about Alex.

SG: Did you have wallpaper in your office with speakers in it?

NA: No, no. I don't know what they were, but they weren't wallpaper. It was polystyrene, about that thick, with what looked like glue, went around like that, looked like a speaker. Couple of wires in the back and you got sound out of them. Look, Magic Alex was okay. He wasn't a bad guy.

SG: When did they realize that Apple was falling apart, that they were throwing away money and stuff?

NA: That's a popular myth, about Apple throwing away money. And maybe we were. But we were all still together. We were all still trucking, we're still a big name. Some turkey might say, "You're throwing your money out the window," we'd say, "Well, yeah, okay. Well, what are you going to do about it." Apple could have kept on for the next ten years at a million dollars a year. So, in retrospect, Apple was fucking cheap compared to what we had to pay to get out of it.

SG: But the Beatles as a group were already in trouble. Paul had met Linda, and John Eastman was in the picture. John Lennon went out and found Allen Klein.

NA: Allen Klein, this little fat guy, seems to be okay, right. But I hated that bastard. Mick or somebody told John, Allen's fine. John signed with Allen and the next day, Mick will say to Klein, "Fuck off," and he'll go someplace else. I don't remember if Mick tried to warn Brian. You know, Mick's not dumb. If you think about it, Apple Records was only going for eighteen months. Everybody seems to think it was going for like, ten years or something. Apple had 7½ percent of the market.

SG: Did Klein intentionally pick the *Let It Be* release date so that *McCartney* would come out the same time as *Let It Be*?

NA: If George wants to put his album out on November 17 with his record company, okay, and John wants to put his album out on November 17, right, why can't they do it? What's the big deal? There's no big deal unless somebody makes it into a big deal. And that's what Klein was doing. He was calling Paul a shit and saying that Paul was doing it on purpose to fuck up *Let It Be*. But McCartney's not doing something to fuck up something else. That's not his nature. He's not going to do that any more than you would or I would.

SG: [Perhaps] if they said, wait a minute, hold off *Let It Be*, and for three months, and you'll double your sales because this other album is coming out, I'd want to be reasonable. Ringo tried to talk to Paul, who yelled and screamed and threw Ringo out.

NA: Ringo shouldn't have done it, for a start. But secondly, you must understand that *Let It Be* had been made between June and July. We arranged the release day for November 10. Then between July and the end of September, McCartney had gone away and done his own album and decided he's going to release that on November 10 . . . or something. *Let It Be* was made in 1969, right. And then because of the movie and putting all that together, and waiting for the movie deal, *Let It Be* had been delayed for eighteen months. In the meantime, the Beatles have gone into the studio and done *Abbey Road*. Done it, pressed it, released it. It was out there, okay. Then all the split-up crap happened, right. And when the movie deal was done with United Artists for the documentary *Let It Be*, it had been like almost eighteen months since the Beatles have split up. In those eighteen months, McCartney had gone away, he'd done his own album and he wants to release it, and his release date happens to coincide with something he'd been part of two years ago. Now you're saying, "Oh, I'm not allowed to release my new McCartney album, because you've got this *Let It Be* album coming out. Well, fuck it. You know. I'm not going to back off." [They] just put 'em both out. Who gives a shit? What happened at the time is like a personality crisis, right, where it was like, you could have put out *Let It Be* three years later, right, when McCartney was putting out *Band on* *the Run*, and if Klein had still been there, he'd have still said, "You can't put out *Band on the Run* [laughs], because we're putting out *Let It Be*."

SG: How'd they manage to record *Abbey Road* when in the movie, um, *Let It Be*, which came before *Abbey Road*, they were at each other's throats already? How did they manage to do that?

NA: I don't know. You know what's amazing about *Abbey Road* for me, right? Is the last track on the last side of the last Beatles album is "The End." Then they followed it with the national anthem—just like when you were a kid when you were leaving the cinema, they played the anthem. If they didn't know it was the end after doing that, man, then nobody did. For me, that is like, amazing. That's why they can never get back together. Because they've done it. 'Cause they've done the end. And the end says you've got to "carry the weight, man." That's what we're all doing here. Whoever was ever associated with them in whatever capacity, including them, right, you've all got to carry whatever the weight is. And, uh, for me, it's part of why they were unique. You know, no other band has ever done the last track on their last album and called it "The End." That's it. So the ball game's over, thank you very much, and do something else.

David Puttnam

Lord David Puttnam was born in North London to a working-class family. He dropped out of school at age sixteen to become a messenger at an advertising agency. Two years later, he had become an agent to some of the top photographers of the 1960s, including David Bailey and Art McCain, putting him square in the middle of Swinging London. He later switched careers again to produce the films The Killing Fields, Local Hero, Midnight Express, *and* Chariots of Fire, *which won the Academy Award for Best Picture. He sat in the House of Lords for over twenty years, and in 1983, Puttnam was awarded the Citizen of the British Empire.*

DAVID PUTTNAM: My career was entirely made by the Beatles. It was 1962, and I was a messenger at a very good advertising agency. I was bright-eyed and bushy-tailed, but I had long hair and always wore a white suit. They figured I would be a turnoff for clients. Whenever they were pitching for business, and new clients came to the office, I was told to go around the corner to a coffee bar and wait until the clients left, and a guy would come get me and say, "All right. They're gone. You can go back to work." Then came '63, and suddenly the Beatles emerged, and people started saying about me, "Oh, really. He looks a bit like Paul McCartney. He's got long hair and maybe that's all right."

Suddenly, after the Beatles, the floodgates opened and they made me a kind of spokesman. I was actually allowed to meet the clients. Within two years, I split and became a photographer's agent. I did very well. I had Art McCain, David Bailey, Brian Guthrie, David Montgomery. I was a lucky man. I met the Beatles at Vogue Studios. David Bailey was doing a book, *David Bailey's Box of Pinups* [portraits of the royal court of Swinging London], and the Beatles were just coming in. David Bailey said, "I've got these boys from Liverpool. I cannot understand a word they're saying."

STEVEN GAINES: Can you explain the Ad Lib nightclub to me and its significance to the whole scene?

DP: The Ad Lib had just started. Max Maxwell, the art director at *Vogue*, took me there the first week it was open.

SG: Was the Ad Lib famous because of the famous people who went there? Why that place and not any other?

DP: God knows. That's the most interesting question of all. It's chickens and eggs. Within two months, there were famous young people there. It wasn't beautiful, particularly. It wasn't even unusual. It was inconvenient to get to. It was cheap, looking back. Even at the time, it was an inexpensive club, whereas all the other clubs were very expensive. It was unique, I suppose in that it catered to a different type of club, the new type. It was the first club that catered to photographers and fashion designers. Let me put it another way. Two hundred people like me broke through in different fields within the same year.

The irony of Swinging London was when I was eighteen, I sort of knew it was going to happen. There was tremendous energy, and once that energy found a place for itself, it was extraordinary. It kind of had to happen. Why it happened the way it happened, and why it happened that year . . . I talked to Paul about this. He doesn't know either, except he's got that story about, "You know, we're going to be the toppermost of the poppermost." He says they always knew they were going to really crack it, the same thing, but how? Why?

I think that if you saw photographs of the Ad Lib you'd see, it wasn't a particularly terrific place. There was not a special table. The only real difference was whether you wanted to be over by a window or nearer the door. It was just a whole series of benches and then the odd occasional stool you could sit on. It was all built like that around a central dance floor, and there was a kind of stage. George was hardly ever at the Ad Lib. Ringo, yes. Pattie Boyd was a young model at the time, going out with a photographer, Eric Swaine. Paul was at the Ad Lib, and John a lot. Ringo and John the most, and Paul sometimes. The media invented people. In Jean Shrimpton's case, very reluctantly. She didn't want it. She found it hard to handle.

There was one incident at the Ad Lib that shook me rigid. It was very late. It was about three in the morning, and the place was three-quarters empty, and a very strange thing happened. John Lennon was sitting there, and there was an almost empty pitcher of water, and a waiter came and took it away. Lennon called out to him, "I wanted that," and the waiter said, "I just want to bring some fresh." The waiter came back with a pitcher full of fresh water with ice in it, and John Lennon stuck his cigarette in it, in the fresh water, and it shook me rigid. I don't know why. I found it such an offensive thing to do. What he did was he looked at the waiter when he did it; just looked at the waiter.

I've never been crazy about John at all. I do think that John was a genuine anarchist who in any other walk of life or at any other period of time, would have just got squashed. Someone would have gone, "What?" The Beatles happened so quickly that John, the type of person that John was, became current. I think at any other time in any other country, John couldn't have happened. He was too big to stop. His insolence, I think rather cruel insolence, but it was insolence.

The first conversation I had with Paul, he was very impressed by the fact that I was married. He was intrigued and we talked about it several times, and then he came by my house a few times. I used to see him. I used to bump into him a lot. Paul was always very polite, and I found him very easy to talk to, but he was always asking about marriage and sex. The first question every time I'd see him, he says, "You and Patsy still married?" It was the first fucking question every single time. Paul, he fucked everything that moved and yet didn't seem to want to. Out of the bunch, they always regarded him as the beauty. I guess I identified with Paul as a person who had any interest in me at all. I liked him, genuinely. I think he liked me because I was straight. I'm a straight, middle-class boy. The happiest I've ever seen Paul, and my best relationship with him, was during the time he was with Jane Asher.

Paul, from the very moment I ever met him, treated me like an equal. Never, ever condescended, was never difficult. I remember a conversation we had one time. We were talking about different decades, and I used to be a little nervous around him. We'd been talking about fashion, and I remember once saying, "Look. We've got through the forties, and not a lot happened fashionwise. I don't even know what happened in the forties." Paul said, "Only a fucking world war, only six million fucking Jews got killed. That's all that happened in the forties." Like I was this real kind of cunt. I remember Paul would steer the conversation right around and not let you.

The other thing was John used to be very defensive about the music, whereas Paul couldn't wait to play you what he'd either just thought of or if they had a demo. He'd always play me demo music, whereas John used to be much more kind of uptight about others hearing it. The other side of Paul is that he wanted the world to believe that he wrote the music, and John wrote the words. I think he very deliberately tried to give that impression about the work. I think there was friction there. The truth of the matter was Paul wrote wonderful fragments, and John was the one that turned the fragments into songs. That's why so many of Paul's songs are still bits of different fragments of songs. They're not really songs. So the interesting thing is that John in a way, I think, supplied the steel in the music. Paul would write marvelous little motifs.

I remember the moment that Brian died. Oh God, they seemed to begin to be entirely self-destructive, entirely. From that moment onwards, I don't remember ever hearing from Paul a sensible word, not one, single . . . I don't remember a cohesive idea was followed through. They were mad. It was like everything flew apart. It was one lunatic scheme after another. There were always schemes. They weren't like scams; they were schemes. They were never moneymaking schemes. Their ideas weren't Allen Ginsberg far-out. They were juvenile because they had never been thought about. If you go around ten restaurants at lunchtime, you will see groups of people meeting and talking about ideas. Nine hundred ninety-nine times out of a thousand, they leave lunch, but somebody is stuck with the bill, and the only thing that ever happens is that there is a bill. That's the only tangible result of that lunch, right? It was like that with the Beatles. Everything was just scattered.

Brian gave some stability to it. I remember him telling me that there was a policy. We're not going to do that. We're not going to do that. I've turned down that. You had a sense that someone had made a series of decisions to which were going to be roughly adhered. There didn't seem to be any central policy.

Magical Mystery Tour was a very interesting thing because, again, schematically it was a perfectly reasonable idea. Commercially, it made sense because they knew they could make money on a special, no matter really what they spent. Musically, I think it was a very strong piece. I thought in many ways it was some of their best stuff. From the moment they started meeting to make the film, there are fantastic stories of total lunacy. You hire a caterer, and you tell him there's going to be one hundred meals and one thousand people would turn up, and then it would be hysteria because there wasn't a thousand meals, and no one had told the caterer. They never knew how many meals they were supposed to be preparing.

I walked in on the recording of "A Day in the Life." I remember it was lunacy. I looked at George Martin, and he went [shrugged]. He was embarrassed. There were a lot of people there, a hell of a lot of people. It was actually a very advanced idea to film a recording session; a very clever idea, except that making anything in life, I suppose even growing a redwood, requires a sort of organization. When it comes to film, you have to actually plan a week ahead, and if you wanted something, you had to book it, and then once you've booked it, that person also has to be fed, and that person as well as being fed to be transported.

SG: Did you have relationships with Linda and Yoko?

DP: I remember when John and Yoko were busted, that Paul made the great gesture of inviting them to stay at his house if they wanted. It was like Paul was saying, "Well, I know the world is against you, but I am still your mate," kind of thing. Linda was there at the time. I felt used, not by Paul but by Linda. She could be very dismissive. She got hooked into the photography thing, and asked me to do some favors, and I did them as best as I could. She is a very demanding girl. In the end, I thought, Hang on a second. One day I got a phone call at home, and my wife said, "It's Paul on the phone, but Linda wants to speak to you." They also used to do this extraordinary thing. One would cover for the other. Most peculiar. They even still do it. We'd reached that point where every single phone call was, "Do you have? Can you do?" and it would always start off very sweet, and then a week later, if you hadn't done it, she could become quite demanding. "Where should I get my color processed?" "Am I getting ripped off with syndication?" She was in fact a very aggressive young lady, who was using Paul's contacts and who he was. I really felt used. It started out as a favor, and then it became an obligation. The relationship I had with them altered. Up to that point, I felt a 50/50 relationship with Paul, where I really enjoyed him asking me anything. It was nice. I never felt pressured by or put on by him, ever.

For some extraordinary reason, I got to know John Eastman. I guess through Paul. John Eastman used to have dinner with us whenever he was in town, which would have been almost every other week. Paul sometimes would turn up, so I used to hear the other side of it. Paul was very anxious to show the opposite of himself. Paul always gave the impression that he thought that John had lost his trolley a bit, and that people like Alex, for example, he wanted nothing to do with.

SG: Was it bitter and vindictive between John and Paul?

DP: Oh yeah. Very. I had no experience with that sort of business in those days. It seemed to be a level of bitterness that I have never encountered. Real commercial hatred, about one person that was ripping off the other. I sensed that Paul would have killed Klein had he bumped into him. Allen Klein became the object of Paul's hatred [instead of John and Yoko]. I think Paul got obviously very, very emotional. I used to hear all sorts of incidents. I remember over dinner, sometimes I'd almost fall out of my chair, half in amazement, half horror, at the fascinating incidents that would be recounted by Paul. There was a whole series of all-day Wednesday meetings that Eastman used to come to, and there were real black comedy stories. They were quite incredible.

I remember John Eastman saying to me, "I fucked it this afternoon [in reference to who was going to buy NEMS]. I blew it. I had Klein and I realized it too late." Klein apparently had very grandiosely said during an argument, "Oh, I'll put up a million dollars of my own money [to buy NEMS]," and John Eastman said no. He thought later, "Klein doesn't have a million dollars. If I had said, 'Right, take it out of your own pocket,' it all would have ended because Klein didn't actually have a million dollars." Eastman said, "I let him get away with it, and now we'd lost it."

Martin Polden

Attorney Martin Alan Polden did not believe in the legalization of any drug, including marijuana. He did believe that in the late sixties, the police were targeting rock stars and other high-profile personalities of Swinging London for publicity purposes, and for the personal glory of the anti-drug zealot Sergeant Norman Pilcher. Polden, whose primary interest as an attorney was environmental causes, found himself representing dozens of prominent young people on drug charges, including artists, fashion designers, hairdressers, photographers, and rock stars—including Mick Jagger, George Harrison, and John Lennon, who was busted on marijuana charges. (Polden told the court, "Mr. Lennon is an artist of note and integrity. He has brought some pleasure to millions. He has stood by his views. He is entitled to some compassion of the court.") Polden grew up in London and received his law degree at London University. He was awarded his OBE for his work against environmental pollution. He was age fifty-one in 1980 when this interview was conducted.

MARTIN POLDEN: I first appeared—*appeared* is right—in connection with clients that I had in the design and boutique world, who were in King's Road area. They were suddenly caught up with drugs issues with the police. I must confess that until I'd had dealings with their problems, I really hadn't known much about drugs and the problems of drugs. Initially, it came to me purely as a question of public rights and personal liberty. Because it all followed rather in the wake of the legalization of homosexuality, so the police had no homos, no queers to be hitting on, and they suddenly discovered this marvelous thing with drugs. The way that happened is because the police, I'm afraid, do not like to lean on certain sections of society, whereas they had a marvelous whipping boy with the queers. When that started to dry up, they were looking elsewhere. That's how I look at it, cynically. The civil liberties issue developed because under the laws as they were then, the police specifically could walk in and search your home, whether or not they had a right to.

Suddenly there was this impact: young, certainly educated—if they weren't educated, they were very vocal people—getting involved with this kind of drug nonsense. That's how I first became involved. I was then acting for a lot of young designers who were mainly operating in Knightsbridge, Kensington, Chelsea. Clearly, I had a, a kind of interest in this sort of issue. There was enormous enthusiasm. Social historians will have to explain why it was. I got thrown into the whole thing for years. It was all rather exciting because they were young, lively people. The pot issue was something aside. It really became a question of, is one entitled to, to smoke as one is entitled to drink? But beyond that, one gets into more serious areas of, does soft lead to hard drugs, and do people who are on hard drugs have first been into soft, and all these bigger problems should one legalize.

STEVEN GAINES: Was the notorious Sergeant Pilcher a righteous zealot or just plain vicious?

MP: Norman Pilcher was on the Scotland Yard Drug Enforcement Squad. All these people started to take shape because the whole thing feeds on each other, the whole process of victim and assailant. Philosophically, one needs each other. As I understand it, the Drug Squad was formed in Scotland Yard, and it didn't know itself how big it was going to become.

The Beatles and friends relax at Brian Epstein's country house in Sussex, June 1967. (*Left to right*): John Lennon, Cynthia, Peter Brown, Pattie Harrison, Paul, George, Jane Asher, Mal Evans, and Neil Aspinall. (*Photo by Brian Epstein*)

(*Below*) Left to right: John Lennon, George Harrison taking a photo of Ringo, Paul McCartney, Peter Brown, Mal Evans (head cut off), Jane Asher, and Ringo Starr photographing George. (*Photo by Brian Epstein*)

(*Above*) Peter Brown (far right) and the staff at NEMS, Great Charlotte Street, Liverpool. (*Photographer unknown*)

A brief holiday in Wales with Peter Brown's parents and Paul McCartney's father and stepmother. (*Photo by Peter Brown*)

(*Above*) In Malmö, Sweden, on their way home after asking the Maharishi to stop promising ABC-TV that the Beatles would appear on a television special with him. (From left: Peter Brown, Paul McCartney, Börje (Peter's partner), and George Harrison.) October 15, 1967. (*Photographer unknown*)

After John and Yoko's wedding in Gibraltar, flying in a private jet to Paris. Peter Brown, Yoko Ono, and John Lennon. March 20, 1969. (*Photo by David Nutter for Camera Press*)

(*Right*) John in newly wedded bliss returning from his wedding in Gibraltar "near Spain." (*Photo by David Nutter for Camera Press*)

Peter Brown and Pattie Boyd embracing each other at an Eric Clapton concert in 1974. (*Photo © Richerd Kleinberg*)

At Peter Brown's Southampton house with Paul, Linda, Stella, and Heather McCartney, who is petting Gary Lejeski's dog. (*Photo by Peter Brown*)

(*Top*) Pattie Harrison at the Maharishi's ashram in Rishikesh, India. (*Photo by Balden for* Transworld)

(*Above*) The Beatles in the early days of their fame with the British Prime Minister Harold Wilson. (*Courtesy of Zuma Press*)

(*Above*) Paul's brother, Mike, Paul McCartney, George Harrison, and John Lennon listen intently to their new guru, Maharishi Mahesh Yogi. (*Photo by Jack Smith/Camera Press*)

The Beatles, Brian Epstein, and Peter Brown arriving in Munich on June 23 at the start of the Beatles' 1966 world tour. (*Photographer unknown*)

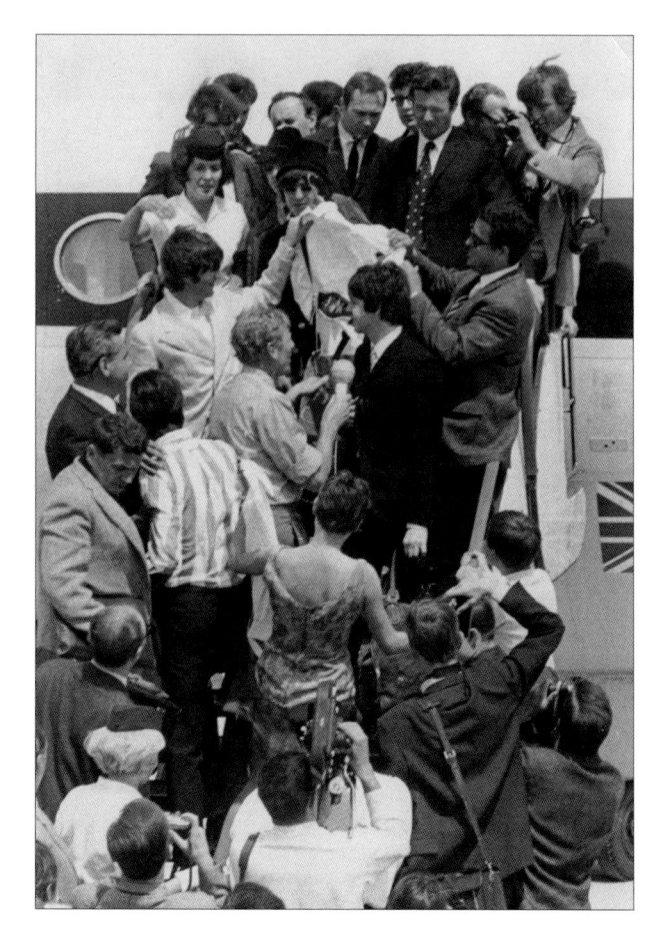

(*Above*) Peter Brown and Queenie Epstein at her house in Liverpool, October 1980. There's a picture of Brian on the table next to them. (*Photo by Steven Gaines*)

The telegram that Brian Epstein carried around with him in his briefcase wherever he went. (*Photographer unknown*)

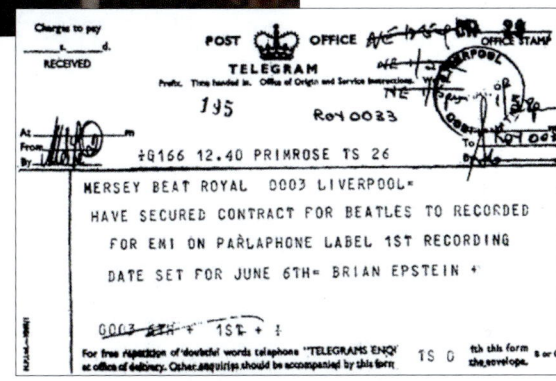

Paul McCartney and Linda Eastman. (*Courtesy of PictureLux/The Hollywood Archive/Alamy Stock Photo*)

Ringo Starr and Peter Brown at the Beatles' office in London. (*Photographer unknown*)

Brian Epstein and Peter Brown watching the recording of background tracks for "All You Need Is Love." (*Photo © David Magnus*)

The men on the squad had previously been on stolen-property duty, stolen-car duty, or whatever. And suddenly, they're the Drug Squad, pushed into that. What the hell do they know about this? All they know is there are these, uh, rich young kids, uh, and older rich people who should know better, because it was very much that time, middle-class upper-class syndrome. It was only developed gradually, that you got the, the working-class type kids into it. Because Pilcher was the detective sergeant in charge of the Drug Squad, it was operating centrally. So he got the big busts. And he also made it his business to get the big busts. He enjoyed it. And suddenly these were people the press were interested in. I remember when John and Yoko were busted, the press were outside waiting for them to be brought out.

SG: How did that happen? Were they tipped off?

MP: Clearly someone spoke. Clearly. Well, it wasn't them, it wasn't us. Guess it wasn't John and Yoko.

SG: Did you represent Mick Jagger or Robert Fraser?

MP: In fact, it was Robert Fraser that opened the door to several other people so that I represented Mick's brother.

SG: [Reading from newspaper] July 1, 1967, Robert Fraser convicted of possession of heroin after raid. Also, Rolling Stones' Keith Richards sentenced to one-year imprisonment for allowing his house at West Wittering, Sussex, to be used for the smoking of cannabis.

MP: Robert Fraser came to me after his case. He had a fantastic art gallery. Then somehow, I got involved in Eric Clapton. I went to see Eric Clapton. I think I got a call one night at the office from George Harrison, asking if I'd go to Eric Clapton. They were very close. I remember picking up the phone, and someone said, "This is George Harrison from the famous Beatles" [laughs]. It was a very strange thing because they treated the Beatles as something separate from themselves at that time. So that's how it started, and then when John was busted, I was brought into that. Um, then after that, there was George.

SG: You said in the newspaper that you hoped "the police will now accept that this is a closed season for the Beatles."

MP: Pilcher finally got charged with perjury and sent to prison for two years and two months.

SG: Did you represent John and Yoko in 1970, when they went to the London Clinic? Were you involved in that at all, them going to the London Clinic for heroin withdrawal? I'm not exactly sure if there was an arrest.

MP: There was no arrest. If they went in, they went in voluntarily. There's one of two things. Either you're so far gone that you're committed because you're not capable of doing it yourself, or you go in as a voluntary patient for whatever your problem is. She was heavily pregnant in the hospital. She lost that baby.

SG: Was she put under stress from the trial?

MP: It's difficult to know. It couldn't have helped. It was a very unpleasant experience because I think they were very private people thrust into enormous limelight. In part, they did it themselves. They attracted publicity, they couldn't help it, but they also wanted to have a private side to themselves. It's not very pleasant when that private side is thrust out. They were going through an enormous crisis at that time. The whole thing was building up. It was just before the film *Let It Be* came out. Which was kind of their epilogue, wasn't it? If you stood back from that, you could see that there were four developing people.

They were each necessary to each other, and then they grew beyond being necessary to each other.

SG: Thoughts on Allen Klein?

MP: They needed someone like him, I'll say that neutrally, because they were dealing with such difficult people and they were being ripped off left, right, and center. And therefore John took the view that they needed somebody that could help them. That was, that was his thinking.

SG: When you say they were dealing with difficult people, you meant that Apple was dealing with difficult people and getting ripped off?

MP: Well, people lived in a remote world, but they were unused to doing the simplest things for themselves. I remember that I'd never been enmeshed in Beatle excitement before, except in the distance. And the day we went to court for the first time with John, there was an enormous crowd outside, enormous. And we managed to get our way through that. When we came out, another enormous crowd. And they got in the car, the doors slammed, they went off, and I was left standing there like an idiot. I remember the last thing I'd said was, "We'll meet at the office," which I meant my office. But no, their thinking it was their office because everybody went to them. They never went anywhere. I came back to my office and hung around, and then they phoned and said, "Where the hell are you?"

They got so far removed from doing things for themselves, from doing the normal things, that in the process, everybody around them is saying, "I'll do that. I'll do that." Then you develop a whole building of people. So Klein came, and he was a kind of carpet sweeper. But the action of a sweeper is to suck things up, and Klein sucked a few other things up.

I remember an occasion at the Harrisons' home, when Klein came there with Phil Spector. Pattie suddenly wanted to play Happy Families, a card game. You have sets of families and sort of pass it around each other and ask questions like, "Do you have Mr. Baker?" Every time, you have to say thank you. If you don't say thank you, you lose a card. Klein played this game as though it was the biggest deal he was ever in. It was fantastic. He lost, he lost, and that was terrible.

I was going somewhere with John and Yoko, I don't remember where, and I suggested at one point that we leave the car and walk. So we walked down the street and the appearance on the road of these two walking together holding hands and dressed in white, always, caused people to stop and stare. People couldn't believe what they were actually seeing. It was an extraordinary feeling, really. It was uncomfortable in a way that people should be so amazed, but that's what the Beatles built up, you see. There was this whole thing around them so that it was like experiencing, uh, royalty or perhaps even more. But to see them walking on the street . . .

SG: Robert Fraser told me a story of a girl in John Lennon's house. She was Fraser's date, and when she got there, she got so overwhelmed by the idea that she was actually in the presence of a Beatle that she couldn't shut up about it. She went off her head, you know, a little, she started calling up people and saying, I don't believe it, I can't believe where I am.

MP: My first meeting with John and Yoko was at Paul's house in St. John's Wood, shortly after their bust. I couldn't get in, because there were girls outside. It was impossible. There were always hordes of people. I couldn't get into the house. I had to go away and telephone. I said, "Look, please let me in." They came out to the gate. One of the minions. It's interesting that John went to Paul's house for shelter because Paul hated Yoko, you know, through all that. But I guess in the time of need . . . There was nowhere else to go. I think in a sense Paul was enjoying a bit of John's discomfort. I think that's perhaps unfair because everybody was rather shocked by it. John and Yoko and Paul and Linda were sitting around Paul's living room. He had that rather lovely sheepdog. Martha, beautiful dog. John and Yoko and I went into a small room and talked it through. Then we sat around talking generally about the problem of drugs and how the case would be handled and who I would need to speak to. It was a very straightforward relationship, I thought. I think by that time, they'd got used to calling an expert and, um, getting the most out of those experts. I think they really sorted people out in terms of "he's good for this, she's good for that." And really, you were put into a kind of segment for that purpose. And, uh, and it was a first meeting, so, um, one wasn't going to be, uh . . . I can't tell you how they responded.

The problem with going to meetings with them at Apple is that the meetings went on and on, and, and if you were there for a two o'clock meeting, they still weren't finished till four o'clock. Because they were never finished. They would never formalize their meetings. People would sit around and the doors would be constantly opening and there was great sharing of rooms. And of course, a key figure in their lives at that time was Derek Taylor. He was the soul of the Beatles. He was the philosopher.

Peter Brown on Apple

By 1967, the Beatles were earning millions of pounds, but the taxman always took the lion's share, approximately 90 percent. Brian was still employing the Liverpool accounting firm that his family used for their furniture stores. The firm recommended a financial advisor named Dr. Walter Strach, who had a thick German accent and could have been played by Peter Sellers if there were a movie. He set up a tax shelter scheme in which the Beatles' royalties would be paid to a company called Beatles Enterprises, incorporated in the Bahamas, a tax haven. The catch was that to avoid British taxes, the money had to stay in the Bahamas for a minimum of two years, and someone from Beatles Enterprises had to set up residence there. This task befell Dr. Stratch himself, who got to live in the Bahamas free for two years. When the Beatles found out about the scheme, they didn't think it was ethical to bend the rules, and they asked that the Bahama company be disbanded and Strach sent home. Alas, the Bahamas was blacklisted as a tax dodge by most European banks, and the loophole allowing income to be paid to a holding corporation in a foreign country was sewn up tight.

On February 6, 1967, the Beatles signed a nine-year contract with EMI which included back payments that EMI had withheld while

Brian negotiated their new rate. Out of this windfall, £2 million was distributed among the four Beatles, who suddenly had a huge pile of money with the taxman standing by. There was a legitimate way to avoid taxes for a corporation, and that was to spend money on expanding the business. The initial suggestion was that the Beatles should expand by opening a record shop, and eventually, a chain of record shops. But the way the four boys envisioned it was they could invest in almost anything if it was somehow connected to the Beatles. They decided that the money was going to be used to finance a utopian venture, called Apple, as in *"A* is for apple," a whimsy on Paul's part. The stated purpose of Apple was "to encourage unknown literary, graphic and performing artists," the incorporation papers said. Simply put, if you had a good idea, Apple might finance it. It was as if the Beatles were suggesting they would become cornucopia of money to ventures that might not seem so worthy if you weren't on LSD. This was how the Fool, a clothing design duo who previously owned a barbershop in Amsterdam, were given £100,000 to start a clothing line that was sold at the newly opened Apple boutique, which was soon buried in mountains of debt and the clothes were given away. There was also Apple Publishing, Apple Films [not to be confused with George's personal company Handmade Films], and Apple Records, the only successful division of Apple.

Perhaps the best investment of all was when in July of 1968 the Beatles purchased a splendid five-story Georgian building at 3 Savile Row, in Mayfair, for £500,000. It was on the National Heritage List and preserved with all the original interior intact. This building became a mecca for thousands of Apple aspirants flocking there from all over the world. Aided and abetted by Derek Taylor, our brilliant press officer, his office became the heart of *The Longest Cocktail Party*, the aptly named book by Richard DiLello that details the never-ending merry days and nights of booze, birds, and LSD at 3 Savile Row. I refer you to Derek Taylor's transcripts for his firsthand account of the Apple madness.

Alistair Taylor on Apple

ALISTAIR TAYLOR: We started to set Apple up before Brian died. I think in April. Brian was very anti-Apple. He didn't like the idea at all. I mean, let's have no illusions. Apple was purely "How do we spend money?" The beginning of Apple was to invest money to reduce the tax bill. This was a business, to be created and owned by Beatles Ltd. The very first concept of Apple was a chain of greeting card shops, and it evolved into Apple. In December of '67, I became general manager and I was on the executive board. When we bought 3 Savile Row, people came from all over the place to visit. Because it was groovy. Where groovy people would all meet, and talk, and discuss the world, and peace, and what was wrong with life.

STEVEN GAINES: Were the Apple offices as much of a *Satyricon* as they were made out to be?

AT: It was ludicrous. I used to check the invoices, and the alcohol bill was utterly farcical. I remember asking the girls who were responsible for ordering to let me see the order before it went off. I wanted to see it. I did this for about three weeks. Peter Brown would order for his own office, maybe a couple of scotches, vodka, gin, a dozen Cokes. Maybe one week, two bottles of gin, a bottle of scotch. Neil would roughly order the same. I am not exaggerating when I say that Derek Taylor's office order was thirty-six bottles of scotch, twenty-four bottles of vodka, twelve bottles of gin, a gross of Cokes. If you entertained Fleet Street every day, could they have been that drunk? I couldn't believe these figures, and we're not talking about the smoke. We're talking about booze.

SG: What about marijuana? Was that charged through Apple?

AT: I presume so. I mean, it would be an invoice they'd probably kept away from me. Because I was the guy that Paul referred to as "the man with the shiny shoes." I was the guy that could always stand in front of fans and crowds, and nobody knew me. If they wanted someone to stand by a door to open it at the last minute, it'd be me. 'Cause I was an unknown. I was a backroom boy. Right? Paul used to say I was the guy in the straight suit, when everybody else was loony in caftans and all that. I always appeared in a dark gray suit with shoes polished. The straight man. So I, as a businessman, objected to the liquor orders. I thought this was ludicrous. You know? This was really taking the boys to the cleaners. And I got told to not be such a bloody drag."

Paul and I talked in the early hours many, many, many times about it. Why should business be such a drag? Why should it be gray? Why should it be always unpleasant and hassling, and arguing? Why couldn't business be fun? And nice, and everybody welcome? But it screwed me up slightly, when I saw the money that was being spent on equipping Apple, with pictures and fantastic furniture. At the time all this was going on, Apple had done nothing. It hadn't earned a penny. We set up Magic Alex, who was still dabbling in his laboratory in Marylebone. Ron Kass [president of Apple Records] had been brought in, but we didn't have a record label set up. Nobody said, "What's paying for it? Where's it coming from? What is the budget?" It was just, whoopee. I was at Apple from December '67 to April '69.

Derek Taylor

Derek Taylor was funny, wise, and slightly drunk. He was the perfect press officer for Apple. Every lost soul who strolled into 3 Savile Row wound up in his office with a smile on their face and a joint or a cocktail in their hands. (Alistair Taylor, in his interview, marvels at the liquor bills.) There was also a serious side to the press office, and somehow business got done. Yet the party seemed to go on nonstop, and Derek's office became the face of Apple. Derek was there when the Beatles smoked their first joint, and he was there when they fell apart in slow motion. When he left Apple, he became the vice president of publicity at Warner Bros. Records in Los Angeles, until he could no longer bear the sun and fake joviality and moved back to London, where he gave this interview. Derek Taylor passed away in 1997 at age sixty-two in Sudbury, England.

The interview begins with Derek kicking down the door to the Beatles dressing room in Southport.

STEVEN GAINES: You were reporting for what paper?

DEREK TAYLOR: *Daily Express* as a theater critic. I went to the Floral Hall building in Southport on a rainy night in October. Together with a lot of other members of the national press, a heavyweight crowd looking to fucking nail the Beatles for saying yes to the Queen Mother [agreeing to appear in the Queen's annual Royal Variety Performance]. Neil Aspinall was apprised of this visitation of the press, and there were a lot of press in those days. We were all there in the bar, wondering how the hell to get past Neil Aspinall and the promoter, who were guarding the door. Neil and the promoter had no relationship 'cause as far as the promoter was concerned, it was just a bunch of kids and another kid looking after them. I was at the front of the line about to form a flying wedge to get in the room. Neil started to argue with the promoter, and while they were busy, I gave the door a big kick and then suddenly we were all inside the room with the Beatles. It was like the Marx Brothers' *A Night at the Opera*.

George was most impressed [that I had kicked down the door]. He asked, "Who are you?" I said, "I'm *Daily Express*, and we're all here with an unpleasant task. We're here to ask you about saying yes to the Queen." John was very grumpy, and he said, "You better ask our manager," and turned away. I said, "Well, we could, but that's not why we're here." There was lots of pressure in the room by now. Ringo said, "Uh, well, I don't mind. I wanna play me drums for the Queen Mum." And that was it. I was off like a shot.

I wrote an entirely favorable story. Ringo wants to play the drums for the Queen, and why not? Although I didn't know, the Beatles read the papers and took note of things. They've all got memories like elephants. They really have.

In November, the following month, I went again to Manchester where they did this huge show, and I met all four Beatles for the first time in the backstage situation. And George said, "Oh, hello, it's you? I remember you kicking the door down." I was sort of an okay chap, because although I kicked the door down, it was rather cheeky. George confided in me that the next single was going to be called "I Want to Hold Your Hand." Which was always of enormous interest, the name of the next single.

In December of that year, the *Daily Express* decided we wanted to hire people to write a column which I would "host" [and ghostwrite for them]. I asked Brian if I could write a column for George, and Brian said, "Oh, this will be very nice for George, it'll give him an interest. The other two have got their songwriting. Then I was not only a Beatle maniac writing *about* them, now I was a ghostwriter for the Beatles and George. The long and short of the thing was, I got deeper and deeper into this thing, more and more trusted. Until, uh, Brian asked me, would I find an author who would help him write his book, and I said, "I'll do it."

He paid me a good amount. He gave me a 2 percent royalty and £1,000 pounds up front. Which was a hell of a lot for a working journalist then. Although I was a theater critic and showbiz columnist of the *Daily Express*, which was then a hot paper in the North, I was making only about thirty-five pounds a week. A thousand pounds was a hell of a lot.

We're calling this book, by the way, *Silver Voice*. Did you know that? That was Paul's suggestion. I think it's a shabby suggestion 'cause it's quite funny. We were in an elevator when John said, "Why don't you call the book *Queer Jew*?" I've never seen Brian so hurt in a [visible] way. It wound him up, unable to speak. It was the worst thing.

The Beatles were making everyone feel good, and Brian was right in the middle of it. Brian was a cheery Christmassy figure. It was all a wonderful thing because everyone was young and in love with life. These were very young men whose dreams were coming true.

So I was interviewing Brian for his book and one day we were having difficulty with the tape. We'd been not getting anywhere. Brian kept saying, "I told this girl and she said, 'It's me or them.'" Finally he said, "Switch the tape off, and we'll have lunch. I have something I must tell you." Well, I wasn't that daft. So this was going to be a big one. And he said at lunch, "Uh, I'm homosexual." I said, "Well, there it is. It's all right." I felt very, very sorry for him that he was having to go through this awful thing and I couldn't alleviate it. But I wanted to have the thing out of the way. I felt like holding his hand. But we didn't do that then. You know, you didn't hug people. It was the Beatles who taught me to hug other men. And I still make the mistake, when I go up North, giving pre-Beatle friends a hug. So I tried to reassure Brian that it was quite all right. So, having said that, he said what a lovely idea it would be if you work for the Beatles. So I moved to London, Joan and the four children and me.

SG: You quit eventually because you took Brian's limousine after a big charity show at the Paramount Theatre in New York and he got furious?

DT: Yes. I took a number of journalists, including Gloria Steinem, in my limousine back to the city from the Riviera Motel, near Kennedy Airport. Dylan was there, Albert Grossman, Gloria Steinem, Steve and Eydie. At least two of the three of the Kingston Trio, all of Peter, Paul and Mary [laughs]. Plus, Princess Obolensky, and the *National Enquirer* haunting the corridors. Brian had had a few drinks. And all the limos were outside, and I took Brian's limo. It was very much on my mind that Gloria Steinem must get back to the hotel. But Brian's response that I took his limousine was quite out of proportion to the seriousness of the event. He went to bed and ripped the sheets and cried and I went to his room and knocked on the door and he said, "Get out." I resigned, the next day on the plane. He sent me a note asking me to rescind my resignation and I said no, I wouldn't. I went to where he was sitting and he had another cry and I had a cry and held his hand and said, "Well, we can be friends, but I can't work with you, I can't take all this." And then I had twelve weeks' notice. I worked the full notice 'cause we were pounded. But he punished me by sending me to L.A. in December with Tommy Quickly, on a twelve-day promotional tour of all the terrible towns and American cities.

SG: Was it also at the Riviera Motel near Kennedy Airport that the Beatles got high for the first time with Bob Dylan?

DT: Not the same night. We were doing the Forest Hills dates of 1964 tour. Turning on was ceremonial, I was the connection. Turning on was ceremonial, Victor Maymudes was there, the Sephardic Jew. He was Bob's psychic friend. Very dignified, wonderful-looking man. Maymudes stood there ceremonially and rolling a joint. Yeah. And, uh, because I think apart from the terrible dangers of, of the thing, you know. It was a rather ceremonial affair. The lights were down, the blinds were drawn, and Victor was doing this. And, uh, this little chap with his hook nose was doing the actual turning on. It was almost like a key. When they got high, Bob was doing the foot-in-the-mouth thing and Brian was doing the, "I feel as if I'm on the ceiling," and Paul was saying, "Come here, I want to hug you." I mentioned all this 'cause my job was just a holding operation further down the corridor. Every fucking disc jockey in New York was there, including Murray the K. The Kingston Trio, Peter, Paul and Mary. If they'd been turning on before then, then I didn't know about it.

SG: Paul says not. What's your take on the maharishi?

DT: I didn't meet him, I was in America, but I never, ever meditated for a second. Never. I was terrifically glad they were doing it, and I swallowed everything they ever told me, all their lyrics. I was a Beatlemaniac. And you know, I had my own followers, who thought I was the bee's knees. And all the way down, this chain reaction of beatitudes, and the deities, and the archangels, and all that. We were all out there with the psychedelic paintings Peter brought in. We believed in our own artwork.

The maharishi, he announced that they were going to appear in some sort of a major concert in Los Angeles under his auspices, and it infuriated them, because they had no such intention of doing so.

He was a bad boy. I think that Magic Alex might have been with the maharishi. I think Alex was, you see, a jealous man. He didn't show it to me, I was too close in to be divided from them, but if there was any way of getting a little wedge in. I think he was paranoid enough to think that he, alone, was the only other. There must be someone jollier, isn't there, to talk about?

SG: Let's talk about the Hells Angels . . .

DT: Who are the Hells Angels, anyway? There was one, very, very heavy dude, who was paralyzed from the neck down. And this hit someone on the jaw. They hit Donald Smith on the jaw. Peter Brown came over . . . And shook his finger in his face and said, "Just look here. Now, behave yourself."

PETER BROWN: *It was Christmas 1968, we were having several parties at 3 Savile Row, including one in my office, where there was a ventriloquist show and children dripping ice cream all over the rug. In residence were also the Hells Angels, drunk and hungry on Christmas Day and impatient for the promised turkey dinner. Frisco Pete, the head of the group, complained loudly. A husband of one of the secretaries asked him to calm down, and he got punched in the face. Now Frisco Pete approached John Lennon, who was dressed in a Santa Claus outfit, and cursed him and everybody else for not feeding them. John, who was not one to back down, even with a Hells Angel, was just about to get into a fight with him when I literally stepped between them. Sounding very much like Brian would have, I admonished Frisco Pete for his rudeness. I explained that the caterers were still laying the table and he would have to be patient. I said he could stuff himself, but to please be patient. Somehow this calmed him down.*

DT: Do you want to know a funny story? Apple received a letter from Squeaky Fromme, who's now in prison after trying to kill President Ford, if you can imagine . . . I was on acid. I made myself ill. They'd get my house and my children. "I shall be calling you," the letter said. Spooky. And within minutes, this is true, there was a call from America, from a girl who was part of Manson's family. "Hello, this is Squeaky Fromme."

I said, "What you're asking for is a personal service. I do the press. The man you want is Peter Brown." She said, "Can I talk to him?" And I said, "Will you hold on a minute, Squeaky?" "Yes, thanks very much, dear." And all very nice, very helpful. I said, "Peter, I'm at the house with someone you know, her name is Squeaky, she's speaking for Charles Manson. It's a personal service. Will you be taking the call?" And he did take the call. "Hello, Squeaky?" he said. I didn't hear what he said, but when he's sober, ask him.

Ah yes, yes. The Peter Brown lunches definitely should be in your book. Peter should interview himself, about the Peter Brown lunches. Because he's . . . a splendid fellow. And all but one of those fellows who came to lunch was a poofter. Nothing but what I call Bertie Woofters coming. But there was lots of them, they were always good company. They always liked me, they were pleasant. I'm not a bigot, you see. Always a liberal.

I have to keep repeating this because it's important—it was only because it was the sixties that such a mad nonsense could have continued like Apple. Because in that climate, the optimistic climate, one was able to maintain one's own Apple almost like a sort of long working vacation where, although you're having a wonderful time, either drinking or doing Peter Brown lunches, or talking about yourself or doing something extremely egocentric and silly, you're also working as well. You're answering phones and taking Beatle messages and fixing up things and making dental appointments, in Peter Brown's case, or arranging interviews in mine. It's the same thing, really. It's a service job, essentially. And in many cases, simply taking famous people, or unknown people, off the street and giving them a gainful job. And making the world a happier place, in general, was what we had in mind, in the sixties. And like I say, in the sixties, in the fog of either liquor or drugs, all these things were possible. They wouldn't be possible now. The great unknown, on the edge of the terrifying eighties. I think in George's book, he uses the phrase the "terrifying edge of the eighties" . . . it's very journalistic.

Neil [Aspinall] is another one. He's as mad as a hatter as well. Isn't he? Neil Must Leave. He's the keeper of dead papers. For guys who keep remembering, he's so bottled up about it. He keeps on saying, "I'm back to square one," when I talk to him about it. And he, personally, is back to square one.

There was a young man who was on a quiz show which had something to do with the Beatles. He was asked, "Which of the Beatles didn't like cabbage," and he said, "It's not in the knowledge. It's not known." And it's a fact that no one in the world knows which of the Beatles doesn't like cabbage. Because it's not in the knowledge.

But it was good at Apple. I was trying to establish that everyone had his own Apple. Long after it should have died, because it was the sixties; we were all having such a time of it. Even when it was all over, in terms of meaning, one kept one's room going as a sort of service to mankind.

PB: Actually, your role was positive, and your office was truly crazy.

DT: It was, yes.

SG: Do you remember Alistair Taylor?

DT: Alistair Taylor was there right at the beginning. The Peter Brown days. He was, I'm telling you, a genuinely nice man. He hadn't a dog's chance amongst all these savage beasts and egos surrounding him. He had his own sense of dignity, but he hadn't got the ruthlessness and drive of the Browns and the Taylors and the dogging sort of "I knew them first" aspect. He was one of the early ones, Alistair, he should have been the last to go. He was a harmless and very worthwhile guy.

No, that man should have been spared. But although we all spoke up . . . He shouldn't have gone, no. I should have gone before him. He wasn't making forty quid. Nor was I.

SG: Who did the firing?

PB: Me.

DT: I was taken to lunch by Allen Klein. I said, "Why are we having lunch in this restaurant, Allen? We've never eaten together before." He said, "There are some things going on in the office." I said, "What kind of things?" He said, some evil work. I said, "Who's doing it?" He said, "Peter Brown." I came back to 3 Savile Row and asked Peter about it, and the worst was yet to come. Peter was irritated, and we were firing people one after another.

PB: The thing was that we had no control over it, at that time.

DT: Paul had been asking me for a list of those being fired, and the list was never forthcoming. Paul wasn't the greatest employer, you know.

PB: He was also very political. It was a standoff situation about us and them. Klein wanted all of us out, everyone.

DT: Did he? I didn't know that.

PB: There were some people that couldn't be removed: Derek, Neil, and me. That's where the line was drawn.

DT: That's the thing about the Beatles. They all knew, roughly . . . They'd never tell George, "So-and-so is okay," if he had decided they were cunts. You could never tell him someone was a cunt if he decided they were okay. And as Brian once said, the boys were very bad judges of character. I don't wish that to imply that my dear friend George was not a good judge of character. Whether Brian was any better judge, of course . . .

PB: I don't think any of us were a very good judge of character.

DT: I mean, let's face it. If you look at the truth, if Brian was accurate is debatable. This has to do with whether it was right for us to be protected, rather than kicked out like dear Alistair Taylor. I'm only glad that I wasn't fired.

PB: Allen told me to get rid of Alistair, Ron Kass, and Peter Asher. The only reason I agreed to do it was because I thought the idea of Klein telling Alistair and Ron Kass . . .

DT: There were a few others who went that day, their secretaries and assistants, who became redundant. A few big ones, and a lot of small ones were fired that day. Alistair Taylor, there was just no justification at all. He had many administrative qualities, and he was fun in a way.

PB: He was very sad. Also, the thing is that he was also a very good friend of Paul, and I expected Paul to protect him. Paul was already kind of saying, "Fuck it," but I also thought Paul would say, "Don't do it to Alistair," which he could've done, and Klein would've said, "Okay." Klein wanted to get rid of everyone, but he couldn't fire me or Peter or Neil.

DT: Why would he want to fire everybody?

PB: What do you *mean*, why would he want that? He wanted his own people. Why would he want you there? You were *them*. So was I, so was Neil. You were the one who told me to take that phone call from Klein.

DT: I got a call saying that Klein was trying to reach John Lennon, and my old buddy, Peter Brown, was blocking the calls, please move him out of the way. I told Klein, "Peter isn't in the way," and then you continued to block the calls. I said let the boys find out whether he is what they say he is, or whether he is not.

PB: It wasn't as if Klein brainwashed John. John was waiting for something like Klein.

SG: For somebody to go get Paul?

DT: I keep saying it is a lot harder to know your true cellmate.

SG: Why was Paul so turned off to Klein?

DT: He didn't trust him. The next thing that happened was the firings had gone on, and we were all then on a ghost ship. I went home in 1970 for most of the year. I used it as a sabbatical to write a song and straighten it out a bit. I was sober with no confidence left at all in the outside world. Shattered. Unbelievable. In 1964, when I joined the Beatles, I was very secure and a promising journalist. And by 1970, I had become terrified.

PB: Derek and I left at the same time.

DT: I left on New Year's Eve 1970.

PB: I gave my notice the same day.

DT: I went to Ringo's party that night at the house in Highgate.

PB: Which I was also at.

SG: New Year's Eve, out with the old, in with the new.

Peter Brown on "Hey Jude"

When Brian was alive, he hardly ever went to the studio, which he considered the boys' domain, even though the Beatles were always eager to let him hear what they were working on and ask for his advice. But Brian was gone, and it was highly unusual when late one Friday afternoon in July of 1968, Paul phoned me in the office and invited me to the studio to hear a new track they had just finished. He and John were nearby at Trident Studios in Soho, and they were thinking about putting the song on their next album—what would become known as the *White Album*, or perhaps they should release it as a single, the very first single on Apple Records. They were hesitant because it was long, seven minutes, too long for radio airplay. It was a song Paul had written for John and Cynthia's son, Julian, telling him not to be sad because of his parents' divorce, but he had changed the name from "Hey Julian" to "Hey Jude." Paul and John wanted me to give them my honest opinion about it.

Trident Studios was outfitted with an eight-track recorder, and "Hey Jude" was the first song they recorded on eight tracks. It's hard to believe that all the music the Beatles had created up until then at the EMI studios on Abbey Road was on a four-track recorder.* I walked

---

* The Beatles producer George Martin and EMI were so alarmed at the thought they might

over to Trident Studios from my office, wondering what I could say to John and Paul if I didn't like it. When I arrived, they sat me in a leather armchair in the control room and rolled the tape. The song brought tears to my eyes. The long, building, repeating coda was like a prayer, the melody was mesmerizing. I wanted to sing it over and over. It could never go on for too long.

"It's just beautiful," I said to them. "It doesn't matter how long it is. It's a masterpiece exactly as it is."

John was in a very happy mood when he asked, "Why don't we all have dinner and celebrate?"

I said I already had plans to have dinner with my close friend, Tommy Nutter, the men's clothing designer. Tommy was a big name in London's fashion scene, and Paul and John knew him well. Paul suggested I invite Tommy to the studio to hear their new song and then we would all go out to dinner together. When I rang, Tommy, who prided himself on being perverse, said he didn't want to listen to a song or have dinner with the Beatles, he wanted us to go away for the weekend. Paul could tell I was having a difficult time and took the phone away from me and said, "Hi, Tommy! This is Paul! We're so excited about this new song! We want you to come over and listen to it and tell us what you think!"

Well, even Tommy couldn't turn down a command performance like that. When he grudgingly arrived at the studio, he sat in the same leather chair as I did and listened quietly to the song. No one moved during the long coda. When it was over, we all looked to Tommy for his reaction.

"Well, it's all right, I suppose," he said and shrugged.

John and Paul looked stunned. I tried to reassure them that Tommy had an edgy sense of humor.

Finally, Tommy smiled and said, "Yes, it's *wonderful*."

---

lose the Beatles to Trident Studios because of their eight-track recorder, George Martin immediately built one by attaching two four-track recorders together.

Then we all went for dinner.

I guess they forgave Tommy, because three of the Beatles were wearing his clothes on the cover of *Abbey Road*, save for George, who insisted on wearing jeans and a denim shirt. That photograph is one of the most famous in the world. "Hey Jude" was the number one song in over a dozen countries including England and sold over ten million copies in the United States, where it became the longest-running number one Beatles song in the US singles chart. It is also the number one fan favorite of all Beatles songs.

Robert Fraser

Paul McCartney called the art dealer Robert Fraser one of the most important figures of 1960s London. Dashing, amusing, and decadent, Robert Fraser was London born and Eton educated, during his apprenticeships in Manhattan art galleries in the early 1960s, he befriended Ed Ruscha, Dennis Hopper, and Kenneth Anger, among other emerging artists and writers. His Mayfair gallery became the nexus of the art and pop music worlds. He also owned a flat at 23 Mount Street that gained its own legendary status as a salon for poets, pop stars, dissolute aristocracy, drug dealers, and rough trade. It was Fraser who art-directed the cover for the Beatles' 1967 album Sgt. Pepper's Lonely Hearts Club Band, one of the most recognizable works of art in the world. In 1966, Fraser became a cause célèbre when he was arrested and prosecuted on an indecency charge for exhibiting eight paintings of penises by American artist Jim Dine. One of the most enduring photographs to come out of Swinging London was the tabloid newspaper front page of Fraser and Mick Jagger both handcuffed in the back of a police car, being taken to jail on charges of possession of heroin. Martin Polden defended them. Fraser died from an AIDS-related illness in 1986.

STEVEN GAINES: When did Swinging London end?

ROBERT FRASER: I would imagine it ended with the breakup of the Beatles, although I'm sure that driving force was gone. That and taxation, I think, a very important factor. People started moving out. The younger people that got successful.

SG: When did you get into the gallery business?

RF: I started in New York in 1958, working for various galleries. Then I came back here in 1962 and opened the Robert Fraser Gallery in Duke Street. But it didn't actually get going for about three years until 1965, because up until then I was showing the school of Paris. I didn't really start getting a group of English artists and American artists for about two years. It took me a while. The pop generation were all more working class than anything else, which is the first time that there had been artists that were all interested in music, and it linked art together with music. That's why artists at the time were in exactly the same way the rock groups were. They were the same people, although the groups were usually not interested in art, the artists were interested in the music.

SG: Why did it turn out that the rock stars were really the high priests of the pop generation, and not the artists, or the photographers?

RF: Music communicated to more people than art. Art is not a mass communication medium. Art is always more limited and appeals to less people. It's not as potent. I met [Rolling Stones] Brian Jones via the DJ at the Ad Lib. Brian, really, was the most interesting. All those guys, the same with the Beatles, they were very nervous of going outside their own. They were totally unsure of themselves, and Brian Jones was the first one that was really keen to see things and meet people, and Mick Jagger was totally very anti-everything at that time. For years, and if you said hello to him, he sort of . . . It was a long time before he became interested in anything except his rock and roll.

PETER BROWN: He met Anita Pallenberg.

RF: Yeah, and she thought, *This is it*. I'm going to be a Rolling Stone. Then she took up with Brian Jones and everything happened. It was probably '65.

SG: Was it through the Stones that you met the Beatles?

RF: No. I met Paul through a guy called John Dunbar, who was a friend of Peter Asher's, of Peter and Gordon. He had a gallery called Indica. It was experimental. I mean, it was sort of a bookshop and a gallery, but Peter Asher was a part of that group that came in, and he was friends with Paul. Peter Asher was Jane's brother. I think he brought Paul over to my place. He made me sorry because he saw a sculpture in my apartment and said, "I want that." It was quite a lot of money for those days, it was like 2,500 quid. Paul never asked the price until he decided to buy something. If he liked it, he wanted it.

SG: I guess they didn't have to think about the price.

RF: No, but most people, even if they don't have to think about it, they want to know the price. Paul was very, very open-minded, but he was also more . . . Well, John was, too, but I mean, John was sort of very difficult to . . . He was more difficult to . . . He was very shy in a way, and it comes out in an aggressive way.

SG: It's an odd decision Paul made to live at his girlfriend's home with her parents.

RF: Paul was a very domestic sort of personality. He liked the idea.

PB: I didn't think twice about it, but looking back on it now, it was pretty ahead of its time to move in with your girlfriend's family.

RF: Even now, he's done exactly what he wants. He's not really like . . . He never really lived a rock star's life.

SG: Did you know Yoko independently as an artist?

RF: No. I knew of her.

PB: Was she considered a serious artist prior to her becoming associated with John?

RF: By some, yeah. I think she was always too serious. A somewhat slightly pretentious approach. She tried to make it in New York for some time. She didn't hit in New York at all, and then they came over here. She was always trying. She was one of these artists that was always up to some project, but first, always slightly second to somebody else's ideas. John Dunbar got very involved because a lot of the stuff he was showing was electronic things moving, some sculptures, the tackiest things. You know? He became more involved in electronics, and then Magic Alex sort of said, "You must start doing art electronics in the future." Then John suddenly sort of—well, there was a lot of acid floating around. John had very heady ideas.

SG: You eventually gave Yoko a show. Why did you do that if you weren't especially fond of her work?

RF: It was not for her. It was for John Lennon. That year, I wasn't doing too much. Every night, they used to come around, and they'd launch balloons with little tags on them. The idea was that people who found the balloons should mail the tag back. It was sort of silly. It was a very youngish idea. It got a lot of press. It was interesting to do, but in the art world, because there's no other world, the bottom line is somebody has to pick up the bill, and John was picking it up. I mean, it's all very well to have a nice art exhibit, but who's going to pay for it?

SG: Her show was a favor to John, and he was paying for it.

RF: There were other things going on at the same time. I mean, John was a very persuasive person. He says that he's chosen you to do the show. It was fun. It was a very frivolous episode at the time. Nothing was for sale. I wasn't selling anything. It was a happening.

Do you know Sam Green? He's very friendly with Yoko. I think he helped her and John with some of their real estate deals. Let me tell you a marvelous story about how Sam engineered his meeting with Yoko. He was going to a psychic, and the psychic mentioned that Yoko Ono was also a client, so Sam made an incredible deal with him. He asked the psychic to tell Yoko that Friday afternoon around three o'clock, she was going to meet a man on Columbus Circle near the park entrance, he would be wearing a muffler and some kind of hat, and she could trust this man. The psychic thought it over and said to Sam, "Well, the first hundred thousand in commissions is mine."

SG: When Yoko arrived on the scene and Paul was already with Linda, do you remember any animosity and contention between them? Was it visible to you?

RF: The animosity, as far as I remember, was entirely created by Yoko Ono. She really made them work at it. I mean, she was always telling John that he should be on his own, and do his own thing, and she was always in the studio, and he would hold her [in his arms]. They were totally inseparable. It was the first time that sort of thing was ever tolerated. It wasn't the way it happened before. She did sort of break— I mean, he was totally the lamb to the slaughter, and he was charmed by it. John was so fascinated by her. He's sort of very naïve, at the same time, a very brilliant mind. I guess it's his first intellectual type of woman that he'd met. John is a very strong person, a very strong hardheaded person, and yet, he chose this very dominating, relatively unattractive . . . utterly charmless person. There is nothing going for her; a supposed artist who was deeply in debt. Well, it's all totally weird, but I think mainly it's the fact that she was a woman, and she was an intellectual, and John obviously had some hunger that he never expressed to the world for another dimension. He couldn't get it from the conversations with the boys.

SG: She wasn't particularly transparent in what she was after.

RF: I remember William Burroughs telling me, "The only hustlers that get through to people that are on their guard against hustlers are really the totally obvious hustlers because anybody who is making a small play, they sort of brush aside.

PB: Like Allen Klein.

RF: Yeah, John was just *mad* about Allen Klein, *loved* Allen Klein. He thought it was the best thing that had ever happened to him. Somebody comes to you trying to [fast-talk into buying] some little thing, but Allen Klein wanted to rape you. He was a terrible thief, and yet he got through. He *is* slightly weird, John. He has a sort of masochistic streak.

SG: In an interview, John was saying that Paul [dropped by] the Dakota about two years ago, and John asked him not to come again, unless he rang first. It was done in a very bitchy way, and I thought, God, after all this time, couldn't you be a little more charming, a little more . . .

RF: Paul told me that when he called up John, he'd get through to the answering service. "Mr. Lennon's not available." He said, "Then the message came back. 'Ask Paul what's the name of the teacher in fifth grade.'" It's quite funny.

SG: Well, probably a thousand people have called John and said, "It's Paul." Although I think Paul was hurt by it. If it was part of John's sense of humor, nobody else understood that. If Paul did, I think he'd still have to be embarrassed by it, because it was Paul's business too.

Ray Connolly

Ray Connolly at the Evening Standard *had the most access to the Beatles of any journalist in London. He was a special favorite of Paul McCartney, who even gave Ray his father's phone number. Ray was present during several critical decisions as they were made before being revealed to the public. His memories about the production of the Beatles' ill-fated TV special,* Magical Mystery Tour, *explain a lot about the disarray in the Beatles' professional life shortly after the death of Brian Epstein.*

RAY CONNOLLY: I came in '67, really, uh, and got thrown into the *Sgt. Pepper* deal, because I was given this job at the *Evening Standard* where my function was really to cover anything pop or young. I was given the page, which I did for twenty-seven years.

STEVEN GAINES: Did you know the boys from Liverpool?

RC: No. I knew Mike McCartney and Paul's father, who were very kind to me. In '67, they wouldn't speak to anybody after *Sgt. Pepper*. But then I met them on *Magical Mystery Tour*. It was really Paul's idea, and Paul was the machine behind it. At that point, nothing could go wrong. After *Sgt. Pepper*, they'd done everything, and they'd proved they could actually even go further than everything. And what next? Everything was open.

I think *Magical Mystery Tour* was a panic thing. John said it at one point when Brian died, "Oh fuck. This is it for us, isn't it? You know, what are we gonna do? We're gonna get shit on now, because there's no leader." I mean, although Brian wasn't the leader, he was sort of the catalyst in the sense that he was almost mothering the boys. Once he'd gone, they sort of panicked, "We'll have to do something quickly. Well, all right, we'll do this film." And without thinking, they did that. After the film, they're all, you know, "Let's do that one next."

SG: Did you go out on the *Magical Mystery Tour*?

RC: I was on a bus. There was a whole caravan. The Beatles bus was in front, and then probably forty cars followed it through Devon. It was an extraordinary sight.

SG: How did the press find out where the bus was going to be?

RC: Tony Barrow [the Beatles' press agent at the time] tipped off people he was friendly with where the Beatles were going to stay that night. Like an idiot, I telephoned the hotel where they were going and said I wanted to book a room. I asked, "The Beatles are going to stay there tonight, aren't they?" The hotel said, "Oh, no. No, we've got Mr. and Mrs. Smith and a party of four young men" [laughs]. And so when they get there, they should have got there in complete silence, because no one was meant to know. But I tipped the hotel off, and they called the police just in case. There were millions of people outside [laughs]. So, from then on, they didn't ever say where they were staying. Anyway, I think then Paul was very kind to reach out to me. That night at the hotel, we got to talking about his father and he gave me his phone number for some reason. And from then on, I could ring him up, or ring Ringo and John, and George too. I didn't know George very well until then.

SG: Do you remember any of the fiasco that happened on *Magical Mystery Tour*?

RC: The funniest bit, and it was hilarious, was that the bus was quite wide and it got stuck over a narrow bridge. There were cars for miles backed up both ways. The Beatles were sort of stuck in the middle in the big bus, carrying all these people and dwarves in the middle of Devon. It looked a wonderful sight and John had a funny hat on and a pink tracksuit. It was bizarre, utterly bizarre. They couldn't shoot anywhere, because the press would hound and follow them. They'd be trying to shoot, and of course we all followed them wherever they went. I think it was in Penzance, or one of those Cornish places, and George was sitting cross-legged, trying to think about something, or meditate, God knows what. And there were thousands and thousands of people taking photographs, and it was just chaos, total chaos. They hadn't planned anything. The funniest line I heard was when one of the Beatles said to an extra, "Come back to my room, and let's have a script conference." There was no script. It's not a bad film, though, when you see it now. It was torn apart when it aired on the BBC on Boxing Day.

SG: You called Paul after the show aired?

RC: What happened was, I kept phoning and Paul's father was staying with him at the time. I phoned about three times, and Jim kept saying, um, "I'm sorry, but he's still asleep." I finally said, "Look. I have to have my story in by one o'clock." Otherwise, we were going to miss it. The front-page picture—the whole lead page was this piece about how the Beatles have made this big mistake. I said, "What shall I do, Mr. McCartney?" And he said, "Ray, God loves a triumph, ring again in five minutes." I rang again, and he said, "I'll wake the bugger up" [laughter]. So, he went in, said, "Wake up, here's the papers. Talk to this man." Paul got on the phone and said, "Maybe we goofed," or something like that. But Paul was so clever, because that night he went on the David Frost show on TV and charmed the whole country by saying, "We made a boo-boo. We goofed and we thought it was all right, and I'm sorry if you didn't like it. It's not that bad." When you see the film now, you think, Well, what's the fuss about? It's quite a good little film.

SG: What was it like at 3 Savile Row, the Apple offices?

RC: It was ridiculous. It was a waste of my life. I mean, it was wonderful, because it was a very elegant building. That was nice. On the second floor was Derek Taylor's office, where people would hang around. It was absurd. People came from the States, no one knows who they were, and they were just sitting there. Then they'd go. The other thing was that all these projects were going on at the same time. All sorts of things were always going on. All those different kinds of Apple, Apple hair, Apple . . . Paul was talking about [turning Apple into] Marks & Spencer. [Some of the people who were there] I think were hopeful people who had an idea, and were able to generate enthusiasm for ideas, which weren't necessarily great ideas. I don't think the Beatles got conned all the time by bad people, but I think the enthusiasm of naïve people was often slightly contagious. I think the Beatles got conned by that. There were a few real eccentrics who were sort of attracted in. But I still think it's unfair to say that all those people were con artists. I don't think they really were, I think they were just naïve. In retrospect, it's too easy to sort of say they were being conned. I mean, what they were doing was spending right, left, and center. They were spending like lunatics, and in Derek's office, there were thousands of girls. And there were thousands of people working at Savile Row, what they'd do all the time? It just wasn't a specific sort of organization, in a sense.

SG: Also people were taking LSD in the office, and in the kitchen they were making hash brownies. It doesn't help to do your work.

RC: I'm sure it didn't. There were a lot of people who were working probably as much as they wanted to. You see, I've always had this belief that in London there were about fifty people, thirty people, doing things, and about three thousand who were hanging around. And I think that because Apple was such a generating source of energy. And it was, I mean, it was quite exciting to be a part of it. It tended to have more than its share of that three thousand than anywhere else.

SG: Do you remember when things started to go sour between the Beatles?

RC: I'm trying to think of the details. I remember going to a recording of the *White Album* one night, and Yoko was there with John and they were mixing "Cry Baby Cry." Paul was there. He was trying to stay well away from Yoko. He went into another room and began to write "Let It Be." You had that sort of feeling that he didn't want to be involved with John and Yoko.

SG: Did you see Yoko as a hustler?

RC: At first, I may have thought she was, but I don't think so now. I mean, we were all hustlers. I was a hustler as much as anybody. We were all attracted to this . . . this . . . But the fact is that Yoko stayed around and she gave John what he didn't have with Cynthia. I think that's the important thing with Yoko. She was wonderful, Yoko. She was very nice and I liked her. I just think that John and Paul had both grown up, and as they grew, they were growing away. John had found a chum, which was what Yoko was. I think that's the best word for Yoko. She was a chum on his wavelength, or she was partly on the wavelength, and she took him with her.

SG: Cynthia had never been a chum in that sense. John thought in abstracts, Cynthia was a very down-to-earth, sensible woman. But Yoko stepped into John's professional life. She moved a cot into the

EMI studios, and she hadn't been a week when she was making suggestions to Paul about how the music should sound. That seems a bit audacious.

RC: Well, it's only audacity if John let it. I mean, John should have said, "Fuck off," if that's how he felt, isn't it? He should have said, "Well, you can't do it. You can't carry on like this." Was she pregnant? Must have been. She was pregnant, wasn't she? She'd just got pregnant or she was about two months pregnant.

SG: They were arrested October 22, 1968, and she miscarried exactly a month later in November.

RC: I can understand how the other three would hate her, especially Paul, but I think that . . . If it hadn't been her, something else would have happened. I think they were going [to part] anyway. On the *Magical Mystery Tour*, they weren't together. In fact, they were very rarely together. Paul was playing the director, saying, "Why don't we shoot this and why don't we do that?" And the people were in the way. John was just looking to go home. He didn't do anything.

I was surprised how they didn't know what each other was doing all the time. You would assume, wouldn't you, that John and Paul would know intimately what they were doing all the time. I remember going into Apple one day, and Paul came in with Linda, and he was surprised John and Yoko were also expected. They just weren't speaking. Or when they did speak, they shouted. Things like, Paul got terribly upset about the way Phil Spector put the strings on the mandolin or the choir. John read about it in the papers months afterwards when the record came out. "Oh, he didn't like that, didn't he?" John asked. "Well, he never told me."

Paul was getting more and more upset at this, and John to tell you the truth . . . may have just blocked himself off purposely.

SG: John knew of Klein's reputation. I asked Paul why he thought John went with Klein, and he said John wanted a dog to say, "Go, get that."

RC: I remember one day when *Abbey Road* was coming out, it was a hell of a row. They had a meeting in the room on the second floor. I was sitting across the hall with Derek Taylor, trying to keep him from getting smashed on whiskey and lots of coke. There was some terrible row. Derek said, "Well, that's fucking it. I'm out. That's it." I remember John telling me when they were finished. John said, um, "I've got something for you. I could tell you, but I promised Allen Klein that I won't tell anybody. If I tell you, you've got to promise not to run it straightaway. When it happens, I'll let you know first. I've left the Beatles." This was in December '69. And I said, "Why?" He said, "Why should I play with Paul when I can play with Frank Zappa?" Or whoever he played with in Plastic Ono. So that was quite early, and it didn't come out until Paul did his album in March 1970.

The day the *Mirror* finally ran the story that Paul wasn't going to record with them anymore, Paul didn't say, "I've left the Beatles." He said, "I'm not working with them at the moment and have no plans to," leaving the door wide open. It's like also a call for help, isn't it? It became world headlines. Paul rang me up. He couldn't explain to the other boys why he'd said all these things. Paul got very anxious about all the—he really got hit with the sort of, "Paul's killed the Beatles." He talked about Phil Spector, and how Ringo had left at one point and George had left at one point and they'd been falling apart. I don't think Paul had the nerve to bring about the divorce himself. [Instead] they did it through the media.

PETER BROWN: Paul will talk endless hours [laughs] without even mentioning George or Ringo. Like they didn't exist.

RC: Ringo knew exactly what his contribution was and how lucky he'd been. I remember him saying to me, "I just say yes. Whenever I listened to them, I just said yes all the time. My answer: yes." But I think he knew how important he was, and how unimportant he was, and that he could be replaced. Not literally. They knew that it could've been anybody, but it was next to nothing. I think he was going to try to work things out. I didn't get to know George, really.

SG: I don't think he was easy to get to know.

RC: Isn't it an interesting thing that George turned out to be the one who has this baronial mansion in the material world?

SG: He gardens all day long. It's very obsessive.

PB: All the years I've known him, I've never felt I was ever close to George. You never knew what was going on in his head. I saw them a lot because I used to go out with Pattie all the time. But I never knew quite what was going on in there. Ticking around in his head.

SG: Maybe nothing. That's sometimes the case. Inscrutable people are sometimes like Peter Sellers in *Being There*.

RC: George was very sharp. Extremely sharp.

[Ray reminisces here about George Harrison's concert for Bangladesh, August 1, 1971, in New York, when he stayed at the Park Lane Hotel with Yoko and John.]

RC: John and George had a row. George said, "I don't want Yoko onstage." I think John tried to explain to Yoko, and Yoko said, "Why, why don't they want me? Why can't I come onstage?" Yoko and John were totally done [with George]. John flew back to England. Yoko was going to follow him home about three hours later. Yoko said, "Look, Ray. You check out of your room now." I left all my luggage on the plane and had kind of lost it. So I had only my briefcase. Yoko said, "Look. You leave your room downstairs and move into our suite." It was a huge suite. I mean, you know, they don't mess around. She said, "I'm gonna follow John back to England. You'll have everything we've got, you see? Whatever you want, just write Lennon, room 1525. You'll have the limo waiting and the tickets for the show. All of John's clothes are there. He didn't take them, they're all there." It was wonderful. For three days, I was a Beatle. I got this limo, and all his clothes.

John Dunbar

John Dunbar was twenty-four years old when he first met Yoko Ono. He was small, attractive, and shrewd. Cambridge educated, he was the son of a cultural attaché to Moscow. He had a lot of cachet with the Ad Lib crowd in Swinging London. In 1965, he married sultry singer Marianne Faithfull, who dumped him for Mick Jagger. Dunbar owned the trendy Indica Gallery in Mason's Yard, which featured pop art works ranging from psychedelic light boxes and perpetual motion machines to poetry readings and a show by an obscure avant-garde Japanese artist, Yoko Ono.

STEVEN GAINES: You're infamous for introducing Yoko to John Lennon.

JOHN DUNBAR: It was my first conceptual work of art, bringing those two together. It broke up the Beatles. Changed the whole course of history.

SG: Yes, exactly. You gave Yoko a show, and John came to the preview.

JD: I mean, they're obviously made for each other.

SG: When did you open the Indica Gallery?

JD: At the end of '65.

SG: It's been written that John Lennon climbed a ladder in your gallery with a magnifying glass, and if you looked at a spot on the ceiling it said, *You are there*, or *Yes*.

JD: It was pretty nice, John Lennon climbing up there. Me and Yoko were sitting around, and it was great fun, really just good energy. It was very entertaining.

SG: I asked somebody, "Did you see Yoko as a hustler?".

JD: She's not a hustler, is she? I've never saw her that way. But that's not how she comes on, you see? I mean, it's not, what, you know, she's a sort of spiritual hustler, if you like. I mean, she's got something to hustle. Listen, not only did she just get John Lennon but she moved in on them. She had a cot in the studio at EMI. He needed her more than she needed him. Yoko was a truly powerful chick. I mean, whether she was hustling or whatever she was doing, she's certainly powerful and magnetic, and she's very interesting. She's not stupid at all. She's got a lot to offer, and obviously she had to offer John what he felt he needed. She was a woman, and she could share his life. She was the first intelligent woman truly on his own level that he'd ever met. So if you think about it in that sort of light, it's not surprising, really. It's not that she didn't have anything to offer. She was one of the few hustlers that hustled what she had to offer, which was herself. And it was a big package. She saved his life. I think that's why I wasn't allowed to see him. She thought that I might sort of encourage him to take drugs or something.

SG: His middle name became her last name. Instead of John Winston Lennon, it's John Ono Lennon.

JD: She can just stake her claim.

SG: How did you know John Lennon?

JD: I knew all the Beatles, because I got to know Paul pretty well. My parents lived just around the corner from Paul, where he was living with Jane Asher. Her brother Peter Asher was also a good, old friend of mine.

SG: Didn't Paul have an affair with your nanny or something?

JD: [laughs] Yeah. It's true.

SG: But that had to be before or after he was living with Jane Asher.

JD: I'm not sure how much I should kiss and tell.

SG: You've already told a writer that for "several years Paul was also close to my kid's nanny. He saw her on and off for ages."

JD: Somebody had a tape recorder on, yeah [laughs]. The author is my friend. He went to Cambridge. I vaguely remember us getting pissed one night and hanging out. You know, Paul McCartney was pretty funny about that nanny thing. I always thought his whole scene was pretty strange. My nanny filled some gap in his needs, I suppose, which is nice because she was really good. She was a very earthy working-class girl.

SG: What year did you marry Marianne [Faithfull]? Do you remember? Was she involved with the Rolling Stones by then?

JD: We got married in 1965, when I was still at Cambridge. I'd introduced her to Andrew Loog Oldham [Rolling Stones manager and producer] the year before. I guess she'd made a record by then, hadn't she? *As Tears Go By.*

SG: If it was '65, then Paul was still with Jane Asher.

JD: Oh. Paul was with Jane from the minute I met him.

SG: You mean even when he was fooling around with the nanny?

JD: Well, the nanny didn't materialize till later. I met Paul when he was a lodger at the Ashers' house, and we lived next door. I suppose I was fifteen or sixteen. We'd spend a lot of time at each other's houses.

SG: Was there a lot of LSD?

JD: In the beginning, they were very puritan about drugs. When I first met Paul and John, they didn't smoke grass, they didn't do anything. And I remember the first time I met John, I was smoking some hash in a pipe. He was really shocked that I was smoking some dope. Then they came around to my place, John and Paul. I remember they also smoked with Bob Dylan, too, but I certainly gave Paul a joint. He was suspicious of it. I remember him doing one of those "I don't feel anything" routines people do when they first smoke marijuana.

SG: They were for a long time taking purple hearts, whatever those things are.

JD: Speed. From Hamburg. But mate, that was different. They were pills. I mean, they were a bit suspicious of smoke. It didn't take long for them not to be, but I remember John being quite funny about it. When he saw me smoking a little pipe of hash, he was shocked. With the LSD, clearly we were in that sort of acid fog. So much, everything got bleached out. I've never done that before or since. There was almost no color left.

SG: When the Beatles were taking all of this LSD, where was all of it coming from?

JD: Owsley.

SG: Owsley? The real Owsley in San Francisco? Owsley was famous in America as the purveyor of the finest LSD in the world.

JD: Oh yeah. I remember somebody kept filling our telephoto lenses with acid to get it past customs. As soon as Brian died, they had no control. They knew they had to do something with all their money, and they had total rein. They told Brian about their idea for Apple, but he had no interest. The Beatles always tried to protect and defend him. Back then, Brian's homosexuality was a terrible thing and kept hidden, probably because the Beatles couldn't have him as their manager [if it were known]. Paul once said to me, "There are always rumors about me and Kenny Everett, or that Cliff Richard and I were gay."

I said, "The only rumor I remember is that you were dead."

SG: I'd forgotten that he was dead.

JD: Yeah, but he remembered instantly. I called him up at his farm in Scotland, and I said, "Paul, I hear you're dead." He said, "Not true."

SG: Were the Beatles generous to their friends?

JD: They never had to pay for anything, like in a restaurant. It was always on the house.

PETER BROWN: They had cash, because I remember always sending money to them by messenger every Thursday, like a pay packet for a laborer or something. All of those years, one sent to them money in a little envelope . . . It was weird, considering how successful they were. But that's what they needed. Everybody would charge. Before credit cards, you had accounts everywhere. They never had any credit cards. None of the Beatles had a credit card.

SG: Paul had an Aston Martin but no pocket money.

PB: It was his great love at that time. And he had it for a long time.

SG: [to John Dunbar] How did things end between you and John Lennon?

JD: John went so overboard accepting everything that Magic Alex said, it was all just a bit too much, you know. It all got rapacious somehow. So I dropped out a bit for my own health. I went to Scotland for a while.

SG: Were the Beatles fools? With Apple? Or buying Greek islands? Or Magic Alex?

JD: No, not at all. It was four people, and with all these things plus dope, and they didn't want to have anything to do with business, you know . . .

SG: Were you around when they started to get angry with each other?

JD: Oh yeah [laughs]. I mean, 'cause that was, uh, about Yoko, really. You can't be in each other's pockets forever without getting . . .

PB: She's, I think she struck the match.

JD: She finally did, yeah. Yeah, all right, well, let me tell you what I can remember is Paul and John were the best pals, really, right? They spent all their time together and stuff, and they had individual lives. But in the end they were the final sort of arbiters of everything, you know, between themselves. Yoko completely took over John. I mean, Paul just really felt left out and just hated it, you know what I mean? It was because John put Yoko right into the work situation. Maybe while they're sort of singing into his microphone, you know what I mean? But that was it, maximum. Yoko was there all the time with John, I mean, all the time.

SG: Magic Alex was very destructive in your friendship with the Beatles—John, in particular. Was it Yoko who introduced you to Magic Alex?

JD: "The Crooked Bubble." *Bubble and squeak* is "Greek"—that's London rhyming slang. Anyway, so the Crooked Bubble was introduced to me by an artist friend of mine, and I introduced him to various people, including John and Yoko.

SG: You unleashed him on the world.

JD: I did, yeah. By the time I realized exactly what kind of a cunt he was, basically, he had already cheated a lot of people. He's a very personal guy. He's got a good line. He was the first guy any of us knew who was into electronics. I had various projects I wanted to do. And I wanted Alex to help me make some machines. That was after I'd introduced Yoko to John Lennon. I gave Yoko a show at my gallery, right? And asked John Lennon along to see it obviously in order to meet Yoko. As simple as that. John got the Beatles interested in a sort of spurious religion—LSD. It was in the middle of acid, right? I sort of made Alex take his first trip. John Lennon and I kind of made him. Alex is a strong guy. He's such a rigid sort of guy. He kind of handled the acid okay, but I never got the impression he really enjoyed it. He apparently did some very nasty things in Athens. It seems that he got people into trouble. You know, he was a TV repairman when I met him. For Olympic Electronics. Nothing he made ever worked. It was so funny. I mean, he couldn't even make a radio work.

This Magic Alex stuff came a bit later, you know? I saw quite a funny little transformation. For a year, I watched him kind of get in there and take over quite a lot of the Beatles' psyches for a considerable amount of time. I mean, he really sort of blinded the Beatles. And by the time you sussed what a drag he was, I think he was really a bit psychotic. I was gathering some of the bills, and he was charging Apple a lot more than the actual price. It was unnecessary, you know. He was eventually booted out of Apple, he wasn't allowed anywhere near the place. All his ideas were secondhand. I mean, every one. The way he kept it going and the delaying tactics and the way everybody was stoned, he got away for a long time with doing nothing at all. I mean, just toys that blinked, and it was all great, it looked fabulous. By the time I sussed him properly, it was too late. By the time he'd sort of managed to completely get between John Lennon and me, that was it, really. After that, it was impossible to get through to John.

SG: He was in love with John Lennon the rock star, I think.

JD: That's not what I call love. It was fascination and using somebody. You know, he was always calculating.

Cynthia Lennon
Twist

Cynthia was a shy, kindhearted soul and one of the least-equipped people to deal with the role into which she found herself thrust, the wife of John Lennon. She was a melancholic figure, wistful, smoking cigarettes and drinking white wine into the small hours. Improbably, she said she was still in love with John decades after their divorce, although he was never very nice to her. She pined for him, and dreamed about what her life might have been if not for Yoko. The interview that follows was conducted in Ruthin, Wales, where Cynthia was running a bed-and-breakfast. It was five weeks before John was killed. His death sent her spiraling into depression, regretful that they had never reconciled. She was also concerned about what would happen to Julian, now that Yoko had control of John's estate, although they later would reconcile. In 1980, when John was killed, Yoko asked that Cynthia not attend the small, private funeral.

Cynthia remarried and divorced three times, legally changing her surname to Lennon. She worked briefly as a television interviewer, designed bed linens, published two volumes of memoirs, and opened a restaurant in London named Lennon. In 1978, she published a memoir, A Twist of Lennon, that John tried to block. Eventually she had to auction off much of her memorabilia to get by. She passed away in Majorca, on April 1, 2015, *of cancer. She would have been surprised to learn that her passing was reported around the world.*

STEVEN GAINES: Ringo was dating the model, Vicki Hodge?

CYNTHIA LENNON: Yes. She was part of that scene when the boys had their first flat in London. She was sort of around. She was the girl that he had to dispose of when Maureen came down from Liverpool. Vicki had to [disappear].

PETER BROWN: Was he always seeing Mo, or was she just somebody he knew and could rely on?

SG: He was serious with her all the way through. Yes. When he came to London, though, and he became famous, he obviously had lots of girls after him.

CL: Right? Yes. He had more opportunities than in Liverpool.

SG: So why did he go back to Maureen?

CL: She was very possessive about him, so she turned up in London and stopped anything that might have been going on, and stuck in there. Maureen's a pretty tough cookie. She wouldn't let go. She turned up in London, and she got pregnant.

SG: The first time you met Brian Epstein, you were pregnant with Julian, and Brian wasn't very happy. You and John went out and had dinner with him that night. You said that John had a great deal of control over Brian, and that if John wouldn't do something that Brian wanted, Brian would stamp his feet and tears would come to his eyes. Was he that possessive of him?

CL: At certain occasions, yes. Because John could be very bolshie. If he didn't want to do something, he didn't do it.

SG: John was the leader of the band, but Brian was also sweet on John.

CL: I wouldn't say no to that. The fact that they went to Spain together.

SG: What was that about? You had just given birth to Julian.

CL: I don't know. He came to [the hospital] to see his son, he hadn't seen him, and he said, "I'm off on holiday. Do you mind?" Then they went on holiday.

SG: Did John ever talk about how besotted Brian was with him? Did he ever say that Brian came on to him?

CL: No, no, no.

SG: You said that Brian was no match for the "international leeches."

CL: He wasn't.

SG: What did those people do? Who were those people?

CL: Whenever you went to Brian's apartment, you'd be surrounded by . . . it was always . . . he fancied that kind . . .

PB: But they were the kind of people who were using John.

CL: Using him, and John liked it, 'cause he was at a certain point a masochist.

SG: Were you and John ever busted? There was a police sergeant,

Pilcher, who was fanatic about raiding the homes of rock stars. George and Pattie got busted, and even Jenny Boyd.

CL: Never got busted. Couldn't believe. I couldn't believe that we got through that period and never had the police. The police were sort of keeping an eye on the place because we were afraid that Julian was going to be kidnapped. They had word from somebody, a tip there was going to be a kidnap attempt on Julian. They had heard from their own sources, but somebody was going to, and the police were following him to school. With the police here all the time, we never got busted. John also did a great amount of acid, he went on hundreds of trips. When we lived together in Weybridge, my mother would come over and she found these colorless pieces of paper. I didn't know about them. I'm terrified of drugs. But my mother knew there was something going on.

SG: The first time you tripped on acid, you were having dinner at the home of a dentist and he dosed you. Was he the guy who fixed everybody's teeth?

CL: Yes. He was George's dentist. He put, he put it in the coffee during dessert. It was in the sugar cube. At the end of the meal.

SG: You all went out to the Ad Lib Club.

CL: Oh, we all escaped the dentist's flat. It hit us all at the same time. Things disappeared and got larger and larger. It was like *Alice in Wonderland*, a matter of fact, and we all looked at each other and said, we've gotta get out. And we just rushed out and got a taxi. We didn't risk taking a car and we just took off to the club.

SG: There was another time you had a bad acid trip, the famous LSD weekend at Brian's country home, Kingsley Hill. Was everybody tripping?

And you were miserable. You went upstairs to the bedroom window. Was it the LSD, or were you just so unhappy at the whole scene.

CL: Well, it was the LSD scene. I think I felt so alone. So isolated. I went to John to talk to him or to try to get some sort of sense. And he dismissed me because he was so high anyway, you know, he just didn't even . . . I felt totally alone and I sat on the windowsill and felt, well, I looked down . . .

SG: Was this the party where John locked himself in the back of his Rolls-Royce with Derek Taylor? They were both having a bad trip.

CL: I wouldn't know. 'Cause if I was high on LSD, I would try des.

SG: Jenny Boyd remembers going to India, to Rishikesh, to the ashram of Maharishi Mahesh Yogi, along with you and John and the other Beatles and their wives. One of the things Jenny thought was complicating things was that everybody had to meditate as long as they could, and John couldn't get it. Couldn't do it. He was unhappy with it. He was suspicious of the moral issue to begin with. But when he got to the meditation, it didn't click with him.

CL: I think it really got to John. It was much easier for George than John. Although John was meditative for days, and I think he was really content. It was when Magic Alex started saying things, and George started getting suspicious, and John was the last.

PB: But again, it was Alex Mardas.

SG: Cynthia, you mentioned a paternity suit against Paul. Was that in London?

CL: Yes. I think it was.

SG: What did they do about that?

CL: I think they got paid off, as far as I know.

SG: When you came home to Weybridge from the vacation to Greece with Jenny Boyd and Magic Alex, Yoko was there in your house, in a bathrobe.

CL: Well, they were having breakfast. It was four o'clock in the afternoon, and they were having breakfast. The curtains were drawn.

SG: He wasn't expecting you back. Was that it?

CL: Yes, he was.

SG: Was this the way he was presenting his relationship to Yoko? It wasn't cool.

CL: I was amazed because he's always been honest with me about other women. But that obviously was the right thing for him. It didn't matter what I felt. 'Cause he knew that their relationship was going to carry on.

SG: Was she that strong or powerful?

CL: She never left him alone for years before. She'd be phoning and visiting the house and writing to him, saying she knew his book, write notes to him saying she would do away with herself unless John helped her. It got through to him, and eventually she met him, and I think it was around the time of Magic Alex.

SG: After your divorce from John, Yoko, she seems to be the one that really ruined the group.

CL: I know the whole thing. I don't know if you can put the blame on Yoko, but it was meant to happen anyway, it was a sort of good–evil situation, and evil got in and was stronger than the good. And that's what dissipated the whole thing. It all went wrong from then. It's very hard to put the blame.

SG: Well, it could have been Linda. I mean, Linda had a similar effect on Paul.

CL: Linda was a different type of woman. She was a liberated woman that came into a situation, took over from the women that were the ordinary girls that they'd known from school. So there was excitement in that.

SG: Alex came to Italy to check up on you. Is that what happened? John sent him there to check up on you?

CL: John was at home, with Yoko at the time. She was sleeping in Kenwood, and he sent, he wanted to get me caught in an affair. He wanted to get me. And he wanted a private detective in Italy to say that he could sue me for divorce.

SG: Instead of the other way around.

CL: The only thing that Alex said was that I was in trouble and that John is going to sue you for divorce and take Julian away from you and send you back to Liverpool.

PB: Obviously, he couldn't do any of those things.

SG: I guess he must have sounded like he could, though, at the time.

CL: Well, it was threatening.

SG: When you came home from Greece and you found Yoko in your bathrobe, then you went back to Italy.

CL: It was okay for a while. John sort of . . . I don't know, it was all a vague, vague time. I sort of disappeared and moved in with Alex and Jenny for a while. 'Cause I couldn't stand it. And then I eventually went back to Weybridge, and things seemed to be okay again. John confessed to everything, to all the women he'd had. We got back together for a short time, and it was nice. And I said, I love you. My love. And then this suggestion of a holiday came, I was really tired. He said, well, I've got a lot of recording to do in the studio. So why don't you go on holiday? So I did.

SG: What about the divorce meeting when you went back to Weybridge and Yoko was there.

CL: I wanted to talk to John alone, and she wouldn't stay out of it. She wouldn't, she wouldn't leave him alone. Wouldn't let me discuss things.

PB: And he wouldn't argue with her. He wouldn't tell her to be quiet.

CL: No, my mother was saying you can't, Yoko was saying you can't talk alone and so anyway, we eventually had the discussion. That was it.

SG: What was the discussion about before?

CL: Well, I wanted to know what was happening because the first thing I knew about the divorce was as soon as I came back from Italy and I went to my mother's house, someone knocked on the door and handed me a divorce petition. And that was the first I knew about it. I mean, I hadn't even been home to Kenwood, so I didn't know what to do. So my mother found my brother, and he took me to a solicitor immediately. Let's see, [to Peter Brown] I phoned you and said, "Could I have a meeting?" I didn't even know where John was. The meeting was just to try and make me say that I'd been having an affair. And I just wanted to know what the future was.

PETER BROWN: *Magic Alex played another nasty role in Beatles personal saga in John's divorce from Cynthia. (I refer you to Pattie Harrison's transcripts, as well as Magic Alex's for their renditions of the following story.) Cynthia was going to initiate divorce proceedings and name Yoko as correspondent. At the time, in English law, one of the grounds for divorce was infidelity. This came as a surprise to no one. John and Yoko's pictures were all over the newspapers, with reporters yelling after John, "Where's your wife?" Cynthia felt humiliated, especially after returning home from vacation one day to find John and Yoko sitting in the kitchen of her house in their bathrobes.*

John was determined that despite the obvious, he didn't want Yoko blamed for the breakup of his marriage to Cynthia. He sent Magic Alex to Italy, where Cynthia was on vacation, with an ultimatum: John was going to sue her for adultery, naming Magic Alex as the correspondent, and Alex was going to cooperate. It was true. Cynthia admitted that sexy, handsome Alex had seduced her one night with wine and candles. Cynthia and John wisely both withdrew their threats and were granted an uncontested divorce, a decree nisi, which became final in May of 1969. John gave Alex a black £6,000 Italian Rivolta automobile for his trouble.

SG: Did John agree to support you? Does he support you anymore?

CL: Yes, he does, to a certain extent, there's a trust set up for Julian, which is now divided because of Sean.

SG: I find it fascinating that Paul was so sympathetic that he came to console you and Julian and that he wrote "Hey Jude" for him.

CL: Oh, it's a lovely gesture. Paul couldn't do much. And I think he was so upset about John anyway, that "Hey Jude" was his token gesture to me. And after that, Paul and John had a row. Oh, they were just getting on to go.

SG: There was one major row?

CL: Well, I wasn't around, but they heard about it. They were in the offices and Yoko was there. She was there all the time, and this was bugging the rest of them. And there's a major row between all of them, with John defending Yoko.

SG: Peter, do you remember a big row they had?

PB: Well, there were several. I think that John and Paul were the main people, but John would bring her too. They were prepared to go along with anything as friends because they would value each other so much. But this to extent where, you know, Yoko had really been shoved down their throat, you know? It wasn't just that she was there. It was that she would be there all the time, and they'd never put up with this from anyone before. You or Maureen would never interfere with the Beatles' creative life. When Paul and George and Ringo had put up with this person [Yoko] coming in, you know, and telling them, being too— It was very hard.

Ron Kass on Yoko Ono

The main thing to remember is that Allen Klein told Yoko Ono that he was going to get David Picker, who was the president of United Artists, to give her a million dollars advance for her films (see Yoko Ono's differing account on pages 225–6). He was talking about the films of John smiling, and of John having an erection, and things like that. Klein really sold her on that. John told me, "Don't feel too bad about Allen Klein, because he's really for us. He's really going to straighten everything out, and he's got a lot of experience. I know people say bad things about him, but don't believe them." John's telling me, I know the guy's a crook. Hello. Klein got in through Yoko, really, Yoko pushing John. Now, she never got any money from United Artists, or anything happened. No distribution of films.

Yoko Ono

Yoko was a small, mysterious figure who could make her tiny voice heard when she wanted. She seemed shy at first, but she was steely in her resolve. The Beatles' inner circle thought of Cynthia as family, and we missed her. Yoko's ascension as First Lady of the Lennons and the authority he gave to her was jarring and uncomfortable for all of us. The bond was at first an intellectual one. As you can read in Yoko's transcripts, her relationship with John was platonic for a long time. Magic Alex asks in his transcripts, "Why her? John could have had the most beautiful or intelligent women in the world, why this odd little Japanese lady?" Perhaps this interview, conducted in the Spring of 1981, will answer that question.

STEVEN GAINES: You met John in November of 1966 at the Indica Gallery, but you've said another year and a half passed before the romance became physical?

YOKO ONO: Oh yes, yes, yes. It was when he got back from India, April 1968.

SG: I remember there was this one story that John said somewhere that he went to your apartment one night and he slept on the sofa.

YO: He slept in the next room. My feeling is that John didn't know how to sort of make a move.

SG: He was that shy?

YO: He was that shy, yes.

SG: In an interview, John said he wanted to take you to India instead of Cynthia.

YO: I know that. In fact, while he was in India, he was writing to me, very nice warm letters, all stolen by the way.* And there's some beautiful letters but on a very sort of platonic way, and one time he did a drawing of me sitting on a globe of the world with a little map on it. I'm sitting on it totally naked, and I thought, how dare he? He thought of me naked. I was blushing and very shy about that. But I think—that's the way he was sort of hinting—and those letters were so precious to me that I always carried those in my handbag when John and I later were living together. And one day, of course, it was in the handbag, and so I'm sure somebody stole them.

SG: During this period of courting, you got to meet Cynthia.

YO: Yes.

SG: What was your impression of Cynthia?

YO: The first time I met her at Kenwood—I thought she was very quiet

---

* In 2006, Yoko accused her chauffeur, Koral Karsan, of threatening to release private audiotapes and photographs he stole if she didn't pay him $2 million. Also missing were John's famous wireframe glasses and the letters from India. Karsan was arrested and deported to his native Turkey. In 2014, 86 of the missing items were sold to a German auction house and returned to Yoko. The letters are still missing.

and sensitive—a nice lady. She had a nice figure and my feeling was in Liverpool, when he went to art school, I think she was like a different class of chick, you know, rather elegant and graceful, and I think that's probably what impressed John. She was probably very intelligent, and when he wasn't doing his homework, he had to get help from her, something like that. She was a strong lady. She had to be strong to be with John. He wasn't a Goody Two-shoes. He was already complex and a boy with a chip on his shoulder.

SG: Did you come to the house in Weybridge to see John and wait by the gate?

YO: No. The only time I came to his house was when I was invited. I thought Cynthia was very nice and she had a quiet demeanor, little things I noticed.

SG: I think Cynthia saw you as a threat immediately.

YO: I wasn't aware—I was looking at them as a couple, and I thought she was not very happy, and I even thought, well, you know this is another male macho guy who's treating her badly. I felt bad because it was lunchtime and I'm seated next to him, and he was complaining [about his marriage]—not in a blunt way—he wasn't one of those blunt macho working-class husbands—but sort of subtly saying . . . That's not the kind of thing you should be saying in front of another woman.

Obviously, their marriage was not going gloriously; otherwise, he wouldn't want to have me around. The thing is, John and I fell in love. But he was a man of the world by then. He wasn't a virgin. I think he's one of those people who took marriage very seriously, and I do too. I was married to my first husband, Toshi, for seven years, and Tony for five years. John and I both had one child each. So to leave that and get together, there had to be a very strong reason for it. But as John said, it was bigger than both of us.

[They make John sound as if he was] sort of manipulated by some strong woman who just comes and grabs him. And the thing is, I don't think he was like that at all. A lot of girls were pursuing him, I'm sure. So I don't think he would have gone for that. I'm sure he was used to a lot of women wanting him, you know, and my feeling was, Oh, I see he's not coming on [to me], that's very interesting, so I started saying, Oh, well, he's probably as shy as I am. It's interesting that I wasn't doing anything about it. In other words, it took over a year, from the end of '66 to—a year and a half later—to April of '68 for us to get together. The fact that it built up so much to the point that we finally had to come together.

John was very shy, unlike everybody thinks, and of course, it was widely publicized then as John was just sort of standing there and I just grabbed him or something. I'm a very shy person—a mixture of being shy and very proud and very old-fashioned maybe—I don't think a woman should make a move, you know, whatever.

SG: You're characterized as having pursued him, as having been very aggressive.

YO: I was not in the position to be. I didn't want to have any difficulty with a married man. I was very much interested in my work. I had my child and my husband. Getting help [from John] on a work level was all right. I probably had this feeling that I just wanted to keep it that way, not getting sticky about it. If the truth may be told, you will find certain people who made sure to make it sound like I was the one who pursued him. But the truth could not be told now, I think.

SG: Why not? You mean it's too late to straighten it out?

YO: No, no, it's not too late to straighten it out. But I wouldn't want to go into it. But I'm sure there are some people who felt that that's how it should sound. I don't know.

SG: Do you remember the moment when Cynthia came home from Greece and found you and John in the kitchen?

YO: Well, it wasn't really like that. Cynthia was in Greece—and she didn't come back on the expected date. We checked and found out that everybody was telling her about [John and me]. She felt embarrassed to come back. She didn't just suddenly come into the kitchen and found us like "What's this?" you know.

SG: That's what she said in her book.

YO: Yes, she might have. Also I don't question anything she remembers, anything she wrote in her book, because the way [John and I] got together must have hurt her a lot. It would have hurt anybody—so anything she says, I'm not going to argue with. And I never have.

SG: When was the first time you were in the studio with them?

YO: The *Sgt. Pepper* sessions just before Christmas of '66, that's the one I was invited to. I was thinking I remembered him having to do *Magical Mystery Tour*, and he visited me in my Park Row [apartment] and told me he was going to do it. He wanted me to join him on that, too, just like he did in India, and later changed his mind about it. The *White Album* was the first time we were openly together—when he was inviting me to come sit in a studio, that time that we were still courting.

SG: Were the other Beatles very rejecting of you? Was John terribly hurt by that?

YO: Yes, John was terribly hurt, but if the Beatles immediately received me with open arms and accepted me, he would have felt very badly too.

SG: How's that?

YO: Because you know, when we were separated in 1973, and we used to talk a lot on the phone—sometimes we met and talked—he used to talk very badly of these people, that just because we were separated, they immediately turned around and talked about me in a bad way, or immediately accepted somebody [May Pang] that he's with, like the new [Yoko]. We sort of compared notes, and he didn't like that sort of thing at all. Now, if that happened then, probably, John would have felt terribly [for] Cynthia and Julian, you know, how dare they do that to them or whatever. I mean, he had that sort of—

SG: Did the others drop Cynthia?

YO: No. No, I don't think so. I think that Paul was always very kind to Julian and Cynthia. George and Ringo too. They were never not civilized to Cynthia and Julian. Also, when I came into the picture, they resisted that much because they saw John and Cynthia and Julian as a family. It's nice, really, it's rather touching that they had that sort of integrity, that sort of feeling for Cynthia.

SG: When you got together with John, had you taken LSD before?

YO: Oh—LSD, yes. But not as much as people think. When we started to live together, at least I knew what he was taking every day, and you know we weren't going on acid as much. The first night or something, yes, we sort of took it, but that's about all. And then what happened was—oh, not just the first night. But when we were living together, we weren't taking acid as much as people think. In other words, he told me he would be just taking it every day or whatever, but we got more interested in sort of discovering each other so that we weren't taking acid so much.

SG: I read in *Rolling Stone* that you said that you and John took heroin as a celebration of yourselves as artists.

YO: We did take heroin later, but John was not into it. I wasn't into it either, except when I went to Paris. That's why George and people like that say, "You know, Yoko put him into heroin." Everything we did in those days, anything that was wrong, was my responsibility. And I was very hurt that's how the relatives saw it, you know. I call them relatives because there's a truth to it in a sense.

SG: Neil [Aspinall] said that in the Montague Street arrest for marijuana in October of 1968 that John told him that the great irony was that when they were arresting him, he was high on heroin, and he had just finished all the heroin that was in the apartment, or he got rid of it.

YO: That isn't true. We were not high on heroin. The great irony was that several days before [the bust] somebody told us that there could be a bust and just be very careful. Of course, we had marijuana in the house, and we cleaned it all. John cleaned it in such a way, you know he's very meticulous about those things. He smelled a bowl and said, "Oh the bowl smells, we have to wash it with soap." We just did everything to make sure that it was clean. [Even after a thorough cleaning then, the police mysteriously found marijuana in a film can.]

I read later it was planted. It was a very strange, it took a long time, they were looking everywhere else, and then the cops went into the room where there were lots of things in storage, the front room, and the minute they went in there, they came out and said "Aha!"

That does not mean that we didn't take H. Of course, George said I put John on H, and it wasn't true at all. I mean, John wouldn't take anything unless he wanted to do it. When I went to Paris [before I met John], I just had a sniff of it and it was a beautiful feeling. Because the amount was small, I didn't even get sick. It was just a nice feeling. So I told John that. When you take it properly—*properly* is not the right word—but when you really snort it, then you get sick right away if you're not used to it. So I think maybe because I said it wasn't a bad experience, maybe that had something to do with it, I don't know. But

I mean so, he kept saying, "Tell me how it was?" Why was he asking? That was sort of a preliminary because he wanted to take it, that's why he was asking. And that's how we did it. We never injected. Never.

SG: You moved to Tittenhurst Park in August of 1969. Was that why you went into the London Clinic that summer, because of the heroin?

YO: No, because of a miscarriage probably. I still can't remember exactly when we took [H], but one of the reasons we took it was the [car] accident we had in Scotland.* I remember John and I were very healthy and eating extremely good food. When we took Kyoko and Julian to live with us, we weren't on anything. And after we came back [after the car accident], I had this back pain and that's when we did [H]. I don't remember if that was the first time. But it seems like it was.

SG: The miscarriage that you had a month after the bust for marijuana [when you lived on Montague Street], and then November 22, it was announced in all the papers that you had lost John's baby.

YO: I don't remember hospitals at all. I was in hospitals so many times, even before we got married.

SG: November 8, you went into the hospital, the bust was October 18.

YO: See, because I remember a conversation in the hospital, John was saying, "Oh, we're not going to go back to Montague Square, we can go back to Kenwood."

---

* The summer of 1969, John and Yoko took a driving vacation to Scotland with her daughter, Kyoko, and John's son, Julian. Although he never drove, he insisted on driving all the way in an Austin Maxi. John drove headfirst into a ditch on the third day. He was the most seriously hurt. Yoko received fourteen stitches and wrenched her back.

SG: John wrote "Cold Turkey" about kicking heroin. Did that happen in the house? Not in the London Clinic?

YO: No, not in the London Clinic.

PETER BROWN: So the London Clinic was nothing to do with withdrawals?

YO: No, nothing to do with it.

SG: And then the following October again, this is something I don't understand, the following October you were in the King's College Hospital for three days. Was that another miscarriage?

YO: Yes. I had about, the ones that I remember at least, three miscarriages.

SG: Here's a really confusing one, as long as we're on this subject. On March 29, of 1970, the London papers announced that you were pregnant. But just a week before that, you were in the London Clinic. Were you in the London Clinic for your pregnancy?

YO: Anytime I went to the London Clinic, [it had] nothing to do with drugs.* We were very square people, you know. We would never allow anyone [laughs] in the hospital to know about it.

SG: No mental health treatment?

YO: No, nothing. We went straight [off H]. But you know, because we

---

* Neil Aspinall, Alexis Mardas, and the author Ray Connolly all remember visiting John and Yoko at the London Clinic that summer, where both were going through treatment for heroin withdrawal.

never injected it, when we decided to get off, I don't think we were hooked. I don't think it was a great amount, do you understand? But still it was hard. Withdrawal was hard.*

SG: H continued when you and John moved to America, he didn't stop it then. Right? He continued on and off [heroin] after that. Do you remember a time, in June of 1972, that George came to America to accept a UNICEF Award, for appearing at the Bangladesh concert. They wanted to see you and John, and John said that you rented a limousine, and drove cross-country, right? The limousine driver drove around while you [went cold turkey] in the back of the limousine? The time that I was asking you about was in 1973, almost a year after George and Ringo came to get the UNICEF award in 1972. In other words, the concert was August of '71, they came back to America long after that.

YO: Oh, I see, I see. Okay. At the time, yes, you're right, we were doing a cross-country drive, and, well—I don't think—I would not like you to write this. We were doing a cross-country drive, and John said that we were getting off something? We were not getting off H.

SG: No? Well, I'm glad I checked that out with you and found out it was incorrect.

YO: But it's really true that we were not getting off H at the time, you know? At the time.

SG: Can you set the record straight from your point of view what happened at the Bangladesh concert that caused such hard feelings between John and the others?

---

* On August 24, 1969, in one creative burst, John wrote the song "Cold Turkey" about withdrawal. The BBC refused to play it. Alexis Mardas remembered seeing syringes casually lying around John and Yoko's country estate, Tittenhurst Park.

YO: When George and Ringo were coming to New York to do the Bangladesh concert with John, we were staying in the Park Lane Hotel [on Central Park South]. That's when one morning, John and I, over breakfast, wrote "Happy Christmas," that song, together. We were just elated writing "Happy Christmas." It was gorgeous. After breakfast, we had a huge fight. And the fight had to do with—suddenly Allen Klein arranged it so everybody else, Ringo and George, were all at the Park Lane, and there was a rumor that Allen Klein was putting all the Indian musicians into the Park Lane, too, and John was very upset about that. He'd say, "What is this? Do we always have to wear the same suit?" That's why John changed his bank account . . .

SG: The story that I've heard so many times, is that George didn't want you to do the Bangladesh concert. He didn't want you to appear onstage.

YO: I didn't know that. Maybe George didn't want it. John felt that probably George would not want me to go there with John, to do the Bangladesh concert [which Allen Klein was promoting]. And John said he would not want to do the concert if that's the way it is. But not because George told us. George is polite about—he wouldn't call us and say, "Hey, we don't want [Yoko]." But we didn't know that, at least John and I in the Park Lane Hotel that morning didn't know that George wasn't asking me. But John felt that George would probably not want me, and John didn't want to do the concert. Not just because of that, but he didn't want to do the concert. That's George's shtick, you know . . . I didn't know that George didn't want me. I said to John, "No, you're just being paranoid, let's go and do it."

STEVEN GAINES: *John knew that George did not want Yoko onstage with the three other Beatles because he called Allen Klein, who was promoting the event, to demand he intervene and have Yoko invited onstage, but Klein said he agreed with George, Yoko did not belong on the stage with the three Beatles. This was a turning point in John's relationship with Allen Klein.*

It was Klein's fatal mistake, not to understand that John and Yoko were a single, inseparable unit. From that moment on, John and Yoko were done with Allen Klein. Incidentally, Klein was later investigated for rerouting the money earned by the UNICEF concert for Bangladesh through his own pocket before it was sent to the hungry and sick.

SG: Can we talk about the Janov primal scream therapy incident? John said that you weren't really into it.

YO: Well, in a way. I was cynical about it. Also, I was watching the relationship between Vivian [Janov] and Art [Janov] as a couple, and I felt that Vivian was rather unhappy. John was excited about the promise. So we both sort of decided that, yes, we think the therapy is beautiful, but the people doing it weren't necessarily perfect, they're not gurus or anything. That's how we were looking at it. I think what [prompted] us to leave was that Art said something like, "This can be done in a month," or anybody could be straightened out in a month, and John likes those sort of "instant coffee" solutions. "Oh! You mean, you can be straightened out in a month? That's sounds great!" And we went there [to California], and months passed. We were saying, "When is it going to end? Then one day in the pool, we said, "Oh! That's what it is—we're the ones who are going to decide it's all okay now, and we're gonna move on." We looked at each other and said, "Let's do it then." Because in the pool, we kept saying—I kept saying to him, remember Art said that it's going to be a month, and months passed, and we were still there. So it's not a miracle cure, is it? John was saying that we're the ones who are supposed to walk out. I suppose that's the idea. You know? Oh, okay, we'll tell them. We just said, "We're cured, thank you, and we're going."

SG: Were you pregnant when you went into therapy with Janov?

YO: I was pregnant when I was going there, and I immediately had a miscarriage there. Number three, I think. The minute we went there, I think before we were going to the classes, I think I had the miscarriage. I did all that and then attended the classes.

PB: Were the miscarriages all around the same time, after seven or eight months?

YO: There was one that went up to seven months, and after seven months if the baby is miscarried, you're supposed to treat it as a person who died. You have to name the child. I was in bed and John explained it to me. I always remember that, very sad and distraught. We had a little coffin, and I had to name him, so I named him John Ono Lennon, and I buried it.

PB: I think it was in Queen Charlotte's Hospital, and you made a recording of the heartbeat.

YO: I think so. And that's John Ono Lennon.

SG: You moved to America in September of '71, when you and John met Jerry Rubin and Abbie Hoffman. Do you think you were manipulated by Jerry Rubin?

YO: I don't think so. I think he probably believed in what he was doing, and he felt he had to manipulate us. He was genuine about it, you know.

SG: For instance, he released an item to *Rolling Stone* that John was going to appear at a concert at the San Diego Republican Convention. It caused John trouble.

YO: I think it was more Rubin being naïve. He didn't realize how dangerous it would have been. In fact, John and I thought about doing the San Diego concert, and I think I probably was the one who said no way.

John also said, well, we don't have to be martyrs. We didn't want to be suicidal about it. But we're the only ones who knew how dangerous it might be for us. I don't think that Jerry or Abbie understood the implication at all. [Jerry and Abbie] were saying, "We'll just have to fly you over the stage with a helicopter." I said, "Are you kidding, the helicopter is going to be shot."

SG: What was the first inkling that there was a [government] plot against John? He thought that the phone was tapped and then he was being followed. But were there actually men following you around? Do you remember that?

YO: But we knew that would happen because immigration told us to get out of this country. When those papers [ordering them to leave the US] arrived, we were in the Bank Street apartment, and we had to decide whether we would actually leave this country or fight. When we decided to fight, we knew that they were going to tap us.

SG: You thought they tapped you because you were fighting the deportation order? The deportation order, the sixty-day warning, didn't come until March 6, and they were already writing secret memorandums about you and John.

YO: Probably because of our connection with Jerry and Abbie, [the Feds] started to tap us.

SG: When did you fall out with Rubin and Hoffman? Was there a point where you said, "Look, you're going to lead children into a violent demonstration?"

YO: John and I took the position of we don't want to do it that way, and Jerry always took the position of, well, you know, sometimes we have to use force.

SG: You poured gas on the fire when you and John recorded *Some Time in New York City*. Even loyal fans of John were going to be confused by the totally political album, songs about Attica and one called "Woman Is the Nigger of the World."

YO: We weren't worried about that. We were more worried about whether the music was, musically, good enough.

SG: It's amazing how much on the forefront of women's liberation you were. You wrote "Woman Is the Nigger of the World" in the sixties. I don't think people have ever given you just due. It's not very well known that you collaborated with John Cage or Ornette Coleman, or that you had your own concerts.

You and John separated and got back together in November of '74. You got pregnant again right after you got together.

YO: The minute I got pregnant, John said, "This time you can't have a miscarriage," so he immediately got a wheelchair and he was wheeling me around.

SG: But Sean was born by Caesarean on John's birthday? Was it planned to be on his birthday?

YO: No, that was a fluke thing. We didn't think we were going to have Caesarean, and the morning when I started to have labor, the doctor said you'd better have Caesarean. But it wasn't the excitement of John's birthday, because it was very early in the morning, I thought it was the day before John's birthday because it started happening like around one o'clock in the morning.

SG: When John went off to Hong Kong all alone, and he realized that he's totally alone in a foreign city, no one knows who he is, it was a major epiphany for him. Did that change him?

YO: Oh, I think that that was very good for him, he was very nervous about going. I knew that astrologically direction-wise, it's a good trip, and I thought it would be very good for him. See, he needed all the luck in the world because he's in this kind of pressured position, et cetera . . . So after he came back, during our—I planned it, you know, mainly that he would just go build up and gradually build up in such a way so he'd be in such a strong position when he puts anything out in the world, you know, whether it's a record or a shovel, it has to be really good. So he would go to all these good-direction places and make his body strong.

SG: What made you and John go back into the studio to do *Double Fantasy*?

YO: I called him when he was in Bermuda and I was working here, and I said, look, all right, we're gonna do—this journey, I would say—because we didn't have very many songs. I forgot what was ready, maybe two songs of John's and two songs of mine. At first, we were going to make an EP [extended play format], but while he was in Bermuda, we started to make so many songs it became an album.

SG: John stopped recording basically to take care of Sean.

YO: But also, to take care of himself, his mind and body and all that, in other words, in L.A. and all that sort of separation and all that, he felt that his body was in a bad shape, and also he felt that his mind was in a bad shape. Both of us learned a lot of lessons from that separation, and we both said, look, we're sort of lighting the candle at both ends and we never thought of tomorrow. I said, "Big people usually plan things, like two years ahead, three years ahead. If we did it that way, we'd probably get something really great going. So let's plan things." It was the first time we planned anything, and it's a very sort of paradoxical suggestion that once we planned it, we planned it to the point of getting all these houses so that for the next forty years, we can go to . . . I mainly concentrated my effort into business.

SG: Is it true that you went to a Beatles' business meeting with all Jewish businessmen dressed as an Arab?

YO: Yes. They hated me anyway, but, yeah, that made it worse. Funny.

SG: What was the reason that John suddenly decided to sue Allen Klein?

YO: Well, I don't think that he ever wanted to sue Klein. The major thing was that we wanted to get out of the relationship.

PB: Why did you decide you'd had enough of him?

YO: When we did the One to One concert [August 30, 1972, for the benefit of the Willowbrook School for Children]. Around that time, we felt that Klein wasn't dealing the way we wanted him to. Despite the fact that John and I brought him into the picture, Klein always felt that he was representing the Beatles, so there was always a conflict, you know? John and I needed somebody who would represent John and Yoko, but he always wanted the Beatles, he always had the dream that one day he would get Paul as well. Because he had three Beatles. So that was the conflict, and finally we realized that Klein just didn't understand John and Yoko, that John and Yoko is a partnership, it's a product. Klein never understood that, and he was always sort of trying to make a Beatles thing out of it.

PB: Didn't he promise you that he would get you a deal on all your films?

YO: No, he didn't. You know, in my life, there were so many paradoxes. I was misunderstood in so many ways, but this is another one. They felt that I brought Allen Klein in because there was some kind of side deal with Allen.

SG: I think that what they believed, that the way that Allen was finally able to sell them on himself was that he said, by the way, I'll fix Yoko up too. I'll get a million dollars from United Artists.

YO: Are you kidding? Klein was such a male macho guy. The reason why we decided was John kept saying to me, "This guy Allen is calling a lot. Do you think that I should see him?" I said, "Well, it doesn't hurt to see him." So we met him in the Dorchester hotel, and Klein started to quote all John's songs. He knows all of the lines. That's a lot, you know. You know for a businessman to remember all the lines. And that's one of the things that Allen was able to do. So we decided there and then that Allen's okay. So that [first] night, I was the only one who could type, so I just typed up this little thing saying that Allen Klein is representing John.

SG: It said, *I don't care what anyone else says, Allen Klein is for me.* It's a famous note.

YO: Nothing was said about my movie. It was good for John, and that's how Allen came in.

PB: But Klein told us at Apple that he was going to get a deal for you and your films. That's what all those people thought.

YO: Allen denied this, but I'll tell you, our next meeting was when we were sitting in Maureen and Ringo's house, where we were sort of staying for a while. John was upstairs sleeping. The bell rang, so I came downstairs. And there was Allen Klein. He came in, and sort of towering over me, and he said, "Listen, if I get John and all, I don't mind if you stick around. You know what I mean?" I'm looking at him saying, well, this is a kind of cheap novel something that you know that I never read, but I've heard about these sort of grade B Hollywood films or something where the producers say, "Listen, chick, I don't mind if you hang around." I was so insulted that I couldn't believe it, I was hearing him say it. Can you imagine? I was laughing when I told that to John.

SG: Did you feel Magic Alex was a well-intentioned person? I always felt that if this was a melodrama, Alex would be the evil person behind the scenes. He had a very small role, but it was pivotal.

YO: I'll tell you what it is. In *Sgt. Pepper*—'67, John and I were communicating in the sense that I was in the session and all that—all that was going on, so the timing was—'66 we met, '67 we were communicating on the level of work, in other words I would be sitting in his session or something, or he'd be saying why don't you put out a record with Apple—that sort of thing. There was some incredible sort of—uh, incredible, as I say—you know some sort of sculptural pieces or also some sort of different discovery or invention of something that I had that, you know, excited him. And he'd said, well, look, tell Magic Alex all this, you know. And I went to Magic Alex and said, well, I had this plan, that plan, all these sort of complicated things that you know need some sort of engineer to create it. And he said, oh, great idea—and next thing I know, I get a phone call from him that he's copyrighting for Apple or something, you know.

PB: What was the invention?

YO: I don't wanna tell the world yet—

SG: But you told Alex. Now that you've brought up Alex, I don't want to get away from this thing about you and John and the beginning of your relationship, but now that you bring up Alex, what was your impression of Alex? Was he a good person?

YO: He was a nice enough person, and I'm sure that what he was doing—he thought that my invention—well, it's flapping—he thought my invention was interesting enough that he wanted to blueprint it and copyright it for Apple in case it makes money. So he was projecting.

SG: Not just in terms of your invention but as a person and the kind of hold he had on John, and who he was in that whole situation.

YO: Well, you see, a lot of people, when they are close to John and later, close to John and Yoko, just the fact that they go to dinner or something like that, they start thinking they have a hold over so-and-so, and they become jealous, et cetera. With Alex, I never thought that Alex had a hold over John. John's extremely not only intelligent but worldly and a very astute observer.

SG: Even then, in 1967?

YO: Even then. Extremely. And he was sort of taken with Alex in a way, and he would say nice things about Alex in front of people, so they all thought John must be taken by him.

Well, look, John was rather—when he wants to be, he can be sort of almost—what's a good word for it? Very emotional and all of a sudden give a car or something to Alex—very extravagant things like that. Then people think, oh, well, he gave a car to Alex, so certainly he must be totally taken by Alex. But it wasn't like that, really. It seemed like a grand gesture, and of course, he gave a car to Allen Klein as well. But his observations about both of them were very accurate in a sense that he knew what they were. In a very balanced way, the good parts and bad parts.

SG: Was that the big black Italian automobile he gave to Alex? The Rivolta, is that what it's called? You were there at that presentation. Did it have a big bow on it, a ribbon on it, as they say? Do you remember that?

YO: I don't think so. Well, look, I probably have to go—I didn't want to ask what time in case you think I was trying to kick you out, but—

PB: It's four fifteen.

YO: Oh, I have to go to studio by four thirty. [Recorder is turned off.]

May Pang

When John and Yoko were not harmonious, sparks flew. They were both very strong people, and no matter what the issue was, they had reached a point where there could be no compromise or resolution. To make things even more difficult, Yoko was going to board meetings and dealing with the lawyers instead of John. In 1973, it was decided that John should move out. (This is one of several times that Yoko decided "John needed to see the world and be alone more." Only John wasn't alone. He spent the next eighteen months with a beautiful young Chinese American girl named May Pang, who was easily mistaken for Yoko. May was hand chosen by both John and Yoko to be his mistress. This eighteen-month period is referred to as John's "lost weekend." May Pang remembers it differently.

May Pang grew up in Spanish Harlem, New York, where her family owned a Chinese laundry. In May of 1969, when she was nineteen, an employment agency sent her for a receptionist job at a Japanese bicycle wholesaler, located in an office building on Broadway. By coincidence, Allen Klein, the controversial and formidable manager of the Beatles, opened a New York office of Apple Records in the same building. May decided to ride up in the elevator and ask if they had any job openings.

MAY PANG: I went up to the fortieth floor, and the receptionist said there weren't any openings that she knew of, and just then, one guy popped out of his office and said, "Can you type?" I started working there in September 1969. Allen couldn't keep a secretary; nobody could deal with him. So I got shifted up over there to answer his phones.

And then one day, I walked into the office at nine thirty in the morning, December of '70, and John and Yoko were standing near the elevators. It was the funniest thing. They had just arrived. They were staying at the Regency Hotel. John said, "What time do people show up?" I said, "Not till ten, ten thirty." They just sat in the clients' office for a bit until Allen [Klein] showed up.

They had come here to make two movies, *Up Your Legs Forever* and *Fly*. Shoot it, edit it, and show it. *Up Your Legs* was 365 pairs of legs, just the pieces from your toes to your thighs, and another with a fly exploring a body. They said to me they needed people to work on it, and somehow, they asked me. It was fun, catching flies. We'd go down to the Chinese restaurant, there were always flies at the back. We had to get a whole bunch because they would die off. I think we shot them with CO_2 . . . to knock the wind out of the fly so that it would crawl all over a body. And the girl's name happened to be Virginia Lust. I have no idea where she came from. She used to lay there nude, sleeping, and this fly crawling over her and they would shoot it.

MP: December of 1971, they came to New York with only two suitcases. They found a place down in Bank Street in November or so, I think it was, and they stayed there. And then I—we worked out of the office, and every so often, we would have to travel down to the house.

STEVEN GAINES: What point did they break up?

MP: [In] '73. It was close to September . . . around the summertime, uh, in '73, somewhere around there. We were all, in a sense, involved in their personal life.

SG: I heard that Yoko was very cool about you.

MP: We were all friends. She used to call us every day when we went out to Los Angeles.

SG: What did you think would become of your relationship with John? Did you think he was going to go back to Yoko? Were you in love with him?

MP: I just wanted to help him and be his friend more than anything else, because he needed somebody to talk to a lot, and I was his friend. And that's what I wanted to, to always be, and that's what we always were. Whatever was going to happen would've happened. I did not say, "Okay, I want this, and I want him to do this with me." I took it as it came. Life is just a little too short to start putting demands on people.

SG: You found a new apartment together. Did he move directly out of the Dakota into a new apartment with you?

MP: Yes. We found a place on East Fifty-second Street.

SG: And Yoko remained friendly with you two all the time.

MP: Yes. She called us all the time. We used to talk.

SG: Did she want him back?

MP: That's something I didn't talk to her about.

SG: Well, you could probably tell.

MP: I'm sure she, you know . . . I just know that we were all just friendly. But she was a very different, very extraordinary woman.

I gathered later from her, and this is after the fact, but that she was hoping he would come back, but she didn't plan to promote him coming back, it had to be when he was . . . if he was ever going to do it, it would have to be when he was ready. I mean, she was that cool.

SG: I just want you to get it straight. I think the most important things are truthfulness and accuracy. That's the most important thing, is not, not for you to guess, you know, on anything that went on.

MP: Oh, I know. It is still hard for me to even talk about it because there are a lot of things, um, that somehow I can't even put into words. It goes so far back and it takes so much out of you. It takes a lot out of me because John meant a lot to me, and we always remained friends and that's what's good. And then I still had that memory. We had great times. There was a year when we were out in Los Angeles, 'cause we were trying to do the rock and roll album and we were having a hard time.

SG: Do you remember the night that you and John went to the Smothers Brothers show at the Troubadour with Harry Nilsson?

MP: John doesn't really like to drink. What happened was Harry and everybody ordered Brandy Alexanders. To John, it tasted like malt, you know, like malt milkshake. I don't drink, I drank Coca-Cola. That's all you would find in my fridge was Coca-Cola. What happened was that he was drinking doubles. Harry was drinking the same thing—and everybody else was drinking, I mean, everybody tried the same drink, so everybody was getting plastered. And Harry started screaming and there was all these people there. We had never been to places like that with Harry. That was our first outing. And it's very strange. John got real drunk.

SG: The night that you're talking about then, the Smothers Brothers were on the stage? And John heckled them or something?

MP: Well, sort of heckled them, and I kept telling Harry to shut up because he was egging him on. And everybody around the table knew. Harry was egging him on, "Go, go," you know?

SG: What did John say?

MP: Oh God, you ask me now. He was just being a heckler. They came over and asked him to be quiet, and of course Harry butted in and next thing you know, all I saw was everything just going up, and I'm going, "Oh God."

SG: They threw him out?

MP: They were surrounded by all the guards at the, uh, Troubadour. We ran out, and then later on, we found out some, of course, some photographer was trying to sue John, saying he hit her. There was no way, because the doors flew open from when we were exiting, anybody who was standing there would've gotten hit by the door. John was meanwhile surrounded by people. He couldn't get at anybody. I was sober and really angry that this whole thing had happened. And I was angry at everybody.

SG: Is it true that he put a Kotex on his forehead?

MP: Oh, that's another night. We went to some restaurant to have dinner. John found the tampon in the bathroom. He started drinking, wine or something, and he forgot it was on his head. That was all, he just forgot, totally forgot.

SG: The waitress came over, and he said, "Do you know who I am?" and she said, "Yes, you're an asshole with a tampon on his head."

MP: There were so many people at the table that would be screaming out. And it was one of those, that finally, um, we started going, "Oh God, here we go again." But we didn't get thrown out of the restaurant.

SG: It's funny because when Ringo and Harry often would get into trouble, that never got in the press.

MP: It's because nobody ever saw John drunk. It was very unlike him because— You see, it only happened two or three incidents that are blown out of proportion, when you talk about—we're talking about two or three times. We're not talking about eighteen months of every weekend being drunk. It was only a couple of times, you know, an incident. And of course, it made such . . . because John, John was a—you know, John was always being watched by people. They want to pick at him, because he's always had a clever remark . . . like, if you watch any, any old news reels, he always had something to say.

We all shared a house one time when we were doing Harry Nilsson's album. There were so many people, and Harry and Ringo and Keith Moon would all go out to drink, John wouldn't go. He'd rather stay home, and he watched television. He . . . It just happened that those are the two or three incidents that, after he got into the press, but it wasn't, excuse me, it wasn't, uh, a full eighteen months of that.

You see, when I was with him, we'd go out for walks. He loved it. He started to get around and have fun and talk to people. We went out to see quite a few people. People would call him and say, "Come on over." We saw Ringo a lot, when we were in L.A., and Elton, and all these people, like Keith Moon.

SG: What got John and Yoko back together again?

MP: That's something that, you know, just happened.

SG: There was no reconciliation visit?

MP: He went to visit her and, you know, he came back, and he told me. And I said that I was [happy for him]. This was the beginning of February '75.

SG: Were you surprised, or did you see it coming?

MP: Um, I didn't expect anything. You know, it was, you know . . . I don't, I don't, I don't remember my reaction at—I mean, it's—it was almost as if it was, you know, okay, going back to Yoko, but it was also, um, it was a bit of both, a surprise and not a surprise at the same time. I mean, I can't explain that feeling. And, uh, you know. I called Yoko immediately and I wished her the best and I hope it worked out for the second time around. Which it did. We got front-page headlines.

SG: Was the time in Los Angeles a healthy change for John?

MP: Well, I don't know if you would call it a good time, because we did a lot of things, we did a lot of recording at that time, we did *Walls and Bridges*. I even got a chance to sing on it, and he wrote a song for Yoko on that album, and he wrote a song for me. You know, John and I had a whole, it was a whole . . . I don't think I could compare whatever Yoko may have had. I know what I had, and everything is different.

SG: During the other times in his life, he experimented with heavy drugs like heroin. John called those eighteen months in Los Angeles his "lost weekend." Was he out of control?

MP: It's only the few incidents, and it just got blown out of proportion.

SG: If this is incorrect, or I would like to explain it if it is correct, that for the, uh, time that when he broke up with Yoko, that he was either so upset or lovesick or he threw her out, or I don't know what the story is, I know that he was down. But the story is, is that he threw her out, that it was his decision, uh, to leave her. I mean, he actually moved out.

MP: See, that—that's something I don't know. You know, I don't know who . . . I mean, at that, like I said, their [inaudible] is I don't know who did what or who said [inaudible] or whatever, I don't know. That's, you know . . . And I'm not gonna, you know, I wasn't about to ask what was happening, you know? But their main—

SG: It's remarkable [inaudible] how you have a part because I couldn't do that. I mean, I would have to know what was going on.

MP: Um, it's only because, you know, I . . . It—it was just at a time, I'm—I'm—I'm always, like, you know, I guess that's the way I am, you know, I—I try to show patience and I try to . . . whatever he wanted as a friend, he needed. He— You know, he . . . we used to go out to Long Island a lot during the summer here. He loved doing things that he hadn't done in a long time, we'd go out to Long Island, we'd go, we would . . . to Long Island, we'd go, we would, uh, meet up with some friends he had, and we'd stay with Peter Boyle a lot.

SG: Then you don't understand what was resolved and what changed when John went back with her?

MP: No. I mean, it, you know, he said to me that he wanted to go home. And I said, "Okay." I don't know, I—you know, I—I didn't—

SG: And you went to the phone and called her and you, and you—

MP: And I said congratulations, you know?

Peter Brown on Allen Klein

When Brian died, Paul was concerned that without management, it would appear the Beatles were floundering. He wanted a manager who was a captain of industry or master of high finance, ridiculous qualifications for managing the Beatles, yet Paul had meetings with unlikely candidates, like Labour politician Lord Beecham and newspaper tycoon Cecil King. Both men were mystified as to why they would be likely managers of the Beatles, and although they took meetings to meet with Paul, they declined any interest.

The one man who wanted to manage the Beatles more than anyone was the notorious Allen Klein of ABKCO (Allen and Betty Klein Company). He was famous in the music business in the United States for being a bully and an all-around shifty character. Klein even looked like a crook. He was sloppy and fat, he wore sneakers and sweatshirts, and everything he didn't like was "for shit." If he were a cartoon character, there would have been flies buzzing around his head. By 1967, Klein had weaseled his way into the Stones management and renegotiated their royalties, getting them a large increase, plus a £1,500,000 advance, a fact that stuck in the Beatles' collective craw. (It would turn out that Klein had withheld royalty payments and neglected to pay their taxes for five years.) Klein's quest was to get his hands on the

Beatles, too, and manage the two top bands in the world at the same time. With the death of Brian Epstein in August of that year, there were few impediments.

I asked Mick Jagger if he wouldn't come to 3 Savile Row and talk to the Beatles about what Klein did to the Rolling Stones. We set a time and date, and Paul, George, and Ringo showed up on time, but when John and Yoko showed up, they brought Allen Klein with them. When Mick arrived, he was horrified to see Klein, and he felt duped and embarrassed by John. He left within a few minutes without saying much.

Dick James on Northern Songs

DICK JAMES: What happened was, Brian died and we all sat down to try to preserve what he had built. We could have actually been a show business entrepreneurial conglomeration. Between us, we had enough experience, we had enough know-how, we had enough basic creative intelligence to make it work.

But when I went down to the film studio at Twickenham, there was John twanging away with his guitar with Yoko sitting right up rubbing knees with him, while he's trying to play. George Harrison was getting up, now and then, walking around, spitting all over the place 'cause he was disgusted with what was going on. Paul McCartney was saying, "All I want to do is get the song recorded."

And they were really falling apart. The writing was on the wall. Apart from that, the various factions were lining up, legally and financially, behind them. And I could see, there was only one thing that was going to happen for Northern Songs. It's going to disintegrate. I was managing director of a public company, and I had allegiance to the stock exchange council.

STEVEN GAINES: The value of Northern Songs was based upon not only an enormous catalog of songs already written but the ability of their songwriting to continue. You saw that partnership was going to fall apart?

DJ: Sure. The Beatles were going to fall apart. It was really Lennon–McCartney. Ringo and George Harrison owned a few shares they bought. They weren't given any shares. They bought a few shares.

SG: They *bought* the shares? At a discount?

DJ: Yes, they bought the shares, at seven and ninepence. They did not have a discount.

SG: You didn't make your move to sell Northern Songs until 1969. Did you feel any responsibility to John and Paul, who had made you a great amount of money?

DJ: Oh, sure. I had a responsibility to go to them, but I had a responsibility as managing director of Northern Songs.

SG: But you didn't turn to them and ask, "You want to buy Northern Songs?" You sold it to Sir Lew Grade [without them knowing].

DJ: Because if I'd have gone to them, they'd threaten me with all kinds of things. They would threaten to sell their shares, wouldn't they? And if they started flooding the market with shares, then it would have sunk down.

So I went to them once I'd accepted [Lew Grade's offer], but with all due respects, I put it to the board of Northern Songs, and [Brian's brother] Clive Epstein was in favor.

SG: Clive wanted to get out because Allen Klein was already in the picture, and nobody could stomach Allen. That's really part of it. Isn't it?

DJ: Well, you said it. I didn't. There were people stacking up behind Paul on the one hand and John on the other, and it was beginning to tear it apart. And when Lew Grade wanted the company, I did not want to sell it, because it was not for sale.

In fact, I will say that at a meeting with John, Paul, George, and Ringo, I said eventually Northern Songs will not be able to survive, because if you don't hold together, it will make us vulnerable for someone to come in and make a bid. It's true that between you and I, we control the shares, but there's no sense in controlling it. And I said, I can tell you here and now that Lew Grade has been romancing me. And a couple of them said, you wouldn't sell out to Lew Grade.

I said, "Why? His money's the same as anybody else's." If I hadn't sold Northern Songs, it would've been destroyed. Not only would have run itself into the ground. He would've had assets, but he wouldn't have had credibility.

SG: It's been written that John Eastman said you were scared that Klein might try to get control of Northern Songs.

DJ: I wouldn't have thought he was very wrong in that assumption, because he did, didn't he? But on the other hand, so did Lee Eastman. The funny part about the sale of Northern Songs was that here in London, a man named Jarvis Astaire owned a little tiny block of stock. Jarvis Astaire was finally the key. Lew Grade obviously persuaded Jarvis Astaire to part with his shares at that point in time. I already had assigned my shares, but I was still emotionally involved, and let's face it, at that particular point in time, I was still managing director. As the press release was being put out, I contacted John and Paul to make an appointment to see them, to explain to them why I did not put it to them first.

SG: John Eastman came to your office and read you the riot act? He was quoted as telling you that you made your fortune on John and Paul and you were a bastard to sell Northern Songs to Lew Grade. The other Beatles were furious with you as well.

DJ: Well, so be it. I set up a meeting with them. I met with them several days later at, uh, Paul's place in St. John's Wood. Linda made tea and John was belligerent. Paul said that he thought that, uh, I had done what I thought was best. It was my decision to make at that particular point in time, I'd apologized for not putting it to them. I think even today that it was definitely the best decision I could have made at the time. They were going to fall apart. I also had two adversaries, I was going to get caught up in the middle. The battle was looming. The troops were gathering on the heights . . . and I was sitting there in the valley, and they're both going to come down on me.

If it was only Eastman, I'd known Eastman for many, many years, very fine man. He knows what a copyright is worth. He knows the value of it. If I had to deal with John Eastman, I am certain that the whole vehicle could have traveled rather well. But to be caught up in the jaws of what was going to become a power game with two Americans. And there is Lew Grade standing there with the money in his hot little hand on nearly £10 million, wanting to hand it over. There was no alternative. And I say this: The decision wasn't made in one minute. The decision was over several weeks. And while the decision was being made, the price was going up and up and up. I think in the last four to five weeks, the price almost doubles.

One day I went to the Twickenham studio to see the Beatles, and one was drinking a Coca-Cola, one drinking a glass of milk. I said, "George, how's it going?" He said, "Well, we've been here since ten o'clock this morning, we haven't got two bars in the can." The camera was rolling and people were effing up lines. They just wouldn't even sit down and look like they were playing. A ridiculous situation. And I'm sitting there, I'm the guardian of the music. And I've got 3,300 people out holding shares.

SG: You mentioned this meeting on Cavendish Avenue. You said Linda made tea. Was Yoko there?

DJ: Yes. John and Yoko. Linda. In fact, before that, I'd had a meeting down at Apple, at which Neil Aspinall was present with, uh, Ringo and George Harrison, and George and I had some very, very strong words. They are never to be repeated. George was possibly reflecting John and Yoko's hurt. Neil threw him out of the room. Neil Aspinall said, "For Christ's sake, George, get out."

SG: I don't understand why you just couldn't have called them up and said, "Listen, I'm going to sign these papers with Lew Grade tomorrow for £9 million. Do you want to do it? If not, he gets it."

DJ: How could I say it, "Hey, Northern Songs is up for grabs. Who's going to grab it?" and then wait for the building to fall in. The real designers in this factory are John Lennon and Paul McCartney. Two wonderful guys that don't know very much businesswise and can be swayed. Can be swayed either by their wives, or their business factors, or anything else. They have equity. They don't realize quite what they've got. If you evaluate it, it's worth over £2 million each. I'm not a dishonest person. I leveled with everybody, always. Whatever else my failings, I always tell the truth. It's the shortest distance between two points. But in that particular case, the moment I tell the truth, I start to get clobbered. So I didn't tell a lie. I just didn't tell anybody anything. I told Northern Songs' board. I told Geoffrey Ellis. You couldn't get a more honest, straightforward, forthright person than Geoffrey Ellis. He couldn't lie. But he also saw the impossibility of leveling with the boys first. It was the one time that I didn't say, "Hey, fellas, what do you think?" I could've been wrong, but let's face it. They made a lot of money. Their continuity with Northern Songs had been preserved with a very good company. I made sure I preserved that. And what has happened since, I think, is fantastic. I only wish that all that could've been a part of Northern Songs. For the same money, it could've been.

But by then, I'd sit back and watch them tear each other apart and not tear me apart. If John and Paul and the Beatles want to tear themselves apart, you had troops lining up on one hill, you had troops lining up on the other hill. Remember, I'd spent months, and months, and months of trying, not only to save Northern Songs but to save NEMS as well. To save Apple, if you like. To tell me they didn't know what they were doing in Savile Row made no sense. Unbelievable. They had an electronics genius, didn't they? He made a nothing box, it was called. It had nothing, but it cost hundreds and hundreds and hundreds of thousands of pounds. If anybody had come to me and said, "Dick, you think this nothing box is worth putting any money into?" I'd have said, "That's what it is—it's worth nothing." The same as opening boutiques and everything else. It's their own money, if they want to open boutiques and lose their money, fine. If they want to make a nothing box, fine.

The funny thing is, it's a tragedy. It was a tragedy. It shall always be a tragedy. The premature demise of the Beatles. Brian, of course, was the first tragedy. That was the real seed that was sown, unfortunately, or the die became cast, that I think effectively guaranteed the coming events. But again, there's the other side of the coin, and that is if they'd had continued, what would they have done? Would they have gone on trying to make their music? Could they have been musically compatible in wanting to change direction? They really went out at a peak. If they hadn't disintegrated, you wouldn't have the legend of the Beatles, because they would've become old hat. Tragically enough, they would've become old hat.

PETER BROWN: You always leave them wanting more, you know.

Ron Kass

Ron Kass casts a gimlet eye on the Swinging Sixties from the singular point of view as president of Apple Records, as well as being married to actress and sixties icon Joan Collins. The record company was the only division of Apple that made sense for the Beatles to finance, as opposed to a clothing store or greeting card shop. Kass supplies a firsthand discourse on the madness and mishandling of the Beatles' record company, the shooting stars it signed, and its ultimate fate when the Beatles felt threatened by it and lost interest. "They were terrible, terrible judges of character," Kass said in his transcript. "They were the kind of guys who prided themselves on 'knowing'—they were boys from Liverpool who thought they couldn't be taken, but they knew nothing."

RON KASS: I was there a little less than two years, but it was like five years anywhere else. There are two things I did with Apple that were vetoed. The really big one was that I signed the Band,* and it was vetoed by John and Paul. But the Band was a big one that really pissed me off because it was . . . no money, no anything. You know, the Beatles had an ego. The Beatles really had an ego. All that stuff that they said

---

* This legendary and influential group was the subject of a Martin Scorsese documentary, *The Band*. Its members include Rick Danko, Levon Helm, and Robbie Robertson.

about wanting to sign artists, I don't think that they really wanted to do that. They just wanted to extend themselves, to extend the Beatles. I know that when we did get successful artists, that they weren't very happy about it.

Peter Asher brought James Taylor in one day. He played me a couple songs on the guitar, including "Carolina in My Mind," and I thought to myself, I don't know if this guy's ever going to sell a record, but he's such high quality. This is the kind of person that Beatles should be associated with, people like James Taylor. So I encouraged Peter Asher to sign him up and do an album. James was only eighteen or nineteen, so we had to have his father sign the contract. I signed him to a five-year contract at 5 percent of the retail sales, a fair rate for new artists. But there was no front money, there was no advances, there was no bullshit. I also signed James to a publishing contract for five years, which was, of course, worth a fortune. James got out of it, because Allen Klein technically breached his contract by not bothering to send anybody accountings. Incidentally, the four Beatles weren't interested in James Taylor at all.

One of the first things I was asked to do at Apple was to fire Peter Asher. Paul asked me to fire him because he said, "I'm breaking up with Jane, and it's embarrassing having her brother [Peter] around." I stalled him. I said, "You know, Peter really has a good ear. He's a musician, and I'd like to have him." Paul grumped a little bit and said he really preferred getting rid of him. He thought I had fired him, and Paul started to see Francie Schwartz, and enough time went that Paul forgot all about Peter. One day, Paul said to me, "Did you sack Peter Asher?" I said, "No." Paul just grumbled and walked away and that was the end of it.

About the same time we signed another artist, the band Badfinger, and we signed Jackie Lomax. With all the bullshit going on, I was quietly, in my way, building up a record company. I was making deals. I had already done two world trips, setting up the distribution in Japan. I remember we were in Japan twice, because I took Alex Mardas with me once.

STEVEN GAINES: You took Alex Mardas with you to Japan? How come?

RK: I don't know. The odd thing was, that when we landed in Japan, thirty-five scientists from Sony were there to meet Alex. Alex is still an enigma to me. He had a way of selling. He had these ideas. Whether he actually was able to execute these ideas is questionable. They were marvelous ideas about how he was going to make blind people see, through miniature television. You know, just a miniaturized microchip television in their eye, mounted somewhere there. All you had to do is get the signal from a camera into the brain.

SG: Alex is selling bulletproof cars now that might not be bulletproof.

RK: He's doing security for the King of Spain. The funny thing about it is that he was so used to being a con that I think it was very hard for him to get into a legitimate business. Hence the bulletproof cars that weren't bulletproof. It's just as easy for him to get the right thing done, to hire people and make the right thing. He's got to be one of the greatest salesman of all time. He's a little bit of a fraud and con artist, but what a great salesman. You know? I mean, he makes it all sound so razzle-dazzle. Some of the things he used to tell us. He said he was going to build the best record-mastering equipment in the world. It was supposed to be a revolutionary mastering machine that was built completely in his laboratory. The day this thing is delivered, I looked at it, and it was built by Siemens, in Germany. It was a very up-to-date computer-driven mastering machine, the latest in German technology, straight from the factory. Alex didn't even bother taking off their nameplate and putting on his own. He was still claiming that he built it himself, as if he went to Germany and built it for Siemens and they were shipping it under the Siemens name.

[Kass turns the conversation to some of the tribulations of trying to launch a record company with the Beatles.]

RK: Apple Records' first release was "Hey Jude." I ordered that the first hundred thousand copies of "Hey Jude" were shipped in a black, glossy sleeve with a lime green apple on it that said, *Beatles on Apple*, so you established the Apple label. The copyright symbol had to have a circle around it. A tiny line around the apple. John insisted this circle be white on both sides. Paul insisted that it be green on both sides. Ringo said he heard that in America, they're now using multicolored, so you can't counterfeit. George didn't give a shit. So I was at an impasse, because John insisted on white and Paul insisted on green. We were two weeks delayed, because they wouldn't agree. Finally one day, I ordered five million labels. I ordered the sliced-open apple side, white, because it matched the thing, and on the green-sided I ordered a green circle. I figured, I can satisfy Paul and John and tell Ringo to go fuck himself. And George didn't care. And that's how it was to get things going businesswise in Apple. In other words, everything that moved ahead . . . Nothing would move ahead. You know Paul and John would get a divergence of opinions and just everything stopped. No decision was made. And, of course, you couldn't run a company that way. So, I just adapted quietly a *modus operandum*. I would just make the decision myself and try and make the two of them happy. They both kind of shrugged when they saw it, because "It's only half what I wanted," that kind of thing.

One day just before the launch, Stanley Gortikov, the president of Capitol Records in the United States, called me and said, "Ron, I know you guys are very avant-garde, but you really shouldn't have done that." It turns out he thought we had an apple drawn that looked like a cunt. I swear to God. The core of it. I called the artist and when I told him, he just died laughing. Gortikov wanted to change the American label. They airbrushed a real apple because they thought it was drawn to deliberately resemble female genitalia. I mean, it was just amazing. Stanley Gortikov called me on the phone and said, "Come on, we're friends." I said to him, "Why don't you get an apple and go cut it open. Then we'll continue the conversation." Madness. Absolute madness.

One thing I would have done differently with John, I would have presented him with a bag of money every once in a while. Money invested was too abstract for him. Tangible money that you can touch and feel. It was my fault instilling in them a sophistication which they did not have. Neil Aspinall was almost like talking to one of the guys. Poor Neil could never figure out who was telling the truth. He was a sweet guy, but he hated to make decisions and he was indecisive. He was naïve. Look, they didn't treat him like he had any bearings. He was just the guy carrying the equipment and things. You know, guys from Liverpool that haven't had any kind of an education. I expected too much of them. Magic Alex was typical of the kind of genre which surrounded Apple. You never knew what was legitimate and what was illegitimate.

On Allen Klein

RK: Allen Klein wanted me out because I would tell the truth about him. I said to him one day, "You know, I'm not going to let you just bullshit everybody." I knew that whatever he'd do, he was going to steal their money. Whatever contract he would renegotiate, it was going to all end up in his pocket, or a good part of it. Which did, you know, luckily it was reversed. Luckily, Paul never signed. You know, Paul never signed any of the agreements. And the British courts stopped it. They really did, they stopped it. But he had a way of siphoning off the money. You see, Allen didn't make them any more money. He renegotiated a contract which we were going to renegotiate anyways. By the way, the contract, you asked how much it was. It wasn't as ridiculous as everybody says. The original contract of the Beatles, with Parlophone, was ludicrous. It was like a penny a record or something like that. Brian Epstein did a seven-year contract, which, I think, showed his insecurity at the time. It was 17 percent of the wholesale price. It should have been somewhere around 20 to 22 percent. When Allen renegotiated, it turned out that in actual figures, it was no more than 1 or 2 percent higher. And Klein took more than that as his part. He was supposed to only take 10 percent of the increase. He always said, "I am only going to take a percentage on the things I get for you." But, of course, when he did the contracts, he was taking 10 percent of everything. Of everything. So, in other words, whatever he did renegotiate, they ended up with less than they had before. It was all based on a lie. He had cheated the Stones. He had cheated Donovan, who told Paul. He had cheated everybody. He's a fraud. I hear that Mick told John about Klein, but he didn't listen. Because with Yoko . . . And, look at how long the Yoko thing has lasted. I mean, look at it. That's much stronger than anything anybody can say.

SG: Klein accused you of stealing?

RK: He had to get rid of me, because I was the truth. I was going to tell them if the new contract wasn't better than your old contract. He was so thoroughly unpleasant. It wasn't only that he was just dirty and unpleasant. He was such a liar. He was the opposite of everything that I had ever stood for. He was dishonest. He had no integrity. *Integrity* was a stupid word to him. Forget about ethics. I could see that the writing's on the wall, and I can't help the Beatles. At first, I wanted to help them.

Anyhow, it's like John would listen to Magic Alex before me. Nobody could prove that Allen Klein was wrong, because there would never be anything specific. The fact that everybody had had trouble with him, they didn't pay any attention to that.

There was a meeting on Easter Sunday, the object of which was to expose me as stealing from them. There was never anything decided. There was never a resolution. It was never said, "Yes." But, where there's smoke there's fire. Klein built the thing. In other words, he really destroyed me there, because he planted that doubt in the Beatles' mind. Like I told you, because they're unsophisticated, the $1,250 could have been $1,250,000. They were just not thinking clearly. To me, also, it was a tremendous disappointment, because I say if the guys are that naïve, that unsophisticated, I don't want to do this anymore. It's upsetting me too much. I wanted to get out of there.

No, they didn't fire me, and I didn't quit. What happened was, I had a contract and Allen eventually had to pay off 100 percent. It was nothing. It was not a large amount.

SG: This house in which we sit was originally leased by Apple?

RK: Yes. My ex-wife had found it, but we had put it under Apple Corps because Apple was supplying the house for me. I wanted to keep this house, but when I was in California, Allen had *moved into it*. That bugged the shit out of me. These are the things that the Beatles will never know. To show you how lightweight Allen Klein was, is that not only did I get him moved out of this house in one day, I got 100 percent on my contract. A lawyer threatened that if he didn't have all of his stuff out of the house and a check for me within twenty-four hours, he was going to expose him to the Beatles. And it was done. Peter [Brown] was the only sane one in the bunch. He signed a release from Apple without telling Klein so I could get the house.

SG: I wanted to ask about something you said earlier. You mentioned that Jane Asher's mother came to Paul's house to pick up her clothes.

RK: Yeah. Jane Asher's mother went over and, Jane told us later on, Francie Schwartz, or whatever her name was, had on her nightgown. Paul was so tacky when it came to breaking up with girls. He just seemed to have no idea how to do it. He was so awkward. When I was staying with him at the Beverly Hills Hotel, he had what I called the black-and-white minstrel show. He was having a three-day love-in. We were sharing a suite with this, a bungalow. He had a black girl and a white girl. Paul was just in there for three days and three nights with these girls. Then Linda arrived. Paul and Linda didn't know each other that well, but she arrived and Paul and the two girls were still with him. Linda stayed in the living room, and Paul got rid of the black and white girls. Linda kind of looked the other way. Paul got rid of the girls and then he took Linda in, so Linda got in there during the night. Meantime, the actress Peggy Lipton was camped out outside. She was already on *Mod Squad*. I was thinking this was so sad. Here's Peggy Lipton sleeping outside, like a groupie. He didn't know how to get rid of these folks. He just didn't know how to end it. They always thought that they were number one.

When we were in New York, by the way, I suggested that we walk back to the hotel from the MCA building. It was only two blocks. It was amazing, because one person would spot and followed behind him and one person became one hundred, and then one thousand. Just walking two blocks to the Waldorf Astoria, suddenly there was a whole crowd of people. We started to run, and Paul was going through a revolving door, and this girl just put her arm in there, put her arm in the revolving door. It got stuck. We had to push Paul back into the crowd in order to get the girl's arm out. It was very dodgy, very tricky. We had extra security people at the hotel, luckily. We had two security guys outside.

I realized that the Beatles just didn't have deep relationships. George would come here every night. He would come here for weeks and hang out here until 3:00 a.m. I couldn't figure it out. Peter [Brown] was taking out Pattie every night. He was here, and I couldn't figure out what the hell. He's got that wonderful wife and he's sitting over here playing old records. There was something, he had to do it if it was, like, it had to be some kind of adventure. Just the straight thing at home, he couldn't quite do it. That was the strange thing about him. That's why Yoko and Linda provided John and Paul with things that they both were missing. They missed some kind of soulful, deep feelings. Their feelings were very superficial.

Linda was always stoned out of her bird. We were flying to London.

It was just me and Paul and Linda. A TWA representative came in and said there was a bomb scare. The FBI was sending somebody over and they were going to have to search all your hand baggage. I looked at Paul, looked him straight in the eye and said, "Do you have anything in your hand baggage that's going to embarrass us?" He said no. So I believed him. I looked at her and I said, "Do you have anything that's going to be difficult?" She had a Gucci handbag that she said was full of marijuana. There was a couple kilos. At that time, I had a great temper. I demanded to see the head of public relations for TWA. I started complaining about how you don't want to search Paul McCartney, and the least you could do is to provide us with a private room so we don't have to be searched in front of all these other passengers. We were in the Ambassador Lounge. They had a little VIP room. So I kicked her bag underneath a chair. I looked at her and said, "Don't touch the bag. Just leave it." She looked at me with daggers, she wouldn't listen very well. I mean, she was just stoned.

I got them all up in the small room, and these two crew-cut FBI guys came in and it was very funny, because they knew it was Paul McCartney. Sure enough, you know they opened our handbags and looked in them. In the meantime, there was Linda's bag under the chair all by its little self. I looked at her and said, "If that bag's got your name on it, you better retrieve it. But I don't want you to touch it until the FBI have left. Just don't go near it." I had her terrified, but that was a large amount of marijuana. That would have been terrible publicity for Paul, Mr. Clean.

Isn't it strange, the chemistry between Paul and Linda and then John and Yoko? Strong women. You can't consider them attractive, by any means. It's another thing. It's completely different. Remember that attractiveness and beauty is something that they OD'd on. They both OD'd on it. They weren't looking for beauty. They were looking for something else. Some kind of fulfillment. You know, both of them were satisfied.

John Eastman

When Brian Epstein died, his brother, Clive, and his mother, Queenie, inherited most of Brian's estate, with Queenie taking the lion's share of 70 percent. NEMS, the Beatles management company, was cash rich, with over £1 million, in the bank. The coffers of NEMS included not only 25 percent of the Beatles' income, including their publishing company Northern Songs, but also a share of the returns of their nine-year recording contract with EMI. A major complication that arose when the Epsteins sold NEMS was death taxes that would be incurred by the Epstein family, gobbling up the million pounds, perhaps more. The Beatles retained Linda McCartney's brother, Ivy League–educated attorney John Eastman, twenty-eight, to represent them. Eastman, with some help from smart British financial advisors, found an ingenious way to buy NEMS with the least cost to the Epstein family. Then the scurrilous Allen Klein arrived on the scene, claiming he would get NEMS for the Beatles for free, and all bets were off.

STEVEN GAINES: Paul met Linda in 1967. Did you start to represent Paul when he became your brother-in-law, or before that?

JOHN EASTMAN: Before that, in November or December of 1968, I think. I was twenty-eight or twenty-nine. Over the years, my father represented a lot of the great bands, like Tommy Dorsey. My first big client in rock was Chicago and Jimmy Guercio, which was in a way as complicated as all the Beatles' stuff was, because the first thing I did was get all their masters back for them and relicensed them to Columbia.

SG: Did the other Beatles, in the very beginning, feel resentful since you were Paul's brother-in-law?

JE: I wasn't his brother-in-law then, but I was Linda's brother. I don't know what went on in their minds.

SG: That was a dilemma that you certainly had to fix, because you had vested interest in one of the people when you were supposed to be representing the interests of all four. Was there already a rift between Paul and the rest of the group when he became your client?

JE: No, our firm started representing *all* of them before Klein got involved. They retained our firm. We represented them for about two months before Klein. [The Epstein firm already represented Beatles & Co. when Klein was brought in as the Beatles' business manager.] The first thing we did was try to buy NEMS [the Beatles' management company] back from Brian Epstein's estate. It was my idea to buy NEMS. Brian had a deal with the Beatles where he got 25 percent of whatever they got, not only during the term of the [management contract with NEMS but from any contracts made during the term of the contract]. Brian was entitled to a quarter of their royalties. There was also a seven-year recording contract with EMI, a quarter of which was vested in NEMS. As well, Brian's estate had a million pounds in NEMS, the corporation, which they couldn't [cash in on] without declaring a dividend to pay estate taxes. So I met with Peter Brown and Clive Epstein and suggested that Brian would want the Beatles to have their rights back, if he weren't around.

So we just traded a million pounds of the Beatles' money for NEMS, which had a million pounds in it, just wash it out. They were getting NEMS for the cash in the bank. That's the deal we did. The Beatles didn't have the money in the bank, and they hadn't had a record out for quite a while either, so I went to Sir Joseph Lockwood and said I was representing the four of them and I asked him for an advance of a £1,250,000. He looked at me and said, "When do you want it?" I said, "Wednesday afternoon." He said, "Fine."

We spent about two weeks negotiating the basic deal with Clive Epstein, when we came down to a simple question of indemnity, which was when Klein came on the scene. I remember a Sunday meeting, around Christmas or New Year's, where Klein said that I was a fool, that it was absurd for them to spend a million dollars of their money to buy NEMS, which had a million dollars in it. It is so dumb, it was a joke. After Klein promised to get it for them for nothing, the other three said, "Let's let him do it." The other three wanted to get it for nothing. I knew it wasn't going to happen. But I tried to cooperate as best I could with Clive. So Klein kills the deal and Clive bolts and sells NEMS to Triumph Investments.

SG: Allen was known to be a crook. How could John, George, and Ringo throw in their lot with him? Could it have been that John was so angry with Paul he was willing to go along with Klein just to irk him?

JE: I think so. I think that John's idea was you need a thief to catch a thief. And Klein talked about how the Beatles had been ripped off.

SG: Who was the thief they were catching?

JE: EMI, Dick James, anyone who did business with them. I think Klein was John's barking dog, as they say.

SG: There was something else that angered the other Beatles very much, which was that Paul had, on his own, been buying Northern Songs stock.

JE: Klein is very good at taking small things like that and just blowing them up. It was just the way he was, the way he operated. Klein always lit fires under everybody. I think Paul had bought 7,500 shares of Northern Songs on the open market, just because he always believed in his own creativity. John and Paul each had a million five [1,500,000] shares. Paul had an extra 7,500 shares. I bought them for him. But the thing is that what's got distorted at the time—and this is where John Lennon was quoted a million times—he thought Paul was going around his back. This was done before the fight. The 7,500 shares were bought before *Revolver*.

SG: You were there at some of those meetings. Did they spit and scream at each other across the table in Peter Brown's office?

JE: I wasn't there. That's the one great meeting, the one that did it all. There was a meeting. I think it was in Lee Eastman's hotel suite, and Lee and Neil [Aspinall] and myself got into an argument with Klein. There were many things it could've been about. But Klein was really baiting us, because he was trying to avoid a proper discussion. That's the way he'd do it. He'd kind of make it crazy. Lee got so infuriated, he shouted. He really lost his temper, and it was bad that he did that, because Lee is discerned as this master of dignity. But Lee was so aggravated by this terrible man that he just walked out. "Fuck this." I mean Lee wasn't really that keen to be involved. He was quite happy with his life.

SG: Did Klein conspire to keep Paul's first album from being released?

JE: He actually stopped it. I know he stopped it, because I brought the masters back [to America] myself in a laundry bag, took them to Sterling Sound, and had them mastered. Paul knew there was just nobody else to do it. I then delivered them to Capitol. Capitol gave them to Klein.

SG: Why would Capitol put the masters into the hands of the enemy?

JE: Because their deal was with Apple [not Paul].

SG: Why did you wind up taking them back to the United States in a laundry bag? Why didn't Paul bring them to his record company?

JE: Because Apple wasn't going to let it out. I was going to give it directly to Capitol and force them to put it out, which I finally did. I remember calling Sal Iannucci, who was president of Capitol, and I said, "I'm just telling you now, if it doesn't come out on Capitol on that date, it's coming out on CBS." And I meant it. I really did. I just couldn't believe that here's one of the greatest stars of all time, one of the great creators of all time, who did his first album all by himself at home, and it's a really lovely album. And not to let it out just blew my mind.

We didn't sue to dissolve the partnership until nine months after the incident with Paul's album happened. They got served New Year's Eve 1970. I wanted to make sure we had our case well put together. It was a case where I just knew we were going to win from the minute we started.

SG: What reason did the others give for not wanting to dissolve the partnership?

JE: They said they were entitled under the partnership agreement to benefits of Paul's individual efforts.

SG: They expected to get income from Paul's individual efforts? Because it was obvious that the Beatles were over, and they weren't going to perform or record together as a group anymore.

JE: The reason Paul held off at the beginning was because that he didn't want to sue the other three. And I don't blame him. I spent some time trying to figure out a way to sue Klein rather than [the other three Beatles.] But since the purpose was to dissolve the partnership, then we had to name the other partners, which is something nobody wanted to do. Klein was mucking about. [Eventually] the others and Klein fell out. We were still litigating. We had not settled with the others when they fell out with Klein. They just couldn't stand him anymore.

When Klein sued the Beatles, we sued Klein. He wanted commissions from them. We sued Klein in England, and then shortly he sued them in New York. Paul was only tangentially named. There were forty-two causes of action, and there was a conspiracy claimed at the end, which was the forty-second, in which they named Paul as a coconspirator with the others to breach the Klein contract. The claim against Paul was dismissed. But since we had a claim against the others, the question was who owed whom what money, whether they owed Klein money or Klein owed them money. It was [Allen Klein's company] ABKCO against all of them.

SG: Was the settlement also Paul getting his own recordings out of it? The Beatles' records stayed at ABKCO, so I assume Paul was still part of that.

JE: Still is. He still owns a quarter of the company. I mean all the Beatles royalties still flow 80 percent to Apple and 5 percent to each of the individuals. And the company still does incredibly well. It was simple stuff I was doing, like the NEMS deal. It worked out that they bought the 25 percent of NEMS back from Triumph. And they paid a fortune for it, and Triumph kept 5 percent.

SG: And they also wound up as shareholders in Triumph, which was a substantial amount of money tied up in their stock.

JE: That's right, which was so stupid. Triumph went bankrupt. What Klein was going to get for them for nothing, which in fact I *really* was getting them for nothing, because I was trading a million dollars in their cash for a million dollars in NEMS's cash. NEMS had in cash, in the corporation, £1 million. They couldn't get it out of the corporation to pay Brian's estate tax without declaring the dividend. Dividends in those days were taxed at a rate of 98 percent, so they had an estate tax that was tremendous.

SG: What I can't understand is why it was so difficult to prove to Justice Stamp what an awful person Klein was.

JE: Well, I'll tell you what. If it hadn't been for Klein's big affidavit, we could well have lost that. Two things happened, two things. Klein was on trial in New York, in the Southern District for ten counts of failure to pay withholding taxes. And he was convicted. I think they're misdemeanors, but he was convicted, ten counts on tax evasion. From employees to the government, which is a crime. I don't know if it's a major crime or not. But obviously we followed the trial pretty carefully, and one day when I got a call from my office that Klein had been convicted on ten counts. I had his certified record sent over to London. In court, our lawyer was telling the judge about taxes and the problems the Beatles faced because Klein had not paid them, and how Klein had no respect at all for England revenue. "I believe Mr. Klein has as much respect for our tax authorities as he does for the American tax authorities. Mr. Klein was just convicted five days ago, ten counts of tax whatever. And I would like to hand up to Your Honor a certified copy of the record of Mr. Klein's ten convictions." And he let the court recess for lunch, really. I think it was all over right then and there. The judge called Klein's testimony that of "a liar or the patter of a used car salesman."

SG: He made a big settlement, didn't he?

JE: But that all went to the company. That all went to ABKCO.

SG: How much was that, $3 million?

JE: I don't remember. I really don't. But everything was paid to ABKCO. You can check their taxes, and you'll see exactly.

SG: Were you in those screaming matches at the Plaza Hotel in New York? Was Yoko a positive force in the settlement? That's who the credit is sometimes given to.

JE: I must say, in all candor, I was dead opposed to the settlement. Because we were running an absolute winner, and we were going to trial. We had a trial date set in England, and we were very anxious to try the case in England. The Beatles decided—the other three decided to settle just before trial. I don't know why.

SG: They wanted Klein to be out of their hair and over with it.

JE: This three-year fight with Klein, and they were just about to go to trial. I mean we had the whole team I had put together for our case. And they decided to settle, and I must say, about that point, I said if they're going to settle their lawsuit, they should do it themselves. I mean we weren't going to oppose it.

SG: Right, but you had to pay part of that money.

JE: Well, Apple paid the money. That's right, but a quarter of that was Paul's, absolutely. I was so dead opposed to that settlement. I hate to say it, but it was not a settlement that should ever have been made.

Alistair Taylor on Allen Klein Having Him Fired

STEVEN GAINES: When Allen Klein arrived on the scene, did he walk into the building and yell, "Stop!"

ALISTAIR TAYLOR: No. I never met Klein. One of my proudest boasts is that I never met him. I'd been fired. I've only been fired once in my life by a guy [Klein] I've never even met. I thought it was beautiful. It's classic. I never had a doubt about it. I just, frankly, head down, carried on. What I was doing. Um, which was trying to run the offices.

I was at lunch when Peter Brown called me and said, "Can you get back to the office? It's an emergency." When I got to the office, Peter was on the phone, and he had a piece of paper in his hand. I heard him saying, "No. It's operative from today. No. It's a settlement." I saw this list, a long list of names. Ah, and I knew instantly. And I was first on the list.* There were about fifteen of us altogether, if I remember rightly. Which I mean, I found astonishing. But I think what bothered me, and still does now . . . I left. I went home, and I rang all the boys [John,

---

* Per his transcript, Allen Klein contends that one of the Beatles specifically asked that Taylor be fired, but refused to say which one.

Paul, George, and Ringo] in turn. I just wanted to make sure that they knew about it. But none of them would speak to me, and I know two of them, for sure, were there. They wouldn't come to the phone. I left it for about two years, and then I wrote to Paul, *"Look, the dust settled, I'm happy, and you know, we did have fun."* I've written about three times, I suppose. I suppose the easy answer is that they don't get mail. I sort of tried to make it clear to whoever opened it that this was not just a fan letter, but it was someone that had been close. Not a breath from them from that day to this, which is eleven years ago, which I think disappoints me, as human beings. I thought we were buddies. Obviously not. I just think it'd be a gas if he picked up the phone and said, "Hi, fella, how are you?" You know? "If ever you're around . . ." I mean, I would have thought, there's not the slightest fear that I'd become a pest, or a nuisance. So it saddens me.

They affected my philosophy of living, to a tremendous degree. There was so much that I thought was right, and I believe now that I'm carrying it on much better than they are. You know, and I'm just sad for them, that they could treat, someone like myself, when I could truthfully say that I never conned them for anything, except at the very end, which, was quite cold-blooded. Revenge. I had a loan out from the company, and I said "Stuff it, they can whistle for it."

[In 1973, Taylor and his wife moved to Darley Dale in Derbyshire, where they operated a tearoom. Over the years, Taylor published several books about his adventures with the Beatles, becoming known as their "Mr. Fixit." He died in June 2004 in Derbyshire.]

Allen Klein

The following interview took place in Allen Klein's office in New York in late 1980.

STEVEN GAINES: What was your first impression of Brian? Was he a brilliant impresario, or was he lucky?

ALLEN KLEIN: He was not lucky. He had taste and he had a dignity. In reflection, I didn't think he was a very good businessman. I don't think that was his primary concern. I can reflect on what John told me—Brian certainly did make a major contribution. [Back then] because the business was so new, the English record companies treated artists [badly]. That's why in judging Brian Epstein in a business that was so totally new isn't fair. No one understood the business. It wasn't there before. So it was really easy for me.

Management is a pretty personal thing. I only bothered with artists who wrote their own material, who were self-contained. In my life, I really managed only five or six people. Bobby Vinton, it was management. With Donovan, it was management. With the Rolling Stones, it was management. With John Lennon, Ringo, and George, it was management. With Sam Cooke, it was management. He was the first one.

SG: Isn't that how you met Brian Epstein? Brian wanted to book Sam Cooke as an opening act on one of the Beatles' tours?

AK: Sam Cooke ignited me to an idea. He said to me, "Look, they're taking our music, my music, and they're giving it back through white kids." They took black music, that little white girls couldn't identify with, and they came at us through cutesy little white boys. In America, a white person imitating a black person was like blackface and almost insulting. But English singers did it with respect. That's where the roots were coming from.

SG: You were a big thorn in Brian's side, because everyone knew you were aiming to manage the Beatles. The boys used to tease Brian when things would go wrong.

AK: Brian died in August of 1967, and the Beatles were loose and needed management. I don't mean to sound ghoulish, but when I heard on the radio going over one of the bridges, "I got them!" I just knew. I just knew there was really no one else around at the time.

SG: You were still managing the Stones at the time.

AK: Oh sure. I brought the Stones up to Apple. The Stones deal was ending with London Records. We were even talking about bringing the Stones to Apple Records.

SG: I thought by '67, you had fallen out with Mick Jagger for some reason.

AK: Oh, no. Absolutely not.

SG: I understood that Mick was against you. That Mick had told John not to go with you.

AK: Absolutely not. In fact, it was the other way around.

SG: How do you mean?

AK: I think it was either Mick or Keith who told him to go.

SG: How did you finally get to the Beatles? There were barricades getting to meet them and speak to them. One was Derek Taylor. I think Peter Brown at one time was a barrier in getting to meet the boys.

AK: I can tell you what I did. I took the time to analyze the situation somewhat Machiavellian and determined the best way for me to meet John. I almost had a meeting and then it got canceled and then another one got made. And then I spoke to you, Peter.* That was the only time. I never called you and said, please, I want to make an appointment. You were just confirming or canceling or reconfirming an appointment. But the appointment that I made was based upon a telephone call that I made to John, followed up by a desire on both John and Yoko's part to protect themselves. Because I think they felt that they were going to lose control if the E . . . See, you're not aware, the Eastmans were already there, signed. And I think he went there to protect himself, just him and Yoko. And I was not aware that someone lived near Derek. And I don't know if it was . . .

SG: You met with John in the Dorchester hotel.

AK: I never thought Derek Taylor was keeping me away or that anyone was keeping me away, because I wouldn't make an overt act. Other than the phone call I made, I would never, I wasn't calling people and

---

* The reader is directed to the interview of Derek Taylor, who presents an alternative narrative of events that led to Klein meeting with John.

saying, listen, I'd like to see [John]. I was doing it more surreptitiously from the outside. I didn't want them to feel pressure, because I felt that they would respond to pressure by running away.

SG: Then, what happened? You finally got to meet with John and Yoko, and there was an all-night session at the Dorchester hotel. And something happened in that all-night session at the Dorchester that totally won their allegiance to you.

AK: This is January '69. Yes, I mean, I've read what John has said. I mean, he said it in *Rolling Stone*. He just felt that he and Yoko both just knew . . . I think they wanted someone who was on their side for them. It was never for the Beatles. John said, listen, the Beatles are represented by the Eastmans, will you represent me and Yoko?

SG: The Beatles' legal affairs were represented by the Eastmans?*

AK: You see, you have to read that piece of paper.

SG: The piece of paper the Eastmans had with the boys?

AK: Oh yes. All signed.

SG: All of them signed it?

AK: Yes. And Apple. It never used the word *management*, but it didn't have to. If you represent all the negotiations throughout the world of Apple and the Beatles, you have it. The import of that particular piece of document was that everything would have to flow through them. The word *management* is such a word that it offends people and it's hard to define. It happened that night [at the Dorchester]. Right? I can

---

* Please see John Eastman's comments on the contract he had with the Beatles.

tell you that evening we just talked. Remember I still represented the Stones, and all he wanted me was for him and Yoko.

SG: You stayed up all night talking?

AK: Yeah. I went to the extent of having vegetarian food made for him, unbeknownst to them, they would have eaten anything. I remember we talked about ourselves. We were just trying to get to know one another. They were very nervous. I was nervous. How do you really get into it then? We just did. Lennon and Yoko, I would rather not say what won them over for me. I would think that a principal thing was the fact that they really wanted someone for themselves. Apart from the Beatles. That's really what it was. John is a very practical human being and the conflict was there, and it was his band and he was losing control, and he didn't want to. He wanted to be protected. It was as simple as that. That first evening that I met with John, he said, "Do you want to represent us?" I said yeah. And they said, "Don't you want anything in writing?" I said sure. And so Yoko sat on the floor with the typewriter and she typed out to the key people, very folksy, nice letters like, "Dear Sir Joe, I've asked Allen to look after me. Would you please give him anything he wants. Thank you."

SG: The letter to Sir Joe says, "As far as I'm concerned, Allen Klein handles all my stuff." That's folksy.

AK: Yeah, well. She wrote it to more than one person. John probably wrote to Clive. He wrote to Harry Pinsker. He wrote to Dick James. We just wanted to make sure. And he wanted it right away, he couldn't wait. The whole thing was like, "What is he going to tell Paul?"

I met with John on Monday night, I met with the rest of them Tuesday. I went over to Apple and I met the other three. The question of the NEMS deal certainly was brought up. That's why I want to tell you about this, because John Eastman had been negotiating to purchase

NEMS and everyone was under the impression that the deal was done. Paul was telling [everyone] how good the deal was. And I said, listen, it's silly. Why don't we get all the liars in the same room? And then we'll find out. And so he brought John Eastman over for a meeting.

SG: Paul was present at the meeting?

AK: Yes.

SG: And how did you get along with Paul?

AK: It wasn't a getting along. Paul was very charming.

SG: He can be, or he can be distant.

AK: Remember, I had never met any others. I was just going to find out where John stood and what's the point in going ahead with this NEMS deal. John says, okay, well, tell me if I should do it. And I said, how can I tell [if it's a good deal]? I don't know where anything is. John said, call Harry Pinsker [the accountant] who happened to represent Northern Songs and the Beatles and NEMS. I said, I'd call him and we'll find out where everything is. In the meantime, I spoke with Clive and asked him if he would please wait [before he closed the deal to sell NEMS], just let us get our stuff together. Then George and Ringo said, "If you're going to find that information for John, do it for me." I met with Pinsker and I went through all of the files. I took everything that I felt would give me the picture. I had to start all the way back. I remember Neil [Aspinall] was in the hospital. He must have had apoplexy.

[Klein addresses Peter Brown] I have to be fair. I didn't think that you were on my side. I certainly didn't.

PETER BROWN: Well, I was in horror that somebody should come in and take my files.

SG: Imagine those people who came from Liverpool and were with them since 1959 and had been along on the whole trip, how they suddenly felt about having a very strong personality come in—

AK: Well, I remember what I did. In speaking with Pinsker, I found out that the NEMS deal is off, that it was turned down.* That NEMS had turned down the Eastmans' proposal. It was off. There was no [deal].

SG: [Didn't you tell them] "I'll get it for you for nothing?" That's been widely quoted, you said I'll get you NEMS for nothing.

AK: If you just read the court record, and all the sworn documents in there, you'll see that not only did they get it for nothing, they made money on it. When we settled with NEMS, you will find that it cost them zip.

SG: Why was the deal off?

AK: You'll have to ask Clive Epstein.

SG: I did. Clive said that he was afraid of you—

AK: Ah, okay.

SG: That he was afraid of you because he knew that you were litigious, and you were a strong person, and that he ran in the other direction. And very quietly, this not might not have been fair to the boys at all, to whom he had a definite responsibility, very quietly sold the company to Triumph.

AK: Yes. I know what he sold for. That's funny. I can show you the quote that he gave.

---

* Disputed in interviews with Dick James and Clive Epstein.

SG: Well, I'm telling you this only so you can—

AK: No, I understand. He blamed it on a letter from John Eastman.

SG: Questioning the proprieties of the contract.

AK: He blamed that. It was a dumb letter to write. That was a John Eastman letter. Not an Allen Klein.

SG: Dick James was also frightened of you. Because I think Eastman had done this deal, and then you said, "This is a stupid deal." And I think John could see that because you explained to him, I remember this clearly, you said, "You're buying a million pre-tax money, and what are you going to pay? What's the point?"

AK: All of them saw it. Everyone was at the table, including Paul McCartney. And they all agreed that I would be the one to look into the affairs of Apple. And I said, "Let John Eastman be the lawyer." And John Eastman said, "I'm not just a lawyer." Paul convinced him. And then Paul called me that evening, it was Saturday, and said congratulations, and then we got on with it.

SG: Then why did Eastman send that stinging letter to Clive at that delicate point in negotiations?

AK: Stupidity. Bad timing. Poor timing. Inexperience. I mean that letter certainly was a gauntlet. He was throwing it down. And I had met with Clive, and said, "Please, would you please give me three weeks?" That's all I asked for.

SG: Did he agree to wait three weeks?

AK: Yes, he really did.

SG: So why did he sign with Leonard Richenberg at Triumph? Richenberg offered them a very good kind of a tax deal.

AK: He offered them funny paper, in the words of Paul McCartney. "You never give me your money. You only give me your funny paper." Richenberg offered them a paper deal. Okay. I didn't know how good Triumph was at the time, but I sure as hell wasn't interested in John exchanging what he had for that paper. And in addition, it would've been selling out, and they would've been working for someone else. And that's not what they envisioned. And so began the battle.

SG: EMI froze the Beatles' royalties. You warned them not to be paid to Triumph.

AK: Since 75 percent of the money belonged to the Beatles, I said, "Would you just pay us ours until we can work out how much is what?" Richenberg then sued because he had a deed to receive all of the money. That's how it started.

SG: The Beatles and Klein asked EMI to pay them directly.

AK: I never asked for the money to be paid to me. I mean, that would've been against everything I ever stood for. I never asked for an artist's money to be paid to me. They froze everything. They figured they would freeze the Beatles out.

SG: Your name was brought up in court during this whole thing.

AK: The London *Sunday Times* wrote a scathing article.

SG: That's right. "Under the influence of Mr. Allen Klein, who has a somewhat dubious record," they said. "The Beatles might be influenced to part with their money to Mr. Klein." And the judge says it was ridiculous to think that anybody's going to have that kind of an influence on them. Richenberg said that you had made "various and vague threatening noises." Do you remember?

AK: I just went in and laid down on the table what I really felt the facts were. It's not that they related in some ways to the business or to the contractual agreements entered into between the Beatles and NEMS. And we were very careful. And that's why you don't see it anyplace. You never saw it ever, because it related to Brian, and I ain't going to talk about it.

SG: I don't understand. What are you talking about? The record contract continuing beyond the management agreement for several years?

AK: No, there were other things.

SG: There was seven years left on—

AK: No, but there were other things.

SG: Like what?

AK: I just don't want to go into it. I really don't.

SG: But in what area?

AK: I just really rather not. I mean it. Because it has to do with Brian, and what he did or what he was advised to do during the time. And I just don't want to go into it.

SG: What you're saying is there's certain things which would've been very embarrassing to Brian's name and his family if you'd have continued with it.

AK: We did file it. I want you to know. But we kept it under seal, and no one ever saw it. And I never used it in the press to defend myself or to defend the action that the Beatles took. We took all of this shit. I always figured that I could take it. Let them throw it at me. But it was something we just really didn't want to do. Let me tell you something. Let me give it to you simply. Clive Epstein sold his 90 percent interest in NEMS for how much?

SG: I heard something like a million again, somewhere around that figure.

AK: Million pounds. Okay. How much do you think the Beatles got for 10 percent? Because they own the other 10. £400,000.

SG: Well, why did he do that?

AK: Because he liked me and I wore a clean shirt the next time.

SG: Queenie got a different price.

AK: The total price for the 70 and the 20 is £900,000. We got £400,000. And if you remember, we paid commission. Because we were paying ordinary income. That £400,000, they got tax-free. Oh, and they got it in cash. It worked out to more than £400 because the stock went up a little. But we got the cash. £400,000 after tax is worth how much?* In 1969, £4 million. And we got all the rights back.

SG: Why did Richenberg have the Bishop's Report done on you and instigate the article in the London *Times*?

AK: Because he was trying to dislodge me.

---

* Approximately $650,000, the equivalent to over $5 million in today's purchasing power.

SG: That sounds like personal vendetta, though. That's more than—

AK: Yeah. I was about to take away . . . Listen, everyone falls in love with the Beatles, whether it's the judges. I mean, they get Beatlemania. I mean, it's sad, but it's true. The staidest, the most respected. They all get affected. Lawyers become advocates instead of—

SG: You're saying because he had an emotional investment in the Beatles, and you were the adversary, so he did this—

AK: Wait a moment. He was going to wind up having paid a million pounds for zippo. And I tried to make it nice. I didn't attack the man after the thing was settled. Everybody was nice. He needed the 5 percent. I took it out of mine. If you really think about it, I mean, I once did a chart, when we finally settled to show what they would've gotten under the Eastman's agreements and what they got under mine, after paying Richenberg's 5 percent. We had him. It was nothing that Brian did deliberately. And when I say to you that even you were not aware, and the complaint was signed by John, and I think George and I think Ringo. I'm not sure if McCartney signed it, but it's very possible because he was in on all the meetings. I want you to know that.

SG: Paul went to all the meetings? Did he always have one of the Eastmans at his side?

AK: John Eastman was there. John Eastman was the lawyer for the company. But we brought in English counsel. It was an English accent. And I just felt that it was not important for them to go to court. And if you really think about it, I mean just think: £400,000 for 10 percent, £900,000 for 90 percent. I mean, that's why when we paid him the million pounds, I was giving him income for capital. I didn't care. We worked it out. Even the judge. Go to Judge Stamp's opinion. All right?

ALLEN KLEIN | 277

When he talks about the NEMS deal, he said it was brilliantly executed. I mean, it's the only thing I got out of the man.

PB: Well, how come they wouldn't pay capital gains on the £400,000?

AK: They didn't have to because the stock which was purchased, I mean, remember they got the stock back. Remember the capital gain law changed. First of all, they held it for a year. I remember. We did that. The capital gain law, if I'm not mistaken, changed in 1964. If you had stock which you had in '64, the value that it had in '64, you only had to pay tax on the difference. And there really wasn't any difference in the value in '64 to date, and that's really how it happened.

PB: So then we come to the next step, is the Northern Songs.

AK: Which happened at the same time.

SG: It happened almost at the same time.

AK: Oh, I mean I was getting killed.

PB: Also let me tell you something, only because it's an interesting part of the book, is while all this was going on, and Allen was getting my files, and Neil was in hospital, we were filming *Let It Be* in the building and on the roof.

AK: Yes, I remember.

SG: During the movie *Let It Be*, they seem incredibly hostile to each other in that movie. What was it like around them? I mean, the four boys. Were the four Beatles really at each other's throats at that time?

AK: I don't think they knew how to be at each other's throats. They might have felt whatever they felt, but they never really emoted it. Really, really, really.

SG: There was no screaming at any of those meetings?

AK: Screaming at the meetings, later. Was there ever screaming? The only screaming I ever know, screaming, Linda Eastman screamed once at a recording studio. For me to shut up. While they were working, because Yoko was in there in the bed. And you have to understand what was going on. John wanted to leave. John wanted it over. Paul McCartney never left the Beatles. He didn't end it. John did.

SG: By the way, just let me ask you then, what was your reaction when you saw the inside column in the London *Times*?

AK: Well, it was really my fault. First of all, it's strange, I became very friendly and later hired, in fact, a year ago, hired the—

SG: The man that wrote the article?

AK: Yeah. John Fielding and I became very good friends. I refused to talk to him. I didn't want to talk to anybody. I really didn't.

SG: Did you sue them, the inside column?

AK: Yes, I did.

SG: The Bishop's file is missing from their files.*

---

* A investigative account report compiled by detectives and forensic accountants, including lawsuits and criminal records.

AK: I have it. Guess what I did? I have it. I have a Bishop. No, but let me tell you. There's one on Proudfoot. Proudfoot is a company similar to Bishop's. And I want you to look at it too. See, I never knew what a Bishop's was in my life. If you would like something, they've changed the laws here a little, but if you want something nasty written about someone, you can get it done. You can have a credit investigative report done. And Richenberg got one. I went out, and a friend of mine had one done in a positive way just to see. I laugh. It's funny. But a lot of it happened to be true. I did have hundreds of lawsuits. And I was broke. I got sued for $32.50. I mean, all of the lawsuits he's talking about is when in 1950s and '60s, I was broke. I had nothing. Do you ever get sued for your typewriter? I paid every nickel. So you can take a bit of truth and just write it the way you want.

SG: It was at that point that [music publisher] Dick James really bolted, because that was April 2, I think.

AK: Dick James was scared to death of me. Dick James knew exactly what I was after. Dick James knew exactly what was going to happen. There was no way that Lennon or McCartney should have remained with their interest in NEMS. Remember Paul . . . part of the NEMS deal— Oh, I have to tell you.

[Here Klein takes off with a torrent of numbers.]

With the £400,000, we got their stock at thirty shillings. It was thirty shillings. And remember the tender for Triumph stock was at forty. So, in effect, we got another—they had 5 percent at the time. They didn't have 105. They had 10 percent of 5 percent. No, remember there was thirty between John and Paul. And Brian got half of ten because they gave somebody . . . We got another 5 percent. But part of that whole NEMS deal in addition, in a separate transaction, which wouldn't attract any tax, we got an option to purchase the stock at thirty. That was part of it. We were really busy as hell at the time. Yoko, I mean, it was really a very, very, very busy time. And then I had to go and negotiate the deal with EMI.

SG: In the meantime, the Apple three-ring circus was happening on Savile Row.

AK: There was no three-ringing circus. Maybe before I came there. Okay. That might have happened. I can tell you that when I came, I didn't find it a circus. I was able to find whatever I needed. The A&R staff was run very, very well. If I did a disservice to anyone, it was Peter Asher.

SG: Did you fire Peter Brown?

AK: No. I never fired Brown. Okay. But I did Peter a disservice in that I didn't give him the attention and allow him to go forward because I had clients who really were divided as to which direction they wanted that company to go.

SG: But when you arrived at Apple, didn't you find waste in spending and freeloaders?

AK: Magic Alex was stopped. It was a question of not allowing him to continue, which we did. But we went ahead with the recording studio [at 3 Savile Row] and got it completed.

SG: He says he got back from vacation and his inventions had been sold for junk.

AK: I never sold any inventions of Alex Mardas. Did I stop that from going forward? Yes. There were some people who were working there, you get a certain redundance.

SG: Alistair Taylor was fired. He had come from Liverpool.

AK: That was a request. I had never met Alistair Taylor in my life. And if I fell over him now, I wouldn't remember him. There were certain requests that were made to let certain people go.

SG: Specific requests from the Beatles? You mean one of the Beatles asked for Alistair to be let go?

AK: Yes. In truth, yeah. I don't know who.

PB: There were two main changes that happened—Ron Kass and Peter Asher left. And the press department was radically axed, which I thought was an extremely good thing. I mean the excess.

SG: Wasn't there a "Bloody Tuesday" where you had to fire five people?

AK: In my life, I never fired one person in my office. I don't think I ever fired anyone. In fact, I don't think I really fired Ron Kass. I just made it difficult for him to stay.

PB: No, no, you didn't. He was fired. He was on that list.

AK: Didn't I say he could stay for £5,000 a year.

PB: Well, considering he was getting £75,000. I walked him around the block, and I said, "Listen." Alistair was at lunch, and I called him. And we found out where he was lunching, and I summoned him back from his lunch. I offered to do it. It's not a job that I wanted to do, but I felt it was better coming from me because I could explain that things had changed. There was a new regime and this is how it is.

SG: Peter, did you think you were going to be next?

AK: Did you? Did you?

PB: I didn't know.

AK: You would've never been let go ever.

PB: I didn't know that.

AK: You never understood it?

PB: I wish I had.

AK: I had always hoped that you would feel that you would be on my side, but I always had this understanding that you were loyal to Brian. That's not bad loyalty. That's good. I don't mean that you would be disloyal to me, but you just couldn't be wholehearted.

PB: Obviously I felt loyal to Brian, but I felt there were a lot of things . . . You didn't tell me everything you were going to do. You didn't tell anyone.

AK: No, but during that period of time, you were being paid by NEMS.

PB: No, I was never paid by NEMS. I hadn't been paid by NEMS since the beginning of '68, when I resigned as director of NEMS. I was being paid by Beatles & Co.

AK: Ah, Beatles & Co. Right, right. Right. I remember that. I remember the Beatles & Co. thing. It doesn't have any significance to you, but it does to me because I think they allowed that as a deduction from the commission. That was their contribution to their continuing.

PB: Beatles & Co. had nothing to do with NEMS.

AK: Oh, NEMS took their money from Beatles & Co. They couldn't take it from Apple. They always had a commission. It's unimportant.

PB: But I had nothing to do with NEMS at the time.

AK: No. What could I tell you?

SG: So Dick James gets scared and bolts.

AK: No, I tell you. The only reason I remember is I had to put it in an affidavit, and I had pretty good records and they were pretty comprehensive. I remember it. Ringo did at the same time [an affidavit]. We all had to do it. Part of the discussion, was Triumph over at the time? Getting there. Yeah. We were going to have the stock. And then all of a sudden, out of nowhere, I got a call from Neil Aspinall saying that Dick James had sold his stock. And I got a call from John and Paul, because John was with Paul. I think we went to Ansbacher [Henry Ansbacher & Co., a merchant banker], and we were going to make a counterbid. I just felt that having 30 at no cost really, plus NEMS's 5, which was 35. We really weren't far away. And we put in a counterbid for like £1,100,00. I mean, it was easy. There was like £4 million in the bank. It was a great deal. I know what happened ultimately.

SG: Which was what? What did happen?

AK: It really didn't matter. I just wanted the Beatles either to . . . The whole key here was that for the first time, the realization became clear. We were crystallizing everything. Ringo and George had nothing. And no one really thought in terms of publishing because everyone thought everyone was splitting everything. Even Neil told me, he thought everyone was going to split everything. But when it really finally came down to it, and Paul had someone representing him, it became clear that Ringo had twenty thousand shares that he bought that he held on to. And that was it. George didn't have anything. And they really didn't own anything. And so the idea was that John put himself on the line. Otherwise, we would've sold out to Lew Grade. We would've made a deal. Get out. Get my money and get out. Get them capital gain cash. We didn't like the price. We didn't like the paper. We wanted a fixed amount. And John was willing to go on the line to try to get control of Northern Songs. Throw Apple into Northern. And then in effect, redistribute and get the four of them equal so that Ringo and George were taken care of. He really felt that he had that responsibility to them. McCartney disagreed. He felt that he would look after himself first. And I think that you'll find—

SG: He withheld his stock.

AK: That didn't matter. I put up stock to replace his. I put up the collateral necessary to replace his. That was not the problem. The problem really was that he was involved with a group of—

SG: There was a coalition of Northern Song stock owners, is that what you're—?

AK: John Lennon was, as far as I'm concerned, one of the most astute businessmen I'd ever met. He could handle anybody from a banker—

SG: But didn't he call them "the men in suits with the fat asses"? It was quoted in the newspaper. Little piggies.

AK: Never to their face. I'll tell you what happened. Once we had Ansbacher on the hook, and they were going to make the offer, Ansbacher said, "Well, I think we ought to go on TV." And Lennon said, "I'll tell you what color Pan-Cake makeup to wear, but I'm not going to go." And Ansbacher really wanted to become the "Beatles banker." And it became "infected again." It was silly. They just couldn't do a job and get it over with. There was no risk in that deal. All I wanted to do was one thing. Wind up with forty shillings in cash. We made an offer. In fact, we offered forty-two, I think. We offered the consortium exactly what we would be willing to take. I wanted Lennon either to have his money or not have his money. And McCartney was involved in it at the time.

SG: Why did they finally go with Northern?

AK: English pride. English pride.

PB: How do you mean "English pride"?

AK: English pride. Why? They went with the bankers. Oh, I know why. ATV said that they were going to dump every one of their shares. ATV. I'll tell you what, if you need it for backup, I have a letter from Jack Gill which says, "If you want it, you got it." After they got it. After they got the consortium shares, they said, "Allen, you want it? You can buy it at our cost."

SG: Why didn't you?

AK: Because Lennon and McCartney, there was a split already. What are you going to do? Try to get in bed with somebody who doesn't want to be in bed with you. And all we wanted was what we had lined up, which was if they offered somebody else forty, they had to give it to us too.

SG: But nobody else knew that the split was that bad and that they weren't going to write songs anymore.

AK: I did.

SG: Everybody knows that the Beatles lost Northern Songs and all the rest of it.

AK: I'm sorry. They didn't lose Northern Songs. They chose not to take it.

SG: Now, after this, after those two incidents were over, then according to legend . . . you get Phil Spector to put strings on "Long and Winding Road"—

AK: I didn't get to put anything on anything. All right? "Instant Karma!"—that's the first time that Phil Spector ever recorded with any of the Beatles. He recorded "Instant Karma!" with John Lennon in one day. First time. No preparation. No nothing. Just all of a sudden. I brought him along. Phil Spector wanted to be involved with the Beatles. You have to understand. You're still in '69. You're skipping. The Northern Songs thing ended in November. You have to understand that there was a negotiation all during this time with EMI. And EMI had, in 1969, seven or eight more years to go in their agreement. And I renegotiated that agreement, and a separate agreement whereby all of the recordings of the Beatles, the masters, were passed into a company in America that the Beatles owned for the United States, Canada, and Mexico, and the Philippines, I think. I don't know why. We worked it out so that, in effect, the Beatles owned the records in America. And they would sell them to Capitol at a price, which certainly gave them more money on every record, including the first record that they ever made.

SG: In order to do this, though, did you have to guarantee more product?

AK: No. Let me tell you what happened. That's a loaded question. It was based upon the deliverance of product. Okay? Yes. But I was aware that . . . Let me see. We're in 1969. That we had *Abbey Road*, *Let It Be*, and the "hits" album. I had the first year covered. The increase in royalty would only be reduced by one-third if you didn't deliver one album, two-thirds if you didn't deliver three, and stay the same. All right? But they also had the right to offer individual albums.

And if Capitol said, "We do not accept that as a Beatles album," then it would've gone through the Apple California at three times the rate.

SG: Apple California?

AK: Yeah. That was a separate company. That was what we would call the non-Beatle records. All right? That was another record company that the Beatles owned, which put out, if you would, "Instant Karma!" which put out "Cold Turkey," which put out *Live Peace in Toronto*, put out the Concert for Bangladesh, which put out James Taylor, Mary Hopkin, all of that stuff. The profit made on each sale is two times, double the highest Beatle royalty rate that we have. So that they were damned if they did or damned if they didn't. Now they—

PB: But the California Apple company was set up by Ron Kass.

AK: Yeah. And we renegotiated that deal. And in making the arrangement, tell me if you don't understand, what we really did was we said, "Look, take all the old masters and put them into this new company, and we'll arrive at a price. And that price is, say for argument's sake, seventy cents net. All right, you'll pay us every month, not every three months. We'll sell you the finished records. We'll give you the album covers. We'll sell you the finished records, and you'll buy it back and you pay us every month. We'll get the public. We'll get everything every month. We don't have to wait every three months or every six months. We'll determine when they're released, what's released, the sequence. You can't repackage. You can't do anything. No clubs, zero. Now, that's for all the past. Now you can have all future Beatle records for just as long as the old contract went. Now, Beatles records are defined as all four. Now, if one of them puts out a record and you want it, then you have to take it in satisfaction of a Beatle record. All right?"

Knowing that each one was going to do at least one album a year. I had no problem. Now Capitol made a mistake. The first single that came out was "Instant Karma!" So instead of getting fourteen cents a single, which is, I think what I renegotiated the Beatle thing up there, I think we got twenty-five because they took it as a non-Beatle. And they said, "Oh, well, that one . . ." Then "Give Peace a Chance." Now "Give Peace of Chance" is the first non-Beatle record. All right. "Instant Karma!" was the first John Lennon, and they still took it as a non-Beatle. "Cold Turkey," they still weren't on. Then we put out *Live Peace in Toronto*. It was an album, first album. One-half Lennon with Clapton, and God knows who else, and the other half was Yoko. Album did 750,000 in America. Now you're talking about the difference between seventy cents or $1.70. They didn't want to take it as a Beatle record. They got stuck. Then all of a sudden, they started taking everything.

SG: When did the legal dispute occur with them?

AK: Oh, Andrew's [Andrew Loog Oldham, the Rolling Stones former manager] suit. Andrew wanted out in 1968, '67. Andrew wanted out. He wanted me to buy him out off the bat. They weren't getting along. And Andrew came and said, please buy me out.

SG: It didn't have to do with money? Didn't the Stones feel you cheated them out of money?

AK: No, listen. The Rolling Stones were paid all of their money directly from London and Decca. I never got their money. But when I say that they were to be paid directly, the Stones arranged for me to receive their payments. I then loaned them the money so that they had to pay only their minimal guarantees each year. The case finally found in their favor in that in effect, they were loans. And they only had to pick up the income as the guarantees came due and that the big bulk payment, which they ultimately got after they sued me, which was they owed me $152,000.

Allen Klein was convicted of the misdemeanor charge of making a false statement on his 1972 tax return, for which he spent two months of 1980 in jail. Klein died on July 4, 2009, at the age of seventy-eight of Alzheimer's disease. Yoko and Sean went to his funeral.

Maureen Starkey

Maureen had big dark eyes outlined in kohl. She looked waiflike, but she was tough and tenacious. Mo started dating Ritchie in Liverpool when she was was a manicurist in training at Ashley Dupre's hair salon near the Cotton Exchange. When she first saw Ringo onstage at the Cavern Club behind his drum kit, he was engaged to a girl named Elsie Greaves. Ringo had given Elsie a ring, but on the eve of their engagement party, she asked him to quit the band and settle down with a real job and raise a family. On the way home on the bus, Ringo decided he would rather be in the Beatles than married. (You can read Ringo's account of the end to this relationship in his transcript.) When the Beatles moved to London, just as Maureen feared, beautiful women were lining up at his door. This threat was ended when Mo became pregnant and Ringo did the right thing for a northern man and married her. (You can read Cynthia Lennon and Pattie Boyd's observations of Ringo and Maureen in their transcripts.) Ringo and Maureen settled into a contented, relatively normal married life. Famously, she always had a roast and potatoes waiting for him in the oven whenever he got home, no matter what time. She was perhaps the happiest of all the Beatle wives, as opposed to Pattie Harrison, who described the Beatle wives being no more than "luggage."

One year, Ringo wanted to get something special for Maureen's birthday. Maureen was enamored of Frank Sinatra, so Peter Brown called Sina-

tra's management and asked if perhaps the singer could send a birthday note, that it would mean a lot to Ringo. Instead, Sinatra asked his friend, lyricist Sammy Cahn, to write new lyrics to the song "The Lady Is a Tramp." A tape arrived in time for Maureen's birthday, with Sinatra singing: "Peter Brown called me to tell me it's true, she sleeps with Ringo but she thinks of you . . ." The tape was transferred to a single disc, the only one that exists. It was quite the birthday gift.

Maureen ignored it when Ringo was unfaithful. She was a loyal spouse and dedicated mother. When they divorced, Ringo gave Maureen a generous £500,000 plus he bought her a house in London for £250,000. He also bought Tittenhurst Park, John's mansion outside Astor, and signed it over to their three children. In 1989, Maureen married Hard Rock Cafe owner Isaac Tigrett. She died on December 30, 1994, due to complications from leukemia after receiving bone marrow from her son, Zak, who was at her side when she passed, along with Ringo.

STEVEN GAINES: Where did you first meet Ringo?

MAUREEN STARKEY: The very first time I met Ritchie for real was outside the Cavern. He was sitting in his first car, a secondhand Ford Zodiac. You want the license plate of the car? NWM 466. I worked at the Ashley Dupre salon of Liverpool near the Cotton Exchange. I was walking home from night school because I was doing a hairdressing course. Rich [Ringo] was sitting in his car outside the Cavern. They were bigger than any other local band. Their first 45 had just come out, and he signed it for me, on both sides, and on the cover. I was fifteen or sixteen years old. I used to have Monday nights off from Ashley Dupre. The salon was down a few steps from the street, and on my first date, Ringo came there to pick me up. All I could see through the window of the door was his black boot and a black pants leg. And at that point in time, people didn't wear boots like that. So it was just like, "Oh, Jesus Christ." You know, it's actually going to happen, I'm dying. We went to the park and then to the pictures. Then we went to two clubs, the Pink Parrot and then the Blue Angel. We used to do everything in the one night. Used to hit everywhere in Liverpool. Once you got into that, it was sort of like a habit.

I hadn't really been out with people before. You know, I was that into the band that I asked for his autograph the first time I met him, but I also thought twice when he said, "Are you coming tomorrow?" 'Cause I really didn't know whether I could. I'd been educated in a convent. I'd just started going into town, only a little bit. When I was first dating him, I still had to be in at the latest ten, and then eleven fifty. He didn't get offstage until, half past eleven. Honest to God. And I [laughs] . . . This is insane, isn't it?

SG: And then you dated him for a while until he moved on to London with the group?

MS: I don't remember him actually going, actually moving. But I didn't come down to London at all then. And he still used to travel around. It was mainly Mondays that I used to go down. A flat on Green Street. With George and Paul. I came down a few times when Ritchie lived in Green Street. First New Year I spent away from my family was in Green Street.

SG: When did you come to London to live?

MS: When I got married, 1965. Caxton Hall in London.

SG: Who went to the wedding?

MS: Just our lot. John and Cynthia. George and Pattie. And parents. Paul was the only one who didn't. At eight ten in the morning.

SG: Did they do that to avoid publicity?

MS: Oh yeah. Well, all of that was all geared to that, but . . . 'cause, I mean, it would've been really terrifying. Crowds still freak me out. Some of those times were really frightening, inasmuch as they used to rock the car as well, you know, grab the car and . . . And it just wasn't nice. The only thing we had to do when we got married was, um, talk to people to do press then, but I didn't . . . I haven't since.

SG: Did Ritchie change any during those years?

MS: Do you mean change in giant ways? No, barely. Everybody changes, I think, but no, he was always the same.

SG: The Beatles were in the center of this big social circle in London, and there were beautiful models throwing themselves at Ritchie. Did you ever feel threatened? Ritchie wound up marrying a girl from home, instead of, you know, Jean Shrimpton.

MS: The reason I didn't feel threatened was because I had no knowledge of that kind of life. It just didn't occur to me.

SG: John was the only other Beatle who was married. Ritchie didn't even know John was married. I read somewhere that he found out when they all went to an accountant and John declared a dependent. Ritchie said, "What do you mean, you're declaring a dependent? How can you do that?"

MS: That must've been real early, because I also remember rumors were going around even in Liverpool. And I said to Ritchie one day, "Is John married?" He said, "If he is and he doesn't want people to know about it, we don't ask." Or words to that effect, basically.

SG: It's a real northern attitude. He didn't know what to say. It must've been hell on Cynthia, though. Right? It must've been, you know, real hard, I mean, to pretend. You know? It must . . . She must've felt really . . . You know?

MS: I remember seeing her a couple of times coming out of the Cavern or going into the Cavern when we were there. But when they moved down here, I was more acknowledged, sort of.

SG: Um, really, you were kept out of the . . . But I've seen millions of photographs of you. I mean, every time you went somewhere with Ringo, you were photographed. You went to the openings of movies and—

MS: Oh, yeah, but it didn't occur to me they would know it was me.

SG: How do you mean?

MS: I wasn't doing anything. It was him.

SG: Were you able to lead your own quiet life when you came to London, your own personal life?

MS: To do with Ritchie, oh yeah.

SG: Where did you live?

MS: We had a flat at 34 Montague Square. And then we moved to St. George's Hill. Yeah, to Sunny Heights. It's called Sunny Heights. And we had builders in for a long time, two years. Sometimes Montague Square was frightening, because it was a basement and ground-floor flat. There was an intercom, you push the button at the front door and I had to answer it. There were always chicks standing outside. And it used to frighten me sometimes because some of them were basically little cows. And they used to do it on purpose to terrorize me when he wasn't there during the day, when he worked or whatever. There was a window, and they used to stand there. The window was really near, and it was weird, that used to be frightening, they used to do it on purpose, you know? Then I got smart. I made friends with a couple of them. And when I'd walk out, they'd row at the ones that didn't like me.

SG: Do you remember the Ad Lib?

MS: It got to the point where, just every night, we would just . . . we would just go to the Ad Lib. The best description I've heard was that it was a party hall. I mean, all of us used to go. I tried to get Ritchie to dance, but the others didn't dance. George and Paul can't dance.

SG: That's astonishing for musicians. I guess, maybe not.

MS: I remember Ritchie coming out there one night so pissed that he bounced off about fourteen cars.
    Yeah. And then we got home to Whaddon House, that was really . . . That was before we got married. Got home to Whaddon House and he drove into the garage and scrunched the hellfire out of Brian's car, as he drove in. And then scrunched the hellfire out of it as he drove out.

SG: I wonder what Brian did?

MS: Well, we went up to tell him.

SG: What did he say?

MS: He was actually wonderful about it. He was having a party and he didn't expect us.

PETER BROWN: I remember you coming up and Brian was a bit embarrassed because there were only boys there. Nobody was doing anything bad.

MS: It was just that he wasn't expecting us either.

SG: What was the attitude towards Brian among the group? The four boys from Liverpool, the four men from Liverpool, were kind of macho. They didn't think it was weird that he was gay, or anything? They weren't embarrassed by it?

MS: They loved him.

SG: The Beatles were a knit group. Was there one point where everybody decided to go their own ways?

MS: What, to do . . . What do you mean? For real? When they split up? The first thing that had anything to do with any split-up, whatever, was Ritchie. Because he left first. In the middle of the *White Album*, we went to the other three and their houses, and that was that.

SG: Why did he want to leave then?

MS: Because he didn't feel that he was with them and he didn't feel he was . . . He thought it was those three, and, and, and it didn't look like he fitted in. It was almost awkward. When we went around to each one, they all said the same, "If you go, I go. No, you can't go." They all said it. They, they came up with, "If maybe you just took a little while from the band, have a break. You know?" I think it freaked him out more. John was panicking, saying, "Ringo, please don't go now. If you go now, that's it. Gone. I'm going. I'm leaving. I don't want you . . ." 'Cause he wanted them to carry on with somebody. But John was really, you know, upset about it, which is the one thing that got to Ritch. And, in fact, Paul as well.

SG: Why was Ritchie fed up?

MS: He wasn't fed up, it was more of . . . it was more of . . . It was a heavy decision that he'd actually made, 'cause he wasn't . . . he's not a flippant person. I mean, he even had a talk with me. And I remember, in Sunny Heights, and he said to me, "I can't do this anymore." I said, "That's okay. If that's the way you feel, you have to go, carry on and do whatever you want." And he said, "I know, but the money will be different." Which I remember about it, because his brain had gone that far, that he's even covered the money because that didn't even enter into anything.

I have never in my life given an interview . . . I've never done it before.

SG: When were you divorced?

MS: Five years ago, in '75.

SG: No, I thought that you were divorced in like '70 or '71. Because at the same time as Pattie and George were divorced. When were Pattie and George divorced?

PB: [In] '72.

SG: Everybody got married and divorced at the same time.

PB: No, Pattie was divorced later. She put up with George . . .

SG: But it's interesting because I think in the beginning, George was the shy one, not the ladies' man.

MS: He always had girlfriends. Even at the beginning, and when I was going to the Blue Angel, the club I told you about, he had a couple of girlfriends then.

SG: Can you explain what happened between you and Ritchie and Pattie and George? George declared he was suddenly in love with you after knowing you for so many years. I was surprised.

MS: So was I. I don't know. I really don't know. It's amazing.

SG: He fell in love with you?

MS: Well, Pattie was there, too, because he came in and said it.

SG: Must have been [terrible for] poor Pattie.

MS: [inaudible 00:11:33] incredible. I was actually cleaning the table because we just had dinner.

SG: He said it at dinner?

MS: Yeah, after they arrived. We just had dinner. I was cleaning the table. It was a twelve-foot table in the kitchen. Ritchie was there. Pattie was there, too . . . because George came into the kitchen and said it. George came in and he was playing . . . He picked up a guitar and started to sing a song, I don't know which. He was singing and then he just turned to Rich and said, "I'm in love with your wife." I was totally stunned. He just came up to me and said it. It was a very difficult time. And even inasmuch as . . . because I believe . . . whatever, but up until that point, I didn't know that it was—

SG: He must have been out of his mind.

MS: Yeah. Jesus Christ, yeah.

SG: It must have been embarrassing for Pattie.

MS: It was incredible. I was actually in shock at the table.

SG: She told us that it was really rough being married to George in the end. It was really a nightmare for her. He treated her badly. It happens to everybody, no?

MS: No, not necessarily. Not in my situation with Ringo. Present company excluded, I think men are dogs anyway. Sorry about that.

SG: Pattie told me how miserable she was. She was faithful to George, she said, which I believe. One of the most difficult things for her to take was that it's one thing if he was having affairs with women that she didn't know, but when he proposed it with someone she knew, I think that was probably . . .

MS: I think a lot of it was also to do with the sex and drugs and rock and roll.

SG: You mean it pushed George over?

MS: No, that was in people's minds at the time. Because when that time I just told you about, when I first knew anything about . . . I was as amazed as Rich.

SG: What, was Rich angry?

MS: Well, inasmuch as . . .

SG: The group was already over.

MS: Yeah, but this wasn't going on then. No, nothing to do with anything like that. My God.

SG: Oh, I thought it was way back then.

MS: Jesus Christ, no, no, no. This was earliest '74, really.

Ringo Starr

People think that Ringo, being the last one in, would be the weakest link, but he was no odd man out. Nor was he a pushover. Ringo grew up in the Dingle, an inner-city neighborhood and the roughest part of Liverpool; it made him tough inside that lovable Beatle persona. Being poor also made him tightfisted. Yes, he had all the rock star accoutrements, the cars and houses and expensive vacations, but he was a mellow young man, good humored, thrilled with his luck. He had an equal say in the Beatles. He wasn't swayed by the others; often his opinion was a dealbreaker in a vote. Ringo felt increasingly disenfranchised by the group, and rumors persisted that Paul was dubbing drum tracks without his knowledge, although Ringo could tell as soon as he heard a track whether it was him playing. He famously quit the band one day and went to the Bahamas. (There were times when every one of them except for Paul thought earnestly about leaving the group.) Another issue was that although John and Paul were making millions of pounds on publishing rights, since they coauthored all the hit songs, they kept George's songwriting contributions to a minimum, and Ringo's to practically nil. They were all multimillionaires and Ringo got his equal share of all other income, but he made the least money of anyone in the group.

Ringo wasn't blasé about his personal fame, but he wasn't very impressed with the fame of others, except maybe Elvis. The height of Ringo's disregard for celebrity was when he and Neil Aspinall were in Los Angeles on business and staying at the Beverly Hills Hotel. When they checked in, the front desk informed him that the bungalow Brian Epstein usually took was occupied by Elizabeth Taylor and Richard Burton. Word somehow got back to the couple that Ringo had been displaced into a different bungalow, and the Burtons invited him to dinner. Ringo mulled this over for a bit and declined. He wanted to stay in and watch TV. The odd coincidence was, when he ordered room service and stayed in, the movie Suddenly, Last Summer *was on TV, starring Elizabeth Taylor, and Ringo wasn't interested in watching that either.*

The interview begins with Ringo reminiscing about where he grew up.

RINGO STARR: Where I came from, you had to be in a gang in the area you lived in, and half the time it wasn't for protection. It got so crazy, they would set up fights, they would rent buses to take you to [them], and if you said no, it was okay, they would beat you up—your own gang. They would just beat you up on the spot and say fine. But you'd usually go because you stood some chance of coming out of it. You had to belong to a gang, because the teddy boys would just beat you up and be done with it.

Hamburg was more dangerous for the fact— I never felt it was dangerous personally to me, because I was coming out of Liverpool, but English people were not used to guns, and there were usually gas guns and you could buy them in the stores. In England, you never saw that stuff, and the people who had the clubs, I'm not saying they were gangsters, but they were a rough element, and so a lot of people who came into the clubs were rough. And I always remember that a couple of people were checking out these guns while I was playing. I mean, I didn't feel they were going to shoot me.

STEVEN GAINES: Do you remember the Beatles being unhappy with Pet Best?

RS: No. I never felt they were unhappy, because they're not going to come and say, "We don't like our drummer." We never got into that before I joined. Brian Epstein came to get me for a onetime session, to play the Cavern, because Pete wasn't well. I was at home, every time he got me out of bed for a onetime session. He knocked on the door. Brian came for me and said Pete can't make the date, the boys have asked me to come and ask, "Will you play?" and I did that like four or five times, just sat in.

If Rory Storm had a gig, I'd be with Rory, but we were playing different [venues]. It was hard. Everyone was . . . we were all friendly then. We went to clubs together and sat around and talked to each other. George was the one who actually took me aside and said, "We would like you to join the group, what do you think?" I said, "I'd love to join the group," but I was always playing with Rory Storm. Then Brian phoned and said, "Will you join?" I didn't know all the politics that went down, because I was playing out of town.

As everyone knows, George Martin didn't want Pete-the-drummer. Then the boys decided on me, and George Martin didn't want me either. I didn't play on the first two singles, but I play on the album. I'm on the album. It's exactly the same thing—it's the way you do it. So Brian phones and said, "When can you join the Beatles? This was Wednesday, and I played with Rory until Saturday. They had three days to find someone, some blond guy, Gibson Kemp. I knew there'd be riots when I joined the band. If you read the newspapers, it was "Pete Forever, RS Never."

I was asked to join to split a quarter of whatever the money was, and before I joined, when I sat in, I used to get a quarter of the money, minus Brian's commission— Well, Brian put us on wages, really, at the beginning. The first time Brian came to get me, it was twenty-five pounds. And that was a lot of money because we all went to play in Butlin's [holiday camps] for sixteen pounds each, for a week. And this was two gigs and I got twenty-five quid.

SG: So you were always an equal partner?

RS: People join the Stones, I don't know if they got an equal partnership. I was there from the [start]. Always an equal partner from the day I joined. Not [song] publishing, but if we did a show, four ways, minus commission. Records, four ways, minus commission. But not the publishing.

SG: What did you do with your first big check?

RS: George and I ended up buying cars, and I took George to pick his up, an Anglia. At that time, I didn't have a driver's license and I wasn't insured either. I failed the driver's test, and the only way to get experience was to drive, so I used to drive all the time. After George picked up his Anglia, I was following him driving home, and George overtook the car in front of him, and I tried to pass, too, when a dog runs out. The car ahead of me pulls to a complete stop, and I smash the back of it. The other driver wanted to see my insurance. I said, I told him I would pay for it because I didn't want to lose my low-claims bonus, when I didn't even have any insurance.

SG: When you were a kid, your appendix burst. I've read that you were in a coma for ten weeks.

RS: Yup. Well, I was out. I remember going into the operating table. I remember always terrible pain and the whole time we were downstairs, and they took me to the hospital, carried out on a stretcher. Took me to the hospital, and a woman doctor examined me first, and it felt like she was punching my stomach. They said I had appendicitis. They got me ready for the operating theater, and I said to the assistant, "Can I have a cup of tea, please?" She said, "Yeah, when you come out." It was ten weeks later. I was there six months, ready to come out, and fell off the bed and was there another six months. Royal Liverpool Children's Hospital, a greenhouse in a field.

SG: Your father left when you were three.

RS: Yeah. He died this year. I saw him about three times.

SG: Were they special occasions?

RS: No. Not. He left my mother, and he went to live in Crew. Fifty miles away. I used to see him, three or four times, because I was close to my dad's mother and father. That's when I met him because he went to see his folks sometimes, and I'd be there.

SG: Who was the first girl you were engaged to?

RS: [can't remember] Geraldine . . . Jerry . . . my God, that's heavy . . . It matters, though, because I think it's because you asked that question that it doesn't come. We were engaged, the ring, all the folks had met, we had an engagement party, and then one night, she said to me that she was fed up with me playing every night, and that she had to go to a dance or a club, anywhere we were playing. She said, virtually, "It's me or the drums." When I left her that night, I got on the bus and it went through my brain, If that's the decision you want, I play drums. I made the decision on the bus. I never went back. Never went back. She gave the ring back to me.

[The conversation turns to his first wife, Maureen.]

The first time I met Maureen, I was with the Beatles, and she was fifteen. She had to be home every night at ten minutes to twelve . . . Well, she played that girl's trick, she always had a friend, and I had a car, and the friend lived like forty minutes from the Cavern and Maureen lived like five. We always had to take the friend home, then get back to her place, by eleven o'clock—no, at twelve o'clock—her father would whistle out the window, "Good night, dear!"

When we moved to London, we used to call her folks and say she was staying with [Jane Asher, the young actress Paul was dating].

SG: When you first moved to London, did you all live together?

RS: No, George and I used to live together. We all lived in hotels together, but when we decided to move to London, Paul went to live with Jane Asher. George and I shared a couple of apartments, one at Whaddon House, where Brian had the flat above us.

SG: What was it like living one floor below Brian? Was it uncomfortable? Did he had a secret life going on?

RS: It wasn't secret to anyone who knew him, and it was not a hassle. He knew we knew. I would have hoped so, because he must have known that George and I knew because we used to play naughty tricks on him. When he had parties, we'd go up there. And everyone would stop dancing. It wasn't a bother, we were just being naughty. It never bothered me. Brian never came after me, and for all that went down about him going after John, I can't actually say it's true or false. I don't think he did. But it seemed a good story at the time. Brian was a great guy, and the four of us— Well, it's just my opinion, I could have signed a toilet roll and he could have filled the rest in. I never felt Brian would ever rip you off. It didn't bother me that he was homosexual, we'd still have a drink or play cards or whatever.

SG: Twenty-five percent was a high commission.

RS: There were no managers these days. Brian supported us in the early years. He didn't know it would be big, neither did we know it would get this big, but he actually paid out of his pocket.

SG: What about when he died, and you found out there were still nine more years left on the management contract?

RS: That shocked us. We went to Clive, his brother, and we wanted to all join in and Clive wanted to sell us. Because Clive couldn't actually deal with our brains. We were all men, and Clive was a different-attitude person than Brian. Brian quite enjoyed the craziness. Not nutsy, but Clive was a shoe salesman.

SG: But it did shock you . . .

RS: Yes, we thought it was all over. But we were a bit pissed we had the contract which the family made continue. I mean, the family could have stopped it. I mean, they could have said, "It's all over, you've got your lives, we've got ours," but it's a problem with contracts, like the one with the four of us, it's easy to write your name, try and break it.

SG: Do you remember signing one?

RS: We had one, it's called "Beatles and Apple."

SG: Do you remember signing that? There must have been hundreds [to sign] . . .

RS: Not really.

PETER BROWN: I remember where you signed the EMI deal.

RS: But the thing with the EMI deal was that it was so many tracks. And nine years, and I thought that if we did the how many tracks—eighty tracks, something like that—if we had done all the eighty in a year, the contract would have been over, but of course it wasn't, it was actually a nine-year deal. But we weren't really looking at the contract so much. We just really wanted to play, and we were pleased we had a record deal, and you know, the deal seemed good from where we came from. We just went along with a lot of it. We never questioned Brian's— If he made the deal, we'd sign it. Brian wasn't the greatest businessman, but he was a great human being.

With Seltaeb, it's always been a fiasco. We signed away the rights, we never got a penny, and it died. People think we made a fortune on it; we never got a penny. Out of wigs, stockings, little dolls . . . Brian did that. He made another mistake. You see, I can't put him down for that. He was new like we were. He came along, people were offering him deals, we just wanted to play, we loved the crowd, we wanted to make records . . .

SG: Did anybody ever confront him about it?

RS: No. I didn't. There was so much done, our accounts at the time, we sent a man to go and live on an island somewhere, trying to save money.

PB: Walter Strach.

RS: I wasn't going to say his name, you said that. We paid him to live there, holding this money, because England was very hard—you have to try and hold it the best you can. We lost the case, he had to bring all the money back, we paid taxes on it, and we had to pay for him living there. There was a lot more better times. I mean, it's easy just to pick out the bummers. If you're talking about Brian, he was with us from the start for about eight years. If you want to pick on, like, five bummers, try to count up all the goodies that went down. The thing I'm always pleased to say is that Brian always supported us, always. Even when we had two number ones, we'd be back playing the shitty little dance halls that we didn't have to, but because we always played out our commitments. Because those people years before it all happened [supported us], and a lot of people, if you make a number one, you're not going to play the Bottom Line, or whatever. We played every gig even though we were making it. I'm real proud about that. We didn't suddenly become big time and say, "No, are you kiddin'?"

SG: Japan. Do you remember when you got to Japan and the right-wing militants were . . .

RS: Against us? Really, very strongly, because we were playing the Budokan, and it was, like, against their heritage . . . So we had a policeman on every aisle, and the most polite audience we ever played to. Very polite. They didn't yell and scream until after we finished.

SG: Was it horrible in America, not being able to hear yourself playing?

RS: We had the smallest amps, the smallest drum kit. When we toured, there was none for them to actually hear it, it was for them to experience us. And we experienced them. I, as like a human, *Homo sapiens* situation rather than, "Hey, George played a good riff" or "Did you hear that song?" Our situation was not that they came to listen—they came just to go mad. And they did, and that's what we were for. We stopped, though, because we as musicians got so bad, and no one was listening anyway and we decided we wanted to just make music, that's why we went into the studio.

SG: Manila? Did you get beaten up?

RS: No, we didn't get beaten up in Manila. We arrived in Manila, and there was a motorcade of cops and security and madness, we played the gig.

PB: I remember we went on a boat first.

RS: That's right, we did go on a boat . . .

PB: And Neil was left behind because they wanted to search his handbag. Or something.

SG: The baggage didn't go on the boat?

PB: That's where they wanted you to stay, we said, "*No*, we're not going to stay on this boat."

RS: I thought the boat was just to have a drink and say hello to Manila.

PB: No, I think they wanted you to stay.

RS: The main point of the story was that Mrs. Marcos wanted to see us, but we said no, because we didn't want to do it. We were doing the gig, and those functions aren't the most fun anyway. But she said, "You're not going anywhere." John and I don't know anything about it. We woke up in the morning and phone down for the newspapers. We want to see what they like about us, and did the show go over well? Nothing. We figured it was just a weirdo town where they don't give you room service. I called down again to get the papers. Nothing. Madness. We turn on the TV and we see the news and they pan up to all these little kids, and they were saying that we didn't show. So it was all over the TV. They hated us, and we were left with one policeman, after coming in with a thousand. We get to the airport, and it was madness, and John and I were hiding behind nuns. We thought because it's a Catholic country, if we hid behind the nuns, they won't get us. They wouldn't let us go anywhere. They sent us upstairs? We sat up there, they hassled us about the tickets, we came down again, they just came, moving us around while people were shouting at us in this weird language. Then we finally got to the plane. They spat on us. No one got punched.

PB: Mal was pushed over.

RS: Okay, you want to make it a big story? Mal was tripped. I didn't see Mal get tripped. I was not punched in the back. None of us were physically hurt—we were spat on, we were humiliated, but we were not physically damaged. So we get to the plane, and there's an announcement that our press man, Tony Barrow, and Mal Evans had to get off the plane. We thought, now they're taking us off two by two to shoot us. We didn't know. But they just took them off for several minutes, they got back on, and we flew off. Anyway, that's how we got out of Manila. We went to India.

SG: When did the group decide to stop touring?

RS: It was not anything official. It was like the breakup wasn't anything official—it took two years. You knew it was going down, but there wasn't one day when everyone said—you know, there was lots of grumbling and moans, you know we're touring . . . The day it came down, I thought we were actually in the middle of a tour of America. In my recollection, when we decided, we were sitting in some stadium and that's when I think it went down. I don't know where it was, because they all get to look the same after weeks. And that was when it finally came, whenever everyone said, you want to kit it, and John actually said, "What do you think, yes or no?" He didn't want to do it, and we all agreed.

SG: Was John the leader of the group?

RS: Yeah. Paul got us to work, but I think . . . For me, John was the leader. I don't know what the others think, I have no idea.

SG: It trailed off towards the end with John being the leader because he was involved with his new wife and his own endeavors.

RS: Well, everyone had their own endeavors. But Paul was the one who would get us to work. John and I used to live very close together. We'd be walking around the garden having a wonderful time, it was like a nice day, and suddenly the phone would ring and it would be Paul. And Paul was always the one who said, "Well, should we make another record?" So Paul was like that sort of leader where he'd get us in there, but I always felt, as leader of the band, John was the leader. Though everyone had equal say.

SG: What about the day you walked out of a recording session?

RS: Well, I walked out because I felt I was playing real shitty and I felt that the other three were very close and I was not part of the group anymore. Paranoia or whatever you call it. I just felt the other two were really close. Just the feeling came over me, I thought I was useless. The story goes, I went knocking on everyone's s door. John was with Yoko then, and they were living in an apartment that I happened to own, and I knocked and I said, "Look, I honestly feel I'm not playing good right now, and you, Paul, and George are really getting on, and I feel out of the band." And John said, "I thought it was you three [who were excluding me]!"

So that blew me away. Then I went to Paul. I'm like one of those people, if you tell me things, I understand it. It's like John and Yoko, she got us all uptight. Because our wives never came to one session, or they came to one session. It wasn't that sort of thing that when the boys would go to work, the wives were there all the time. Suddenly there was Yoko there all the time, and I was getting as uptight as everyone else, and I went up to John and said, "John, it bothers me. Okay? I don't understand, Yoko is here all the time." And he gave me his reasons and I was fine. After that.

His reasons were, "You know when you go home and you say this happened today or that happened today, you're encapsulating, and you give like three minutes of your twenty-four-hour day. This way both

[Yoko and I] know exactly what's going on, all day. And that's how we're living." It didn't matter if she laid in bed in the studio, whatever . . . and they were doing that . . .

That bothered me so much. Barbara [Bach] and I usually spend twenty-four hours together, because we don't have to tell each other what happened, we both know.

SG: At the time, you were four northern men . . .

RS: Macho . . . Women cooked and the men go out to work.

[Yoko] weirded everyone out. But [later I told] him it was fine, that's what you're doing. It was easy then.

SG: Was touring a grind?

RS: The flying was great, didn't bother me, the problem with the touring was the group got so big, no one understood that you're on tour twenty-four hours a day. From the minute you woke up, you were on tour, people trying to get in, pressure. See, we weren't a band that just went out to do the gig. Doing the gig was the [good part] because it was just the four of us onstage and we were together. We used to take suites in this hotel [the Plaza], floors in this hotel, and we would end up the four of us in the bathroom because there was always traffic, and that's what drove you crazy, never the gigs . . . the gigs were always okay.

SG: One night you disappeared and went out by yourself, with some cops?

RS: Indianapolis. These two cops, they let me drive the police car [late at night]. In fact, we had to hide from the police because I was driving too fast, and I'm in the cop car, and there's two cops hiding in the back, ducking down. Suddenly there was a cop car chasing us . . . and we stopped on some back alleyway, turned all the lights off, waiting for this cop car not to find us.

I just wanted to go around the Indianapolis racetrack. There was one time that we played there, and I just wanted to go around the course where they have the big race. One of the cops said he'd take me around the track in his car. He said, "Do you want to drive?"

SG: You drove the police car around the Indianapolis course?

RS: Yeah, and he said, "Why don't we go to our place?" So I said okay. One of the cops had a ranch, and we ended up on this ranch, and all we had was cognac and Coke for breakfast until his wife . . .

SG: You were out all day and night?

RS: I was up three days and nights, and I was with the cops, and then I got onstage and lost the use of my legs. That was frightening.

SG: From being up so long?

RS: Then they put me to bed. Because the bass drum, this leg started hopping, I couldn't control it. It frightened me.

SG: Do you remember smoking grass for the first time?

RS: [Journalist] Al Aronowitz. Him and Bob [Dylan] came together, but it was Al. I always remember because it was how it should always be. You get hysterical. You know when pot used to make you laugh? So we went into the bedroom, we were all a bit hesitant, you know, it's one of those meets, and we're in a hotel.

SG: Is this the first time you ever met Dylan?

RS: Yeah. So we went in the bathroom and I happened to be first in and first out. Earlier John had ordered room service, and six meals had arrived, whose is whose, and it was so silly because who knew . . . doesn't happen all the time . . .

Bobby [Dylan] was ahead of his time.

SG: Tell us about LSD.

RS: I won't tell you. I don't want to just talk about dope [laughter].

RS: We went to see Elvis. It wasn't as exciting as going to see Cliff Richard. I don't know who set Elvis up. We walked in, we were nervous, he was still the King. The main recollection was that he was playing bass to the television . . . bump bump . . . he was playing the bass guitar watching TV, and I had this discussion with him why didn't he have musicians playing with him, because I really didn't like his music then . . . I loved all his earlier stuff, by then I wasn't buying his records . . . but he was still Elvis.

SG: What about Allen Klein? I met him, and I thought he was bad news.

RS: Not me. I thought he was a real nice man. Never bothered me to have dinner with him. Things changed very rapidly when he came in because they knew . . . the difference with Allen and, say, someone else—I really don't want to name someone, because they get on my case—is that Allen is, he's got a bad reputation and there were people worse than him that got away with the same murder as Allen did. They were frightened of Allen because Allen knows what they were doing.

Allen sues.

SG: He even ripped off Mick Jagger.

RS: Did he? He did?

SG: I thought they had that well documented.

RS: I didn't. Mick didn't come forward and say "Hey . . ." because they were suing him. No. And after we'd finish with Klein, I was on the plane with Pete Townshend. The Who was going to sign up with Klein after we finished with him.

PB: He did have a silver tongue.

RS: The thing Allen did was get rid of everyone around us, including Peter.

PB: He didn't get rid of me.

RS: In his way, he did. I mean he moved out everybody so he could be in control.

SG: What about the people who felt they had been there from the start, like Alistair Taylor?

RS: I mean, it's not a [down] on Alistair, he didn't have a job. Peter came to my house to say he was leaving, and I wanted him to stay just for me personally but he was off to a better situation. I understood perfectly why you were leaving. You came over and said, "There's more I can do." You didn't want to be a nursemaid anymore, and half the time the babies wouldn't listen to you anyway.

PB: That's true.

RS: But Allen Klein didn't move out anyone who was close to us, or Neil.

SG: What about Apple, when you were spending all that money?

RS: We had no idea of money. The main concept of Apple was you didn't have to pay. We were naïve. We thought if you came to us and have this idea, the greatest example was the Punch and Judy show on the beach. A guy came [to Apple], and [unintelligible] Paul suggested this guy, because it was nice, we were trying to make it nice. We lived during the sixties . . . We knew that there was a ton of money, it didn't mean that much, it was just a loan, taxes, we didn't even think about it. The idea, the basic principle, was that you didn't have to pay. We found a few artists. James Taylor, Billy Preston . . . if nothing else . . .

SG: Were there are a lot of leeches and hangers-on?

RS: Yes, yes.

SG: You begin to develop a sixth sense about those people . . .

RS: Yes, but it takes years . . .

SG: That was '67–'68.

RS: If you come up with a great idea, yeah, go ahead and do it, we'll give you the money. The problem we have is that most of the people who came to us didn't fulfill the idea. If they were going to make a movie . . .

SG: What about Magic Alex?

RS: Magic Alex is either a genius or the greatest con man on earth.

SG: I thought the greatest con man on earth.

RS: I thought he was a genius. He showed us paint that lit up. He showed us that. Then we had to bring someone in who was a patent writer . . . I don't even know what happened to him.

SG: I do. We saw him. The patents went to EMI, and they looked after trying to file them. What happened was all of the patents that Alex came up with turned out to be already patented . . .

RS: I don't show you drums. You going to show me a patent . . . fine . . . you know . . . he showed me a few things, he showed me the paint that lit up . . . I didn't know if he invented . . .

PB: It was the wallpaper that you plug in.

RS: He showed me his talking telephone thing where it raises the level the further away you are so you didn't have to shout when you walk away. I walked out the door and the same level voice. I went outside his house, and the volume raised the further you get away . . . He was a genius to me.

PB: What we don't know was that he had done it before.

RS: That's right. We don't know.

SG: Let me ask you another story. It's a famous story, I heard it many times, it's about when you went to Cavendish Avenue to have lunch with Paul and Linda.

RS: It's a famous story?

SG: It is, it's in the court case too.

RS: It was all about that we both had records to come out, and just before Christmas Eve, Paul sent us a man with a whole lot of papers because he was suing us. And I was upset mainly because it was just before Christmas, and we and I phone-called and we went to dinner at his house, and every time I would try to talk, trying to get him not to sue, Linda would cry. And he would take Linda out of the room and we would have to start again. It ended up where nothing was resolved, and at that time Linda stopped the whole situation. She wanted it one way and I wanted it another. I didn't want to get sued. I didn't want to fight Paul ever.

SG: Let me ask you something, if that hadn't broken up that way, what might have happened, do you ever think about that?

RS: Well, I'm pleased it happened because in so many ways, I'm glad it's not going now. It was time. Things last only so long.

SG: The Rolling Stones are going.

RS: Yeah, but they're old men. If you want to take it the other way, Dylan, again, is very bright, he was mentioned in *People*, and in the interview they asked, "What about the Beatles?" and he said, "There was four of them."

SG: John once said he didn't want to play Vegas.

RS: But that's only *Imagine*. You know what I'm saying? Paul with his *Band on the Run*. We all started on a bus and small clubs and things like that, but Paul is that type of person. Paul wanted to do it all over again, and he did. And he went through hell. He went through hell. I mean, now he's not talking to me and that's too bad, but he started again from the bottom to do the Paul McCartney show. I don't wanna do it anymore. I did it once.

SG: Did you want the group to break up?

RS: It broke up anyway.

SG: What does that mean?

RS: It was time for everybody. Still the best band that ever was. Still the best band.

Afterword

The dissolution of Beatles Inc. wasn't formalized until December 29, 1974, almost three years to the day after Paul first sued the others. Some business interests could not be separated, so the Beatles (or their estates) are still very much connected.

It's important to remember that the preceding interviews (save for Yoko Ono's) were conducted only weeks before John was killed in New York on December 8, 1980. It's doubtful that Paul, among many others, would have been as candid about John after his passing. These unfiltered transcripts are the last we'll hear from the key interviewees in this book, most of whom are no longer with us, among them George Harrison, Maureen Starkey, Cynthia Lennon, Neil Aspinall, Derek Taylor, Allen Klein, Ron Kass, David Puttnam, Martin Polden, John Dunbar, John Eastman, Geoffrey Ellis, Nat Weiss, and Alexis "Magic Alex" Mardas.

Why did the Beatles break up? The consensus in the transcripts is that the time had come, an annoyingly philosophical answer yet accurate. "The energy dissipated because we grew and we fulfilled the certain desires that we must have had," George said in his interview. They had spent ten years stitched to each other's side. They were boys when they started and had grown into men. Realistically, how long could they go on being a Beatle and feel creatively satisfied? John and Paul's discontent might have manifested itself as Yoko or Linda, but the fact was that John and Paul had already had enough of each other through a very intense and consuming experience. It is also true that John weaponized Yoko and deliberately used her to alienate the others, and in response, Linda became a worthy opponent. Another factor that's clear from the transcripts is the poison that both Magic Alex and Allen Klein added to the brew. Finally, there was also an issue that is discussed in Yoko's interview that was truly a dealbreaker in the Beatles' existence, and that was John's debilitating use of heroin, which Yoko refers to as *H* in her transcript.

Another refrain in the transcripts is that it was better for the Beatles to end it while they were on top—although with the Beatles, who was to judge what their top was? With each new achievement, Brian Epstein would always say, "Can it get bigger than this?" In the very beginning, when the four of them were feeling discouraged, or broke, or driving home from a gig in a snowstorm, Paul used to cheerlead the other Beatles. "Where are we going, Johnny? Where are we going?" The others would respond, "To the toppermost of the poppermost!" They had reached the toppermost of the poppermost many times and managed to push even higher. Maybe there was a peak, and it was best to let it be. Or as Neil Aspinall said, "The ball game's over, thank you very much, and do something else."

Acknowledgments

The authors would like to thank Dan Strone, Marc Resnick, Jeff Sharp, Tony D'Alessio, Lily Cronig, Claire Romine, Carl Richey, Ana Ban, Emma Fingleton, Alice Berndt, Sara Pearl, Jennifer Enderlin, Sally Richardson, Tracey Guest, Kathryn Hough, Rob Grom, Steven Seighman, Paul Hochman, Martin Quinn, Kenneth J. Silver, Catherine Turiano, Laura Clark, Joshua Rubins, and Eliani Torres.

Index

Abbey Road, 286
   Connolly on, 187
   Let It Be and, 140–41
   McCartney, P., and, 25
   Nutter and, 173
Abbey Road Studios, 44, 49
ABKCO. *See* Allen and Betty Klein Company
Ad Lib Club, 120
   Dunbar at, 190
   Harrison, G., on, 100
   Lennon, C., at, 201
   McCartney, P., and, 29
   Puttnam on, 143–44
   Starkey at, 295
alcohol
   at Apple, 158–59
   Lennon, John, and, 233–35
   Maharishi Mahesh Yogi and, 116
Allen and Betty Klein Company (ABKCO), 238, 260, 261–62
American tours
   Epstein, B., on, 59–61
   McCartney, P., on, 37–40
   Starr on, 309, 313–14
Anger, Kenneth, 174
the Animals, 43, 45
Ansbacher, Henry, 283
appendicitis, of Starr, 304–5

Apple
   alcohol at, 158–59
   Aspinall and, 139, 159
   Brown at, 4, 156–59
   Capitol and, 259
   Connolly and, 184–85
   Epstein, B., and, 82, 158, 194
   Fromme and, 165–66
   Klein and, 268–69, 280
   Lennon, John, and, 30–31
   LSD at, 184
   Mardas at, 159
   marijuana at, 159
   McCartney, P., and, 30–31, 33, 157, 317
   Northern Songs, Ltd., and, 284
   Polden and, 155
   Starr and, 307, 316–17
   Taylor, A., on, 158–59
   Taylor, D., at, 159, 160–70
Apple California, 287
Apple Publishing, 157
Apple Records, 157, 159
   Harrison, G., and, 249
   "Hey Jude" on, 249
   Kass and, 246–54
   Klein and, 230
   Lennon, John, and, 249
   McCartney, P., and, 249
   Starr and, 249

Apple to the Core (Schwartz), 42–43
Aronowitz, Al, 314–15
As Tears Go By, 193
Asher, Jane, 41–43, 48n
   Dunbar and, 192, 193
   Kass and, 252–53
   Maharishi Mahesh Yogi and, 111–18, 122
   Starkey and, 306
   Taylor, A., on, 48–49
Asher, Peter, 32, 176
   Dunbar and, 192
   Klein and, 280
   McCartney, P., and, 247
   Taylor, J., and, 247
"Ask Me Why," 75
Aspinall, Neil, 2, 25, 322
   on *Abbey Road*, 141
   Apple and, 139, 159
   Epstein, B., death and, 65
   interview with, 130–41
   Klein and, 258, 283
   in Manila, 85, 87, 95
   on Mardas, 138–39
   McCartney and, 33
   Northern Songs, Ltd., and, 244
   Starr and, 302
   Taylor, D., and, 161, 167
   Wooler and, 71

Bach, Barbara, 313
Badfinger, 247
Bag o' Nails, 44–45
Bailey, David
   at Ad Lib Club, 100
   Puttnam and, 142, 143
   in Swinging London, 142, 143–44
"The Ballad of John and Yoko," 11
the Band, 246–47, 246n
Band on the Run, 140–41, 319
Barrow, Tony
   Magical Mystery Tour and, 182
   in Manila, 311
Bassanini, Roberto, 126
Bassey, Shirley, 89
Beatlemania, 71, 164, 275

the Beatles. *See specific topics*
Beatles & Co., 4, 256
   Brown and, 282
   NEMS and, 282
Beatles Enterprises, 156
Beatles Ltd., 12
   Apple and, 158
bed-in for peace, 11
the Bee Gees, 12
Being There, 188
"Bell Bottom Blues," 121
Best, Pete, 69
   Starr on, 302–3
Black, Cilla, 24
   James and, 76
   Lewis and, 89
   on marijuana at Cavern Club, 68
   NEMS and, 3, 4
Blake, Don, 90–91
Body Count (Schwartz), 48n
Borja, Jacinto C., 84
Boyd, Jenny, 107
   interview with, 120–29
   Jagger and, 113
   Maharishi Mahesh Yogi and, 111–18, 202
   marijuana and, 113, 125–26
Boyd, Pattie. *See* Harrison, Pattie Boyd
Brown, Peter, 1–14
   at Apple, 4, 156–59
   Beatles & Co. and, 282
   Dunbar interview by, 190–97
   Epstein, B., and, 282
   Epstein, B., death and, 63, 65
   Epstein, Q., interview by, 52–57
   Fraser interview by, 174–80
   Fromme and, 166
   Harrison, G., interview by, 93–106
   Harrison, P., and, 253
   Hells Angels and, 165
   on "Hey Jude," 171–73
   James interview by, 73–76
   Klein and, 238–39, 270, 282–83, 316
   Klein interview by, 265–89
   Lennon, C., interview by, 198–207

Let It Be and, 277
Lewis interview by, 89–92
lunches of, 166
on Maharishi Mahesh Yogi, 119
on Manila, 84–88
Mardas interview by, 107–18
McCartney, L., and, 43
McCartney, P., and, 4, 8–9
McCartney, P., interview by, 18–45
NEMS and, 3–4, 256, 282–83
Ono interview by, 209–29
resignation of, 11–12
Sinatra and, 290–91
Starr interview by, 301–21
Taylor, D., interview by, 169–70
Burroughs, William, 179
Burton, Richard, 302
Byrne, Nicky, 77

Cage, John, 223
Cahn, Sammy, 291
Capitol, Apple and, 259
Capitol Records, 34–35, 249
   Klein and, 258–59, 286–87
Carbitral, 8
"Carolina in My Mind," 247
Cavern Club, 37
   Epstein, B., at, 3, 47
   marijuana in, 68
   Starkey at, 290, 291–92, 294
   Starr at, 303
   Taylor, A., at, 47
   Wooler at, 71
A Cellarful of Noise (Epstein, B.), 4n
Chandler, Chas, 45
Chariots of Fire, 142
Chicago, 256
Clapton, Eric, 12
   Harrison, G., and, 126–27, 151–52
   Harrison, P., and, 121
   on *Live Peace in Toronto*, 288
   Polden and, 151–52
Cleave, Maureen, 15–16
"Cold Turkey," 287
Coleman, Ornette, 223
Collins, Joan, 246

Columbia, 256
Concert for Bangladesh
   Apple California and, 287
   Connolly and, 188
   Klein and, 219–20
   Ono and, 218–19
   Starr at, 219
Connolly, Ray
   on *Abbey Road*, 187
   Apple and, 184–85
   Concert for Bangladesh and, 188
   Harrison, G., and, 182, 187–88
   interview with, 181–89
   Lennon, C., and, 185–86
   Lennon, John, and, 185–86
   Magical Mystery Tour and, 181, 182–83, 186
   Ono and, 185–86, 188–89
   Sgt. Pepper's Lonely Hearts Club Band and, 181
   Taylor, D., and, 187
Cooke, Sam, 265–66
Cox, Kyoko Ono, 13, 216, 216n
Cream, 62
"Cry Baby Cry," 185
the Cyrkle, 89

Daily Express, 160–61, 162
the Dakota, 12
   McCartney, P., at, 179
   Pang and, 232
Dale, Darley, 264
Dalí, Salvador, 13–14
Danko, Rick, 246n
Dave Clark Five, 38
David Bailey's Box of Pinups (Bailey), 143
"A Day in the Life," 147
"Dear Prudence," 111
Dick James Music, 75–76
DiLello, Richard, 157
Dine, Jim, 174
Donovan, 89
   Klein and, 251, 265
   Maharishi Mahesh Yogi and, 111–18, 125

Dorsey, Tommy, 256
Double Fantasy, 224
Drug Squad, 150–51
drugs. *See also* heroin; LSD; marijuana
   Epstein, B., and, 6–7, 21–22, 55–56, 60–61
   Polden and, 149–55
Dunbar, John, 108, 176, 177
   at Ad Lib Club, 190
   Asher, J., and, 192, 193
   Asher, P., and, 192
   Epstein, B., death and, 194
   Faithfull and, 192–93
   interview with, 190–97
   Lennon, John, and, 191–92, 195
   LSD and, 193–94
   Mardas and, 196–97
   marijuana and, 193
   McCartney, P., and, 192–93
   Ono and, 190–91, 195–96
Dylan, Bob, 164, 193
   marijuana and, 314–15
   Starr and, 314–15

Eastman, John, 28–31, 139
   Epstein, C., and, 272
   interview with, 255–62
   James and, 242–43
   Klein and, 148, 268–72, 268*n*
   McCartney, P., and, 255–56
   NEMS and, 255–62, 268–72, 276–77
   Northern Songs, Ltd., and, 242–43
   Puttnam on, 148
Eastman, Lee, 9, 139, 258
   Mardas on, 109–10
Eastman, Linda. *See* McCartney, Linda Eastman
Elizalde, Don Manolo, 85–86, 87
Elizalde, Fredrick, 86
Ellis, Geoffrey, 244
   Epstein, B., death and, 63
   interview with, 77–83
   NEMS and, 7, 77–83
EMI, 22, 35
   contract with, 156–57
   Klein and, 257, 273
   Mardas and, 318
   Martin at, 81
   NEMS and, 80–83, 82*n*, 256
   Northern Songs, Ltd., and, 286
   Ono at, 191
   royalty rate of, 80–81
   Starr and, 307–8
   Triumph Investments and, 273
"The End," 141
Epstein, Brian. *See also* North End Music Stores
   Apple and, 82, 158, 194
   Brown and, 2, 3–4, 282
   at Cavern Club, 3, 47
   contract with, 3, 22–23, 25–26, 80, 82–83, 137
   drugs of, 6–7, 21–22, 55–56, 60–61
   early life of, 19, 52–53
   Ellis and, 77–83
   EMI and, 157
   Gillespie and, 58–61
   homosexuality of, 19, 55, 58–61, 162–63, 296
   interview with, 15–16
   Jagger and, 139
   James and, 73–76
   Klein and, 265–66
   Lennon, C., and, 199–200
   Lennon, John, and, 3, 4, 5–6, 19, 199–200
   Lewis on, 89–92
   management contract with, 3
   in Manila, 84–88, 95
   McCartney, P., and, 18–25
   memoir of, 4, 4*n*
   Northern Songs, Ltd., and, 73–76
   personal life falling apart, 81–82
   personality of, 6
   Puttnam on, 146
   Sgt. Pepper's Lonely Hearts Club and, 20–21
   Starkey and, 295–96
   Starr and, 303, 306–8
   suicide attempt by, 6
   Taylor, A., and, 47–51
   Taylor, D., and, 162–63, 169

ten-year contract with, 25
25% commission of, 22–23, 75, 82*n*, 83, 255, 256, 306–7
Weiss on, 58–61
Williams, A., and, 66, 68
in World War II, 53–54
Epstein, Brian, death of, 7–8
Brown on, 65
Dunbar and, 194
Ellis on, 83
Epstein, Q., and, 56–57
Harrison, G., and, 240
Harrison, P., on, 122–23
James and, 240
Klein and, 238–39, 266
Lennon, John, and, 123, 182, 240
McCartney, P., and, 24, 238, 240
Northern Songs, Ltd., and, 245
Ono and, 240
Puttnam on, 146
Starr and, 307
Taylor, A., on, 62–64
Epstein, Clive (brother), 54–55
Eastman, J., and, 272
Epstein, B., death and, 63–64, 255
Klein and, 271, 271*n*
Lennon, John, and, 269
NEMS and, 256–57, 275
Northern Songs, Ltd., and, 241–42
Starr and, 307
Epstein, Harry (father), 55–56
Epstein, Queenie (mother), 6, 8
Epstein, B., death and, 64, 255
interview with, 52–57
NEMS and, 255, 275
Evans, Mal, 51
Epstein, B., death and, 65
in Manila, 85, 87, 95, 311
Evening Standard, 181
Everett, Kenny, 194

Faithfull, Marianne, 40
Dunbar and, 192–93
Farrow, Mia, 111–18, 124*n*
Farrow, Prudence, 111–18
Fielding, John, 278

Fly, 231
the Fool, 157
"For You Blue," 121
Fraser, Robert, 154
heroin and, 151, 174
interview with, 174–80
Jagger and, 174, 175
Jones and, 175
Klein and, 179
Lennon, John, and, 176, 177–78
McCartney, P., and, 174, 176–77
Ono and, 177
Polden and, 174
the Rolling Stones and, 175–76
Sgt. Pepper's Lonely Hearts Club Band and, 174
on Swinging London, 174–75
Fromme, Squeaky, 165–66
Frost, David, 183–84

Gaines, Steven
Dunbar interview by, 190–97
Eastman, J., interview by, 255–62
Epstein, Q., interview by, 52–57
Fraser interview by, 174–80
Harrison, G., interview by, 93–106
James interview by, 73–76, 240–45
Kass interview by, 246–54
Klein interview by, 265–89
Lennon, C., interview by, 198–207
Lewis interview by, 89–92
Mardas interview by, 107–18
McCartney, P., interview by, 18–46
Ono interview by, 209–29
Pang interview by, 230–37
Polden interview by, 149–55
Starkey interview by, 290–300
Starr interview by, 301–21
Taylor, A., interview by, 47–51, 62–64, 158–59, 263–64
Taylor, D., interview by, 160–70
Weiss interview by, 58–61
Williams, A., interview by, 66–69
Wooler interview by, 70–72
Garland, Judy, 77
gay. *See* homosexuality

Gerry and the Pacemakers, 24, 37–38
   James and, 76
   Lewis and, 89
   NEMS and, 4
Gill, Jack, 285
Gillespie, John ("Dizz"), 58–61
"Girlfriend," 40
"Give Peace a Chance," 288
Gortikov, Stanley, 249
Grade, Lew, 23–24, 241–43, 283
Graham, Bob, 49
Greaves, Elsie, 290
Green, Sam, 178
Grossman, Albert, 163
Guercio, Jimmy, 256
Guthrie, Brian, 143

Haight-Ashbury, 129
Hamburg, 37, 41
   Starr in, 302
   transvestite in, 67–68
   Williams, A., on, 66–69
Hammond, John, 39
A Hard Day's Night, 22–23
   Harrison, P., and, 121
Harrison, Dhani (son), 94
Harrison, G.
   on Ad Lib Club, 100
   Apple Records and, 249
   dancing of, 295
   Starr and, 306
   in Swinging London, 120–21
Harrison, George
   Ad Lib Club and, 100
   American tours and, 38
   Apple and, 30–31
   on the Beatles' influence, 99–100
   cancer diagnosis of, 93–94
   Clapton and, 126–27, 151–52
   Concert for Bangladesh of, 188, 218–19, 220, 287
   Connolly and, 182, 187–88
   death of, 94
   early life of, 19
   on end of sixties, 102–5
   Epstein, B., death and, 65, 240
   at Haight-Ashbury, 129
   India and, 97, 99, 102–5
   interview of, 93–106
   on Jones, 100–102
   Klein and, 35, 139, 239
   Lennon, John, and, 93, 105, 106, 188–89
   LSD and, 95–97
   Maharishi Mahesh Yogi and, 98–99, 111–18, 119
   in Manila, 94–95
   Mardas and, 110, 112
   McCartney, P., and, 19, 94, 94*n*, 106, 128, 187–88
   NEMS and, 3
   Northern Songs, Ltd., and, 241, 244
   Ono and, 188–89
   Polden and, 149, 151–52
   songwriting by, 301
   Starkey and, 127, 297–99
   at Starkey wedding, 292
   Starr and, 303
   Taylor, A., and, 51
   Taylor, D., and, 161
Harrison, Olivia (wife), 94
Harrison, Pattie Boyd (wife), 100, 290
   at Ad Lib Club, 144
   Brown and, 253
   Clapton and, 121
   divorce of, 297
   on Haight-Ashbury, 129
   interview with, 120–29
   Maharishi Mahesh Yogi and, 111–18, 122–24
   Starkey and, 298–99
   at Starr wedding, 292
   in Swinging London, 120–21
Harrisongs Music, Ltd., 35
Hells Angels, 165
Helm, Levon, 246*n*
heroin
   Fraser and, 151, 174
   Jagger and, 174
   Lennon, John, and, 152, 214–18, 218*n*, 236, 322
   Mardas and, 218*n*
   Ono and, 152, 214–18, 218*n*

"Hey Jude," 171–73, 206
  on Apple Records, 249
Hodge, Vicki, 199
Hoffman, Abbie, 221–22
homosexuality (gay)
  of Epstein, B., 19, 55, 58–61, 162–63, 296
  legalization of, 150
  rumors of, 194
Hopper, Dennis, 174
Horn, Paul, 111–18

I Be Me (Harrison), 93, 105–6
"I Need You," 121
"I Want to Hold Your Hand," 161
"If I Needed Someone," 121
Imagine, 319
India. *See also* Maharishi Mahesh Yogi
  Harrison, G., and, 97, 99, 102–5
Indica Gallery, 108, 176, 190–91, 209–10
"Instant Karma," 286, 287–88

the Jacaranda, 71
Jacobs, David, 77
Jagger, Mick
  at Ad Lib Club, 100
  Boyd, J., and, 113
  Epstein, B., and, 139
  Fraser and, 174, 175
  heroin and, 174
  Jones and, 101
  Klein and, 35–36, 139, 239, 251, 266–67, 315–16
  Maharishi Mahesh Yogi and, 122
  Polden and, 149, 151, 174
James, Dick, 75*n*
  Black and, 76
  Eastman, J., and, 242–43
  Epstein, B., and, 73–76
  Epstein, B., death and, 240
  Gerry and the Pacemakers and, 76
  interview with, 73–76
  Klein and, 257, 272, 279, 283
  Kramer and, 76
  Lennon, John, and, 269
  "Love Me Do" and, 74
  Martin and, 73, 74
  McCartney, L., and, 243–44
  NEMS and, 75
  Northern Songs, Ltd., and, 73–76, 240–45
  "P.S. I Love You" and, 74
Janov, Art, 220–21
Janov, Vivian, 220–21
Japan, 90. *See also* Ono, Yoko
  Kass and, 247–48
  McCartney, P., in, 106
  Starr in, 309
Japanese Jailbird (McCartney, P.), 106
Jesus Christ Superstar, 12
John, Elton, 235
Jones, Brian, 44
  Fraser and, 175
  Harrison, G., on, 100–102
  leaving band, 101
  Pallenberg and, 176

the Kaiserkeller, 68–69
Karsan, Koral, 210*n*
Kass, Ron, 159, 169
  Apple Records and, 246–54
  Asher, J., and, 252–53
  interview with, 246–54
  Japan and, 247–48
  Klein and, 250–54
  Mardas and, 247–48, 250
  McCartney, P., and, 252–53
  on Ono, 208
Kemp, Gibson, 303
The Killing Fields, 142
King, Cecil, 238
the Kingston Trio, 163
Klein, Allen, 20, 25–27
  ABKCO of, 238, 260, 261–62
  Apple and, 268–69, 280
  Apple Records and, 230
  Asher, P., and, 280
  Aspinall and, 258, 283
  Brown and, 238–39, 270, 282–83, 316
  Capitol Records and, 258–59, 286–87
  Concert for Bangladesh and, 219–20
  death of, 289
  Donovan and, 251, 265

Klein (*continued*)
  Eastman, J., and, 148, 268–72, 268*n*
  EMI and, 257, 273
  Epstein, B., and, 265–66
  Epstein, B., death and, 238–39, 266
  Epstein, C., and, 271, 271*n*
  Fraser and, 179
  Harrison, G., and, 35, 139, 239
  Harrison, P., on, 128
  interview with, 265–89
  Jagger and, 35–36, 139, 239, 251, 266–67, 315–16
  James and, 257, 272, 279, 283
  Kass and, 250–54
  Lennon, John, and, 25–27, 35–36, 139, 170, 179, 187, 225, 239, 266–69, 278, 284–85
  Mardas and, 280
  McCartney, L., and, 278
  McCartney, P., and, 25–27, 33–35, 139–41, 148, 170, 187, 239, 250, 258–60, 270, 272, 276
  NEMS and, 255, 257–79, 283
  Northern Songs, Ltd., and, 241–42, 277–78, 285–86
  Ono and, 208, 225–27, 251, 262, 267–69, 288
  Pang and, 230–31
  Polden on, 153–54
  the Rolling Stones and, 239–40, 251, 265, 266, 288
  Starr and, 239, 315–16
  Taylor, A., and, 263–64, 280–81
  Taylor, D., and, 168, 169–70, 267–68
  Taylor, J., and, 247
  the Who and, 316
Kooning, Willem de, 9
Koschmider, Bruno, 68
Kramer, Billy J., 24, 41–42
  James and, 76
  Lewis and, 89
  NEMS and, 4
Krishna, 94, 102–3

"The Lady Is a Tramp," 291
"Layla," 121, 127

Lennon, Cynthia (wife)
  at Ad Lib Club, 201
  Connolly and, 185–86
  divorce of, 11, 108, 204–6
  Epstein, B., and, 199–200
  interview with, 198–207
  LSD and, 201–2
  Maharishi Mahesh Yogi and, 111–18
  Mardas and, 108, 116–17, 126, 204, 206
  on McCartney, L., 204
  Ono and, 4*n*, 198–207, 210–14
  pregnancy of, 5, 199
  Starkey and, 293–94
  at Starkey wedding, 292
  A Twist of Lennon by, 198–207
Lennon, John. *See also* Northern Songs, Ltd.; Ono, Yoko
  at Ad Lib Club, 144
  alcohol and, 233–35
  American tours and, 38
  Apple and, 30–31
  Apple Records and, 249
  the Band and, 246
  bed-in for peace, 11
  Cleave and, 15–16
  concert for Bangladesh and, 218–20
  Connolly and, 185–86
  Dunbar and, 191–92, 195
  Epstein, B., and, 3, 4, 5–6, 19, 199–200
  Epstein, B., death and, 65, 123, 182, 240
  Epstein, C., and, 269
  as everyone's favorite, 4
  Fraser and, 176, 177–78
  Gerry and the Pacemakers and, 37–38
  Harrison, G., and, 93, 105, 106, 188–89
  heroin and, 152, 214–18, 218*n*, 236, 322
  "Hey Jude" and, 171–73
  at Indica Gallery, 191
  insolence of, 144
  James and, 269
  Jesus statement of, 38
  killing of, 1, 13, 321
  Klein and, 25–27, 35–36, 139, 170, 179, 187, 225, 239, 266–69, 278, 284–85
  as leader, 311
  Lennon, S., and, 13, 224–25

on *Live Peace in Toronto*, 288
LSD and, 177, 193–94, 196, 201
Maharishi Mahesh Yogi and, 111–18, 123
Mardas and, 107–9, 112, 115, 126, 195, 197–98, 228–29, 251
marijuana and, 149, 151, 193, 215
McCartney, P., and, 10, 27–32, 35–36, 46, 148, 179–80, 186–87, 196
NEMS and, 3, 279
to New York, 12
Pang and, 214, 230–37
Polden and, 149, 151, 152, 154–55
Puttnam on, 144, 148
in *Rolling Stone*, 214, 221, 268
the Smothers Brothers and, 233–34
at Starkey wedding, 292
Starr and, 13–14, 311–12
as suspicious, 30
tampon and, 234–35
Taylor, A., and, 51
at the Troubadour, 233–34
U.S. government plot against, 222
Williams, A., on, 67
Wooler and, 6, 70–72
Lennon, Julian (son), 199, 200, 214
birth of, 5
"Hey Jude" and, 171–73, 206
Ono and, 216, 216*n*
threat of kidnapping, 201
trust for, 206
Lennon, Sean (son)
birth of, 223
Klein and, 288
Lennon, John, and, 13, 224–25
Ono and, 13
trust for, 206
Let It Be, 32–34, 139–41, 286
Abbey Road and, 140–41
Brown and, 277
Polden on, 152–53
"Let It Be," 185
Levinson, Charles, 11
Lewis, Vic
interview with, 89–92
in Manila, 86, 87–88, 90–92

Liberace, 77
Lipton, Peggy, 253
Live Peace in Toronto, 287, 288
Liverpool. *See also specific individuals and topics*
Connolly in, 181–82
Lennon, John, in, 4–6
McCartney, P., in, 18, 18*n*
in World War II, 3
Local Hero, 142
Lockwood, Joseph, 80, 82*n*, 257, 269
Lomax, Jackie, 247
London Records, 266
"Long and Winding Road," 286
The Longest Cocktail Party (DiLello), 157
"Love Me Do," 35
first radio play of, 3
James and, 74
LSD
at Apple, 184
Apple and, 157
Dunbar and, 193–94
Harrison, G., and, 95–97
Lennon, C., and, 201–2
Lennon, John, and, 177, 193–94, 196, 201, 202
Maharishi Mahesh Yogi and, 122
Mardas and, 196–97
McCartney, P., on, 45–46
Ono and, 214
Starr and, 31
Taylor, D., and, 165–66, 202

Magic Alex. *See* Mardas, Alexis
Magical Mystery Tour
Connolly and, 181, 182–84, 186
McCartney and, 4, 8
Ono and, 213
Puttnam on, 146
Maharishi Mahesh Yogi
Asher, J., and, 111–18, 122
Boyd, J., and, 202
Donovan and, 111–18, 125
Farrow, M., and, 111–18, 124*n*
Harrison, G., and, 98–99, 111–18, 119
Harrison, P., and, 111–18, 122–24

Maharishi Mahesh Yogi (*continued*)
  Jagger and, 122
  Lennon, John, and, 111–18, 123
  LSD and, 122
  Mardas and, 107, 111–18, 123–25, 165, 202
  McCartney, P., and, 111–18, 119, 122
  Starkey and, 111–18, 123
  Starr and, 111–18, 123
  Taylor, D., and, 164–65
The Man Who Gave the Beatles Away (Williams, A.), 66–67
Manila
  Aspinall in, 85, 87, 95
  Barrow in, 311
  Brown on, 84–88
  Epstein, B., in, 84–88, 95
  Evans in, 85, 87, 95, 311
  Harrison, G., in, 94–95
  Lewis in, 86, 87–88, 90–92
  marijuana in, 95
  NEMS and, 86
  Starr on, 309–11
Manson, Charles, 166
Marcos, Ferdinand, 84
Marcos, Imelda, 84–87, 310
Mardas, Alexis ("Magic Alex"), 10, 99
  at Apple, 159
  Aspinall on, 138–39
  Dunbar and, 196–97
  EMI and, 318
  Harrison, G., and, 112
  heroin and, 218*n*
  interview with, 107–18
  Kass and, 247–48, 250
  Klein and, 280
  Lennon, C., and, 108, 116–17, 126, 204, 206
  Lennon, John, and, 107–9, 112, 115, 126, 195, 197–98, 228–29, 251
  LSD and, 196–97
  Maharishi Mahesh Yogi and, 107, 111–18, 123–25, 165, 202
  Ono and, 209, 227–29
  Starr and, 111, 113, 317–18

marijuana
  at Apple, 159
  Boyd, J., and, 113, 125–26
  in Cavern Club, 68
  Dunbar and, 193
  Dylan and, 314–15
  in Hamburg, 67
  Lennon, John, and, 149, 151, 193–94, 215
  in Manila, 95
  McCartney, L., and, 253–54
  McCartney, P., and, 8, 22, 32, 193
  Ono and, 151
  Polden and, 149–55
  Richards and, 151
  Starr and, 314–15
Marima, 85–86
Martin, George
  "A Day in the Life" and, 147
  at EMI, 81
  James and, 73, 74
  Starr and, 303
  at Trident Studios, 171*n*
Maymudes, Victor, 164
McCain, Art
  Puttnam and, 142, 143
  in Swinging London, 142, 143
McCartney (album), 32–33, 139
McCartney, Jim (father), 74
  Connolly and, 183
McCartney, Linda Eastman (wife)
  Connolly and, 186
  Harrison, P., on, 128
  introduction to, 9, 43–45, 253
  James and, 243–44
  Klein and, 278
  Lennon, C., on, 204
  marijuana and, 253–54
  McCartney and, 32
  Ono and, 322
  Polden and, 155
  pregnancy and marriage of, 9–10
  Puttnam on, 147
  Starr and, 318–19
McCartney, Mike (brother), 181

McCartney, Paul. *See also* Asher, Jane; Northern Songs, Ltd.
   Abbey Road and, 25
   at Ad Lib Club, 144
   Ad Lib Club and, 29
   on American tours, 37–40
   Apple and, 30–31, 157, 317
   Apple Records and, 249
   Asher, P., and, 247
   the Band and, 246
   Band on the Run by, 140–41, 319
   Brown and, 4, 8–9
   Connolly and, 181–88
   at the Dakota, 179
   dancing of, 295
   Dunbar and, 192–93
   early life of, 18–19
   Eastman, J., and, 255–56
   Epstein, B., and, 18–25
   Epstein, B., death and, 65, 238, 240
   Fraser and, 174, 176–77
   Gerry and the Pacemakers and, 37–38
   on going to the top, 36–37, 322
   Harrison, G., and, 94, 94*n*, 106, 128, 187–88
   "Hey Jude" and, 171–73, 206
   interview with, 17–46
   investments of, 28–30
   in Japan, 106
   Kass and, 252–53
   Klein and, 25–27, 33–35, 139–41, 148, 187, 239, 250, 258–60, 270, 272, 276
   Lennon, John, and, 10, 27–32, 35–36, 46, 148, 179–80, 186–87, 196
   Let It Be and, 32–34
   on LSD, 45–46
   Magical Mystery Tour and, 4, 8
   Maharishi Mahesh Yogi and, 111–18, 119, 122
   marijuana and, 8, 22, 32, 193
   McCartney (album) by, 32–33, 139
   NEMS and, 3, 279
   Ono and, 10, 27–28, 154–55, 178–79, 186, 196, 207
   paternity suit of, 202–3
   Polden and, 154–55
   Puttnam on, 144–46, 148
   Starr and, 32, 33–34, 140, 187–88, 301, 311–12, 318–19
   suit to dissolve Beatles Ltd. by, 12
   on Swinging London, 36–37
   Taylor, A., and, 47–51, 159, 169
   Taylor, D., and, 168
   Williams, A., on, 67
Melly, George, 120
Mersey Beats, 37
Midnight Express, 142
Minford, Leslie, 86
Mod Squad, 253
the Modern Jazz Quartet, 4
the Monkees, 16
Monroe, Matt, 90–91
Montgomery, David, 143
the Moody Blues
   Lewis and, 89
   NEMS and, 4
Moon, Keith, 236

NEMS. *See* North End Music Stores
Newfield, Joanne, 7, 76
Newsweek, 46
Nilsson, Harry, 233–34, 236
Nizer, Louis, 80
North End Music Stores (NEMS), 2–3
   Beatles & Co. and, 282
   Brown and, 4, 256, 282–83
   Eastman, J., and, 255–62, 269–72, 276–77
   Ellis at, 7, 77–83
   EMI and, 80–83, 82*n*, 256
   Epstein, C., and, 256–57, 275
   Epstein, Q., and, 255, 275
   James and, 75
   Klein and, 255, 257–79, 283
   Lennon, John, and, 279
   Lewis at, 89–92
   Manila and, 86
   McCartney, P., and, 279
   Northern Songs, Ltd., and, 255
   Seltaeb and, 79
   Stigwood and, 24
   Taylor, A., at, 47–51
   Weiss at, 58–61

Northern Songs, Ltd., 27–32
  Apple and, 284
  EMI and, 286
  Epstein, C., and, 241–42
  Harrison, G., and, 241, 244
  James and, 73–76, 240–45
  Klein and, 241–42, 277–78, 285–86
  McCartney, P., buying stocks in, 257–58
  NEMS and, 255
  Starr and, 241, 244
  value of, 240–41
Nutter, Tommy, 172–73

Oldham, Andrew Loog, 192–93, 288
Ono, Yoko, 1
  bed-in for peace, 11
  Concert for Bangladesh and, 218–19
  Connolly and, 185–86, 188–89
  Dalí and, 13–14
  daughter of, 13, 216, 216n
  Dunbar and, 190–91, 195–96
  Epstein, B., death and, 240
  Fraser and, 177
  Green and, 178
  Harrison, G., and, 188–89
  Harrison, P., on, 128
  heroin and, 152, 214–18, 218n
  interview with, 209–29
  Kass on, 208
  Klein and, 25, 27, 208, 225–27, 251, 262, 267–69, 288
  Lennon, C., and, 4n, 198–207, 210–14
  Lennon, S., and, 13
  letters to John in India, 117–18, 123
  on *Live Peace in Toronto,* 288
  LSD and, 214
  Mardas and, 109–10, 209, 227–29
  marijuana and, 151
  marriage of, 10–11
  McCartney, L., and, 322
  McCartney, P., and, 27–28, 154–55, 178–79, 186, 196, 207
  miscarriages of, 186, 216, 217, 220–21
  to New York, 12
  Northern Songs, Ltd., and, 244

  Pang and, 214, 230–37
  Polden and, 151, 152, 154–55
  Puttnam on, 147
  scream therapy of, 220–21
  Starr and, 312
  stolen articles from, 210n
  as suspicious, 30
Owsley, 194

Pallenberg, Anita, 176
Pang, May
  interview with, 230–37
  Klein and, 230–31
  Ono and, 214, 230–37
  the Smothers Brothers and, 233–34
Parlophone Records, 73, 250
Peter, Paul and Mary, 163
Peter and Gordon, 176
Picker, David, 208
Pilcher, Norman, 149, 150–51, 152, 201
Pinsker, Harry, 269, 270, 271
"Please Please Me," 75
Polden, Martin
  Apple and, 155
  Clapton and, 151–52
  drugs and, 149–55
  Fraser and, 174
  Harrison, G., and, 149, 151–52
  interview with, 149–55
  Jagger and, 149, 151, 174
  on Klein, 153–54
  Lennon, John, and, 149, 151, 152, 154–55
  on *Let It Be,* 152–53
  marijuana and, 149–55
  McCartney, L., and, 155
  McCartney, P., and, 154–55
  Ono and, 151, 152, 154–55
  Swinging London and, 149
  on Taylor, D., 155
Preludin (Prellies), 7
Presley, Elvis, 80
  entourage of, 100
  Starr and, 301, 315
Preston, Billy, 317

Proudfoot, 279
"P.S. I Love You," 35
   James and, 74
Puttnam, David
   on Ad Lib Club, 143–44
   on Eastman, J., 148
   on Epstein, B., 146
   on Epstein, B., death of, 146
   interview with, 142–48
   on Lennon, John, 144, 148
   on *Magical Mystery Tour*, 146
   on McCartney, L., 147
   on McCartney, P., 144–46, 148
   on Ono, 147
   in Swinging London, 142, 143–44

Quickly, Tommy, 24, 163

Radio Times, 41
Ramos, Ramon, 86
Revolver, 258
Rice, Tim, 12
Richard, Cliff, 102, 194, 315
Richards, Keith
   Jones and, 101
   Klein and, 267
   marijuana and, 151
Richenberg, Leonard, 273–74
Roam, Dorothy, 41
Robbins, Harold, 30
Robert Stigwood Organisation in
   America, 12
Robertson, Robbie, 246*n*
"Robin Hood," 73, 89
Rolling Stone
   Lennon, John, in, 214, 221, 268
   Schwartz and, 48*n*
the Rolling Stones. *See also* Jagger, Mick;
   Jones, Brian; Richards, Keith
   at Ad Lib Club, 100
   As Tears Go By by, 193
   Faithfull and, 192–93
   Fraser and, 175–76
   Indica and, 108
   Klein and, 239–40, 251, 265, 266, 288
   Lennon, John, and, 28

McCartney, L., and, 44
McCartney, P., on, 20
Starr on, 319
Rubin, Jerry, 221–22
Ruscha, Ed, 174

Saturday Night Fever, 12
Schwartz, Francie, 42–43, 48, 247, 252
   Rolling Stone and, 48*n*
Scorsese, Martin, 246*n*
scream therapy, of Ono, Y., 220–21
Sellers, Peter, 156, 188
Seltaeb, 77–79
   Starr and, 308
Sgt. Pepper's Lonely Hearts Club Band
   Connolly and, 181
   cover of, 20–21, 174
   Epstein, B., and, 20–21
   Epstein, B., death and, 65
   Fraser and, 174
   launch party for, 9, 43
   Ono and, 213, 227
Shankar, Ravi, 94
Shrimpton, Chrissie, 100
Shrimpton, Jean, 144, 293
Silver Voice, 162–63
Sinatra, Frank, 290–91
Smith, Donald, 165
the Smothers Brothers, 233–34
Some Time in New York City, 223
"Something," 121
Spector, Phil, 154, 186
   "Instant Karma" and, 286
   "Long and Winding Road" and, 286
Starkey, Maureen, 51, 199
   at Ad Lib Club, 295
   Asher, J., and, 306
   at Cavern Club, 290, 291–92, 294
   death of, 291
   divorce of, 291, 297
   Epstein, B., and, 295–96
   first meeting with, 305–6
   Harrison, G., and, 127, 297–99
   Harrison, P., and, 298–99
   interview with, 290–300
   Lennon, C., and, 293–94

Starkey (*continued*)
  Maharishi Mahesh Yogi and, 111–18, 123
  Sinatra and, 290–91
  wedding of, 292–93
Starr, Ringo. *See also* Starkey, Maureen
  at Ad Lib Club, 144
  on American tours, 309, 313–14
  appendicitis of, 304–5
  Apple and, 31, 307, 316–17
  Apple Records and, 249
  Aspinall and, 302
  Bach and, 313
  on Best, 302–3
  on Brown resignation, 12
  at Cavern Club, 303
  at Concert for Bangladesh, 218–19
  dubbed drum tracks and, 301
  Dylan and, 314–15
  EMI and, 307–8
  Epstein, B., and, 303, 306–8
  Epstein, B., death and, 65, 307
  Epstein, C., and, 307
  in Hamburg, 302
  Harrison, G., and, 303, 306
  Hodge and, 199
  interview with, 301–21
  investments of, 29
  in Japan, 309
  Klein and, 26, 239, 315–16
  Lennon, John, and, 13–14, 311–12
  on Lennon, John, first marriage and child, 5
  Let It Be and, 33–34
  LSD and, 31
  Maharishi Mahesh Yogi and, 111–18, 123
  on Manila, 309–11
  Mardas and, 111, 113, 317–18
  marijuana and, 314–15
  Martin and, 303
  McCartney, L., and, 318–19
  McCartney, P., and, 32, 33–34, 140, 187–88, 301, 311–12, 318–19
  Nilsson and, 236
  Northern Songs, Ltd., and, 241, 244
  Ono and, 312
  parents of, 305
  Presley and, 315
  on the Rolling Stones, 319
  Seltaeb and, 308
  Strach and, 308–9
  Taylor, A., and, 50–51, 316
  Taylor, D., and, 161, 170
  walking out by, 312–13
  White Album and, 296
Steinem, Gloria, 163
Stigwood, Robert, 24, 62–63
Storm, Rory, 303
Strach, Walter, 156
  Starr and, 308–9
stroboscope, 108
Suddenly, Last Summer, 302
Swaine, Eric, 144
Swinging London. *See also* Ad Lib Club
  Bailey in, 142, 143–44
  Fraser on, 174–75
  Harrison, G., in, 120–21
  Harrison, P., in, 120–21
  McCain in, 142, 143
  McCartney, P., on, 36–37
  Polden and, 149
  Puttnam in, 142, 143

tampon, Lennon, John, and, 234–35
Taylor, Alistair
  on Apple, 158–59
  on Epstein, B., death, 62–64
  Harrison, G., and, 51
  interview with, 47–51, 62–64
  Klein and, 263–64, 280–81
  Lennon, John, and, 51
  McCartney, P., and, 47–51, 159, 169
  Starr and, 50–51, 316
  Taylor, D., and, 167–68
Taylor, Derek, 25
  Apple and, 157, 159, 160–70
  Aspinall and, 161, 167
  Connolly and, 187
  Epstein, B., and, 162–63, 169
  Harrison, G., and, 161
  interview with, 160–70
  Klein and, 168, 169–70, 267–68
  LSD and, 165–66

Maharishi Mahesh Yogi and, 164–65
　　McCartney, P., and, 168
　　Polden on, 155
　　Starr and, 161, 170
　　Taylor, A., and, 167–68
Taylor, Elizabeth, 302
Taylor, James, 247, 317
Thank You Lucky Stars, 23
Tigrett, Isaac, 291
Town & Country, 44
Townshend, Pete, 316
Transcendental Meditation, 93, 95, 111–18
transvestite, 67–68
Trident Studios
　　"Hey Jude" and, 171–73
　　Martin at, 171*n*
Triumph Investments, 257, 260
　　EMI and, 273
the Troubadour, 233–34
A Twist of Lennon (Lennon, C.), 198–207

United Artists, 140, 208
Up Your Legs Forever, 231

Vapnick, Reginald Leon Isaac.
　　See James, Dick
Vinton, Bobby, 265

Walls and Bridges, 236
Warner Bros. Records, 160
Weber, Andrew Lloyd, 12
Weiss, Nat, 7
　　interview with, 58–61
Wheeler, Cecil Joseph, 11
White Album, 171, 185
　　Starr and, 296
the Who, 316
Williams, Allan
　　Epstein, B., and, 66, 68
　　on Hamburg, 66–69
　　on Lennon, John, 67
　　The Man Who Gave the Beatles Away by, 66–67
　　on McCartney, P., 67
Williams, Tennessee, 9
"Woman Is the Nigger of the World," 223
"Wonderful Tonight," 121
Woofters, Bertie, 166
Wooler, Bob, 6
　　interview with, 70–72
World War II
　　Epstein, B., in, 53–54
　　Liverpool in, 3

Zappa, Frank, 187

About the Authors

PETER BROWN is the former COO of Apple Corps and has been a Beatles intimate since their earliest days in Liverpool. Their passports were locked in his desk drawer, he was best man at John and Yoko's wedding, he introduced Paul to Linda Eastman, and perhaps the most charming of his credentials is that he's the only real person ever mentioned in a Beatles song, 'The Ballad of John and Yoko'.

STEVEN GAINES is the *New York Times* bestselling author of *The Love You Make: An Insiders Story of the Beatles* (with Peter Brown). His journalism has appeared in *Vanity Fair*, *The New York Times* and *New York*, where he was a contributing editor for 12 years. He is also cofounder of the Hamptons International Film Festival.